THE NEW HYPNOSIS
IN
FAMILY THERAPY

THE NEW HYPNOSIS
IN
FAMILY THERAPY

By

Daniel L. Araoz

and

Esther Negley-Parker

BRUNNER/MAZEL, *Publishers* • New York

Library of Congress Cataloging-in-Publication Data

Araoz, Daniel L., 1930–
    The new hypnosis in family therapy.

    Bibliography: p. 261
    Includes index.
    1. Family psychotherapy.   2. Hypnotism—
Therapeutic use.   3. Family psychotherapy—Case
studies.   4. Hypnotism—Therapeutic use—Case studies.
I. Negley–Parker, Esther.   II. Title.   [DNLM:
1. Family Therapy—methods.   2. Hypnosis.
WM 430.5.F2 A662n]
RC488.5.A73   1988   616.89'156   87-25960
ISBN 0-87630-491-9

Published by
BRUNNER/MAZEL, INC.
19 Union Square
New York, New York 10003

To our children
Cheri, Brad, Andrea
Lee and Nadine
who taught us much about
family therapy

Contents

Preface

The American Association for Marriage and Family Therapy started in 1942 as the Association of Marriage Counselors. Although the concepts were not clearly defined, it was understood, nevertheless, that the new therapeutic approach—unlike the psychoanalytic method—centered on the relationship between husband and wife. The psychological system created by the interaction of two people, not the intrapsychic dynamics, was the special focus of therapeutic attention.

As time went by, the same professional group which had started with a handful of practitioners and has grown now to several thousands throughout the world, for political reasons changed to its current name. Agreeing with the general concept, we also refer to family therapy meaning interactional-system-focus-therapy or counseling. Therefore, as some of our clinical case examples will show, we believe that family therapy may take place without the whole family. Often the couple alone is seen (indeed, the couple may not be married). However, the focus of intervention is the relationship, the system established by it, and the ways in which it affects the individuals who make up the whole family system.

Because of our clinical, practical orientation, the book follows a pragmatic format. Ideally, application follows theory. Therefore, the organization of the book is uncomplicated, the first part focusing on theory and the second on how it is applied. The theoretical chapters are practice oriented, illustrating many points with verbatim clinical excerpts. Theory justifies our practice. However, the "theory" we refer to is "functional," in William James's expression. Although our theoretical orientation stresses practice, we do not intend to build new theory about family functioning or about family therapy. We apply hypnotic theory and practice to family therapy. Our theoretical chapters, then, are an expansion of hypnotic principles to helping families function more effectively according to their own evaluation of functioning.

The case studies are lengthy, emphasizing the actual transactions during the therapy sessions rather than our impressions and understanding of each case. We are inviting you to attend our family hypnotherapy sessions, to watch and hear what goes on while we interact with the families who come to us for help. We hope that this candid revelation of our work, with all the mistakes and shortcomings, will serve nevertheless as a model to other family therapists who want to adapt our hypnotherapy to the families they treat. We should mention here that, while we work as cotherapists (as the case transcripts reflect), our method is, of course, appropriate for use by individual therapists.

It is important for you, the reader, to approach this book with a beginner's mind. Don't believe a word we say until you have mulled it over—until you have used your critical faculty, your intelligence, to understand both what we are saying and the context in which we operate. What we do *within our framework* (our years of experience, our theoretical background as it developed through those years, our cotherapy team, the types of families we see, and so on) may be disastrous in a different framework. This is our rationale for presenting detailed, step-by-step interventions in the second part of the book.

After you have critically and open-mindedly thought about family hypnotherapy as we present it here, select one family with whom you feel comfortable and start using family hypnotherapeutic techniques with them. You must be intellectually satisfied with this approach. But you must also feel comfortable using these techniques. This is the reason we recommend that you begin practicing them with an "easy" family and slowly build your self-confidence as a family hypnotherapist in this method. We would gladly receive your written comments and questions elicited by your professional experience. And we thank you in advance for them.

OUR RESEARCH

We would like to teach you basic clinical (hypnotherapeutic) *principles*, out of which techniques are born—or out of which *you* create techniques. What we give you in this book is based on the evidence we have gathered through many years of practice and on our own follow-up. The evidence that family hypnotherapy has merit comes, then, from our repeated use of it and from what families have reported about its advantage. Of families seen since 1976, we employed 50 for this research. Sixty-six families were contacted by telephone and asked whether they would fill out a questionnaire about their family therapy experience X number of years before. Only after they promised they would cooperate in this project were they sent a brief questionnaire covering five general items. They were called again 10 days after the mailing. About 20 families had to be called two to three times. Finally we obtained 50 responses. The questionnaire sent to the families follows:

Please read the five items carefully before starting to write. After discussing them with your (spouse, family) decide who will put down the answers in writing.

1. What do you, as a (couple, family) believe you gained from the family therapy sessions we had together? Explain in as much detail as possible.

2. What was *especially helpful/useful* to you as a (couple, family) in family therapy that you have been able *to use afterwards?* Please explain in detail.

3. Was there anything in family therapy *that did not help you?* Please explain thoroughly.

4. Please comment on your reactions to the mind exercises, use of imagination, and self-hypnosis you practiced in family therapy.

5. If you had to advise us regarding what could have been done differently or what would have been better for you, what would you tell us?

For this book, item 4 is especially significant. All the families were positive about hypnotherapy, many mentioning it also in items 1 and 2. Comments ranged from "very helpful" to "I still practice it by myself" to "It helped us become a better family team." The less positive responses were in the nature of "It was useful in family therapy but I never did it again."

The responses were ranked along two 5-point scales, one from "very positive" to "very negative," the second from "clear and concrete" to "confusing." We interviewed face to face two families at the extremes of the two scoring scales, and one each whose score fell toward the middle of each scale, 10 families in all.

In the book we attempt to use the information gathered from this research by specifying circumstances that will condition what we present. Aware of our limitations and conscious of the many mistakes made in our work with families, we want to warn you at the very outset of this book that we do not believe in panaceas. We don't want to encourage a preoccupation with technique which will distance us from the family we are supposed to help, as Walters (1985) so aptly put it. We are not proposing *the* answer to anything in family therapy. We are humbly and respectfully sharing our experience of family hypnotherapy with you, as colleagues and fellow professionals. And we assume that you have a humble and respectful attitude to learn from our experience.

Introduction

Orthodoxy is the inevitable destiny of many ideas, both good and bad. Family therapy has not escaped this fate. In spite of the loud protestations against rigid Freudian tenets or the inflexible nonsystemic involvement of individual therapy, many schools of family therapy show the same closed-mindedness they attack.

The "schools" become dogmatic. As the field of family therapy in the mid-1980s witnesses, there are first churches of object relations and second churches of strategic interventions and third churches of paradoxical therapy and fourth and fifth churches ad nauseam. They all form a new dysfunctional family. And in this uneasy council of churches, gods and demigods continuously emerge. We all recognize the new mythology: Ackerman, Bowen, Minuchin, Selvini Palazzoli, Satir, Whitaker, and a legion of others. This absurdity also has its sacraments: the genogram, the one-way mirror, family sculpting, live supervision, the team approach—way past the traditional seven sacraments. They even are supposed to act on their own, like the seven. Salin (1985), Schwartz and Perrotta (1985), and Wright (1985), among others, have courageously complained about the rigidity of many family therapists, which prevents them from being effective.

Although the analogy with organized religion could be developed further, our point has been made. We are against dogmatism and final answers—either purely theoretical or founded on research data presented by the proponents of a particular school or orientation to validate their dogmas.

Our contribution is humble and pragmatic. This is a book on a method of family therapy that can be applied within any specific theoretical conceptualization. It presents an approach involving principles and basic techniques for effective change in family interaction. This approach helps family members change perceptions within the system, as well as improve communication and engage in "inter-actions" that work. Family hypnotherapy is not a new dogma. We could class this method as *experiential*, according to Levant's (1984) classification of family therapy: historical, structural, and experiential. Without subscribing to any of the "experiential" family therapists, such as Kempler (1968,1981), Laing (1961,1969), Satir (1967,1972), or Whitaker (1976a,b), who each formed schools of family therapy, family *hypno*therapy can be grouped with them. It uses genograms, live supervision, the therapist team, and many other techniques as long as they are useful to enrich the inner experience provided by hypnotherapy.

Our view of family interaction is systemic. We consider the individual *in* the family and as *part of* the family, both influencing it and being influenced by it. The family, when functional, helps the individual's growth and individuation. In fact, it makes individuation possible. In a true sense, then, the family *serves* the individual, but the individual makes the family possible and has responsibilities in the system as well as obligations toward the other family members. Only thus will the individual grow in the system and benefit from it. These truisms are needed to avoid the overemphasis on the system at the expense of the individual person, which "tends to devaluate or depersonalize individuals," as Salin (1985) puts it.

The construct of right hemispheric activation to understand how hypnosis is conducive to human change from within should not be dismissed lightly (Watzlawick, 1978; Watzlawick, Weakland, & Fisch, 1974) simply because it is a useful hypothesis. Evidence to support the theory that hypnosis is mostly right hemispheric functioning or that the former activates the latter is far from conclusive.

However, we use this language as a heuristic short cut. We intend to emphasize experiential mental activity as opposed to logical, abstract thinking. We hope to bring to family therapists' attention a method that can help any approach to family therapy by *adding* the right hemispheric dimension, thus enriching the effectiveness of the historical or structure–process approach, following Levant's (1984) terminology. As a matter of fact, the effectiveness of the successful approaches in family therapy, we believe, comes from hypnotic elements, present even in interventions not considered hypnotic by those using them, such as paradoxical interventions. Several groups commonly recognized as effective are rooted in hypnotic principles. Just to mention three, this is the case of the Brief Therapy of the Mental Research Institute and the Milwaukee group; of the paradoxical methods of the Milan group; and of the experiential artistry of Carl Whitaker. Even Jay Haley, who supposedly abandoned hypnosis after having become the most erudite early scholar of Milton H. Erickson, uses many hypnotic principles in his family therapy (Haley, 1980).

NEW VERSUS TRADITIONAL HYPNOSIS

To understand what we mean by hypnosis, hypnotic elements, or family hypnotherapy, you might read *The New Hypnosis* (Araoz, 1985). In that book hypnosis is conceptualized as "reaching beyond the scope of traditional hypnosis by being more experiential, more client-centered and less involved with experimental concepts carried over from the laboratory" (from the Introduction). Because of the differences with traditional methods, this is, indeed, a *new* way of conceptualizing and applying hypnosis.

As a matter of fact, we agree with T. X. Barber (1985b) when he states "that [before the intensive research in hypnosis from the 50s to the 70s] hypnosis had been seriously misconceived and misrepresented and was *not* what it was generally thought to be [namely, a mental state] in which [hypnotized subjects] had either lost the ability or could not make the effort to initiate their own cognitions and behaviors and, consequently, their thoughts, experiences and behaviors could be guided by the hypnotist" (pp. xiii–xiv). This general misconception is still believed by the public at large and, unfortunately, by many health professionals not trained in hypnosis. T. X. Barber categorically states that "it [the misconception] is not accepted by any serious present-day researcher in hypnosis" (1985b, p. xiv).

What the last 30 years of research have demonstrated is that in "hypnosis" there are interacting variables at work so that what is accomplished by using hypnosis "depends far less than had previously been supposed on the hypnotist's formal or ritualistic trance induction procedures and far more on many other complexly interrelated variables, most of which pertain to the subject rather than the hypnotist" (Barber, 1985b, p. xiv). Araoz (1982) summarized these subject variables in the acronym TEAM (trust, expectations, attitude, motivation). Clients have to *trust* both the nonconscious processes of their mind and the therapist they are working with. They must also have the right *expectations*, according to *their* existential reality. If hypnosis is always ultimately self-hypnosis, as the previously mentioned research shows and we believe, then it is a mental skill that people must learn to use through practice. Therefore, there is no panacea in hypnosis; there are no miracles. The expectations must be related more to mastering this mental skill than to obtaining quick results. Clients must also have an *attitude* of curiosity about themselves, a desire to learn more about themselves, as Erickson (Erickson, Rossi, & Rossi, 1976) emphasized repeatedly. When learning self-hypnosis with the help of a clinician, clients must have an attitude of voluntary cooperation with the therapist. Finally, they must be self *motivated*. Hypnosis being a goal-oriented means to an end, it is practiced in order to improve, to change. This motivation is essential, so that using hypnosis to please a spouse, let's say, is not effective.

As the members of the New Nancy School in the early part of the twentieth century insisted, the core of hypnosis is self-suggestion, rather than any rituals employed to assimilate these suggestions. This has led T. X. Barber (1985a) to refer to "hypnosuggestive procedures" rather than to hypnosis as such. The practice of the *new* hypnosis in family therapy (Negley-Parker & Araoz, 1985b) has been mentioned, emphasizing the *client's work* in hypnosis, rather than the hypnotist's ministrations. Therefore, when we refer to hypnosis, we mean the New Hypnosis, according to the preceding explanations. We do not refer to the Svengali-type caricature of hypnosis which still prevails in many people's minds. In this book we apply the New Hypnosis to family therapy.

NEW HYPNOSIS IN FAMILY THERAPY

Family hypnotherapy, then, is the integration of New Hypnosis techniques and, especially *principles*, with any form of family therapy. The flexibility of the New Hypnosis allows it to be used in psychodynamic approaches, such as those of Boszormenyi-Nagy and Spark (1973), Bowen (1978), and Framo (1982), as well as in any other method of the structure–process or experiential groups (see Levant, 1984), which currently are the most popular. We emphasize hypnotic *principles* rather than techniques, believing that the latter must be constructed by the sensitive therapist as the situation of the session demands. These situational techniques, however, are drawn from the four basic hypnotic principles which characterize the alternate mental state called hypnosis and are interrelated. When a person is in hypnosis, these principles are at work, as long as the clinician uses hypnosis for the benefit of the individual. As will be seen, this "hypnosis" is not the rigid, ritualized, and narrow shortcut justly criticized by Wright (1985).

As we explore the vast literature on clinical hypnosis, there emerge four nuclear principles around which revolve all the notions on clinical hypnosis and on which depend the effective use of this powerful therapeutic tool. These four principles are 1) the principle of inner (nonconscious) dynamics, 2) the principle of suggestibility, 3) the principle of positivism, and, 4) the psychosomatic principle.

Inner Dynamics

There are obviously many modes of consciousness. I know that I know, but I also don't know that I know. Hypnosis deals frequently with the mental modality of what I know but am not aware that I know. This can be called *the inner mind*. To contact this vast reservoir of what is part of my knowledge but is not immediately available to my consciousness, hypnosis relies on *imagination*. It takes seriously the productions of imagination, allowing the mind to spontaneously come up with mental images. These are internal representations, mirroring the external senses with which we are familiar. Thus images may be visual, auditory, tactile or kinetic, gustatory or olfactory. By allowing and encouraging imaginative involvement through hypnosis, one gets in touch with one's inner mind. As a historical note, it should be remembered that Freud developed his concept of *Das Unbewusste* (for which the strange English translation of "the unconscious" was chosen) only after his exposure to hypnosis, as it was practiced toward the end of the nineteenth century in France.

The principle of inner dynamics extends the realm of human experience. It is not merely the things that happen to us which make up our existence and experience but the things which we "happen to ourselves" in our imagination. We make things happen in our own mind: beliefs that shape our choices and behavior, self-fulfilling prophecies, even health and sickness—all are to some extent affected by our inner dynamics. This principle helps us understand our total human experience, as it is comprised of the events we live through and our unique reactions to those events: our interpretations, our associations, our hopes, our fears, our projections, and more. Hypnosis provides the means to get in touch with these nonconscious aspects of ourselves. And because this nonconscious world of our human existence is not rational, imagination becomes the key to unlock that wealth.

Suggestibility

Suggestions, either direct or nonverbal, have been always part of healing, both in medicine and in psychology, according to the extensive investigation of T. X. Barber (1985a). Clinically, we operate on the practical assumption that suggestions become such when the individual accepts them or believes in them. In this sense, we are always dealing with self-suggestion since all the ideas in the world suggested to someone have no effect until that person has owned them (see Baudouin, 1922). The principle of suggestibility in hypnosis flows from that of inner dynamics. When the individual activates imagination, two important phenomena are possible. One is that negative self-suggestions in the form of self-defeating images are identified. The other is that constructive and positive imagery can be used to instill effective perceptions, attitudes, ideas, values, and behaviors. Our view is that suggestions are not only words but images (Pratt, Wood, & Alman, 1984). Experienced hypnotists always have been very careful about the use of words because of the images words elicit. These images influence the person; they *are* suggestions. When the mind is in the right hemispheric mode, it becomes more suggestible because the critical faculties are less active. Fromm (1977), as is her wont, has researched in depth this aspect of hypnosis. The principle of suggestibility is therefore very important in family therapy. Thanks to it, many negative expectations and negative beliefs people have about each other (what in general constitutes negative self-hypnosis) can be transformed into constructive and effective mental activities, as Ritterman (1983) pointed out.

Negative self-hypnosis (Araoz, 1981) is a good illustration of the principle of suggestibility, although in this case individuals are giving themselves *negative* messages which are affecting their thinking and behavoir and are not fully aware of what they are doing to themselves. Ineffective worrying is a good example of negative self-hypnosis. In family dysfunction negative hypnosis is at work, as Ritterman (1983) has indicated and we shall explain further on.

Positivism

In clinical use, hypnosis has always been a means to activate inner strengths and resources of clients. Positivism simply means that the goal of clinical hypnosis is improvement, enrichment, and enhancement of the individual. The message conveyed in many indirect ways, through words and imagery, is "I can, I have the resources, I must channel my energy more effectively." Because the New Hypnosis underlines the goal-directedness of its use, the principle of positivism is of extreme significance. It is true that hypnosis could be used for the individual's harm. Therefore, positivism is not an *essential* principle of hypnosis. There is nothing in the essence of hypnosis which demands positivism—contrary to the other principles. However, *in clinical use*, at least since Mesmer (see Eden, 1974), over two centuries ago, hypnosis has been used positively—for the benefit of the clients. In family therapy, this means a constant focus on strengths and attainable goals of improvement, as the book will explain.

Psychosomatics

Hypnosis has always been concerned with the body–mind relationship, unlike nonhypnotic psychotherapies. Diamond (1986) considers this emphasis one of the factors characteristic of hypnotherapy and uniquely enhancing the therapeutic process. In his words, "Hypnotic suggestions have traditionally been oriented towards accessing bodily experience through mental ideas (i.e., ideomotor suggestion). Consequently, accepted hypnotic ideas alter bodily experiences . . . such as . . . pain (Barber & Adrian, 1982). Alternatively, in hypnotherapy the body is often used to access the mind" (Diamond, 1986, p. 241). He goes on to give as an example the case of a person with a conflict she cannot put into words. Through hypnosis she can represent that conflict in her body, like a lead ball resting inside her stomach. This mind exercise may give her a new awareness and understanding of her conflict and the relationship it has with other aspects of her life and family.

By using the body in this way, hypnotherapy is truly experiential, providing what in Spanish is called a *vivencia*, a uniquely and total (mind–body) inner experience of something. *Vivencias* are powerful means of changing because they go to the very soul of our beliefs and perceptions. Hypnotherapy, because of its psychosomatic principle, is more likely to produce *vivencias* than other, more intellectual or merely verbal, psychotherapies.

These four principles lead to a central model of intervention in family therapy. This seems to be connected with de Shazer's (1985) search for "master keys" in therapy—techniques that can be applied regardless of differential diagnosis to innumerable therapeutic situations. (We deal with these "master keys" in Chapter 2.)

At this point, suffice it to say that these four hypnotic principles can be used to determine whether a technique is truly hypnotic. Unless the technique addresses itself to the nonconscious dynamics, to what the person believes or wants to believe (suggestibility), to the positive aspects of the person's personality, and to the mind–body interaction, the technique is not truly hypnotic. Sherman and Fredman (1986), in their handbook on family therapy techniques, remind us that a technique is a "complex move, prescription or suggestion made by the therapist, . . . a means for converting ideas into practical use, . . . [a] carefully designed plan of action founded on theory and observation of behavior" (p. 4). As such, techniques are truly scientific means to attain particular ends.

A FAMILY THERAPY PARADIGM

The OLD C model can become a grid for family therapy, making it possible to apply the previously mentioned principles in clinical practice. This acronym stands for the four therapy steps to be taken in order to utilize right hemispheric or inner experiential forces for the benefit of the family members as a living group. These four steps are:

1. *Observe* the process within the family and between family and therapist.
2. *Lead* to inner experiencing.
3. *Discuss* what happened in 2 above.
4. *Check* experientially to integrate 2 and 3.

Observe

In family hypnotherapy this step is twofold. The therapist must observe the communication process among family members: the actions, words, interruptions, contradictions, somatic reactions to each other, and so on, as we shall explain later. But family hypnotherapists must also observe the communication process of each family member with the therapist(s).

Regarding both processes to observe, it becomes easy to consider three main areas in each: *language style, important statements*, and *somatics* (bodily reactions, mostly nonconscious, to what's happening in the family therapy session). Although separated for didactic purposes, in practice the three areas overlap and modify each other. When these three areas are paid attention to, it is easy to understand Ritterman's (1983) concept regarding family members "using hypnosis" with each other, "inducing trance" on each other, or changing mental channels on each other. By observing these aspects of family members' behavior with each other, one discovers the power family members have on each other, affecting perception, mood, and behavior, and often prolonging faulty communication.

Language style. Therapists can develop a refined sensitivity to nonconscious choices of words (especially adjectives, adverbs, and verbs), figures of speech, and analogies used, as well as to the timing or context in which language style elements appear. Therapists need merely be attentive to this aspect of their family therapy session. After two or three meetings with the same family one becomes sensitive to the fascinating and often surprising aspects of the family language style and to the way the family members react to certain words and expressions.

Important statements. The other area of language to be observed carefully is that of statements with special emotional charge, made often in passing and as part of the general conversation. These important pronouncements are useful in family therapy if their affect is utilized rather than their content. Examples of these important statements will be found in the next section explaining the second step of our therapeutic paradigm.

Somatics. This area includes every nonverbal component of communication, such as voice volume and inflection, emphasis expressed by gesture and facial expression, body movement and changes, direction of eyes, and slight alterations in skin tone (the client becoming a bit redder or paler), which are observed during the family therapy session. The concentration on somatics is not to discover (or invent) a hidden meaning known by the clinician, but rather to help the family become aware of it and to use it as a point of therapeutic entry—a door to inner, right hemispheric processes, as we shall explain next. The work of Cameron-Bandler (1985) is relevant in this respect and shows creative possibilities to the family therapist.

Lead

At this point, therapy per se starts. Language style, important statements, and somatics are used as points of therapeutic entry. Which one of the three areas to choose is up to the preferences of the family therapist and is determined by the therapist's understanding of this particular family's process and experience, by the therapist's sensitivity at the time, and by similar factors. "Lead" is the most prolonged and involved step in the family hypnotherapy process. The lead injunction to utilize one of the three areas of observation is an invitation to "get more into it," "to stay with it," for instance, by repeating an important statement to oneself while checking what effects it has on the body or on feelings and memories. Another possibility is to utilize a figure of speech, let's say "he acts like a lord and master," in order to invite the wife to allow this image to develop in her mind, no matter how absurd or frightening or comical it may become. She is asked not to talk yet (that comes in the next step) but to get fully involved in her inner experience of her husband as a "lord and master." Finally, with respect to somatics, while the daughter is talking, the father may start to move slightly in his chair away from her. The father is invited to "get into" this movement, to allow it to develop fully, to repeat it, paying attention to his feelings, to exaggerate it while exaggerating his inner affective sensitivity. This opens up a new level of personal experience which becomes more meaningful to the individual-in-the-family than an intellectual insight. In the next step this is discussed, but first the father is encouraged to fully experience it by leading him into it from the entry point used, in this case the non-conscious movement away from his daughter while she was talking.

At any given moment any family member is offering more therapeutic material to the observant therapist than is possible to work with or utilize. The more experienced the therapist, the more trained in observation of the client's three areas described above, the more effective the therapy will be.

Discuss

This is the time to return to left hemispheric mental activity. As mentioned earlier, these four steps are heuristic and do overlap in practice. The important point is that in this view, discussion, analysis, evaluation, and the like must *follow* the inner, personal experience. Most therapists agree that clients must get in touch with their feelings as part of successful therapy. The OLD C paradigm is an elegant method to do this. Therefore, the emphasis is on feeling, experiencing, "getting into," not on talking, as many clients insist on doing. We insist on the second step and only then encourage discussion.

Check

This is a final cautionary measure to ensure that an integration has taken place between feeling and understanding or between right and left hemispheres. The intellectual discussion having finished, the therapist asks the family members who were involved in it to go back to the experiential mode and again get in touch with whatever is happening "inside." In the case of the father who was moving away from his daughter, he understood during the discussion that he was afraid of the daughter hurting him by leaving him, as his wife had hurt him by dying two months previously. He recognized the foolishness of his reaction because his fear of being hurt and left might deprive him of the enjoyment of loving his daughter. In the "check" step he concentrated on the joy of loving his daughter until he felt calm and at peace.

These four steps represent a practical clinical method to use hypnosis and to benefit from its four basic principles outlined earlier.

Whatever is experiential, right hemispheric, and inner reality–oriented is hypnosis, in our view. In our public presentations and teaching, we explain the New Hypnosis and its four principles, deemphasizing the rituals of hypnosis. The dramatic effects of hypnosis, which most laymen are concerned with, are minimized in order to emphasize the naturalness of this alternative way of using one's mind.

Related to the four hypnotic principles mentioned earlier is our point of departure in work with families. We start from what constitutes healthy and ego-enhancing interaction for the particular family we are working with. Here, hypnotic principles become functional, since individuals have a mental image of what their families could (should?) be like. We shall discuss this more fully in Chapter 3. At this point, it might be useful to indicate that one of our initial interventions is to ask the family members to spend a few moments imagining the ideal family they could have. This exercise, hypnotic in nature, lends itself to a useful exchange of expectations coming from each family member. It is especially helpful to understand the background (family of origin) of the spouses, thus leading to intergenerational issues as well as to sexual roles. It is also beneficial in our task-oriented work since it leads naturally to behavioral changes: If I want to have this type of family, my behavioral contribution should be thus and thus. But this is merely one of the many hypnotic techniques which, as can be noticed, may well fit in many different family therapy orientations.

Returning now to our departure point, we emphasize wellness over pathology, effective over ineffective family functioning; assuming that even the most disturbed families have healthy traits and patterns of interaction, we build on them to enlarge and deepen the wellness environment. This benefits the individual, contributing to more alternatives and choices in all interpersonal relationships. Likewise, the individual family member becomes a more responsible contributor to the well-functioning of the whole system through a heightened awareness of self and the other family members.

THE TOMATO EFFECT

Now that we've told you where we stand as family therapists you are invited to try this approach. What Goodwin and Goodwin (1984) called the tomato effect is directly connected with the quasi-religious attitude in some family therapy practices mentioned earlier. Before 1820 tomatoes—indeed any fruit from the nightshade family—were thought to be poisonous in the United States. It was a mystery, explained perhaps by climatic differences, that some Europeans ate this fruit without immediate damage to their health. But Americans? Never! Until one good day in 1820, Robert Gibbon Johnson, on the steps of the Salem, New Jersey courthouse, ate a tomato—and Robert Gibbon Johnson did not die. He appeared as healthy as before his feat—and he survived. Only then, and slowly, did the people of the United States begin to add tomatoes to their diet.

We hope family hypnotherapy does not have the same fate as the pre-1820 tomato in the United States. We hope that what Robert Gibbon Johnson was for the tomato, this book will be for the use of hypnosis in family therapy.

THE NEW HYPNOSIS
IN
FAMILY THERAPY

PART I

The Method

Even though we are presenting a clinical method to make our family therapy work effective, the theory underlying it must be understood. This is our rationale to situate family hypnotherapy in the context of family psychology. All scientific endeavor comprises two elements: facts and explanation or data and theory. The same fact—thunder, for instance—can be explained in many diverse and contradictory ways. It may be God's ire, the gods fighting, cosmic warnings of the end of the world, or electric charges. The facts are evident, the explanations are not. People believe whatever they want, given their biases, culture, and other subjective factors.

We prefer to start with a theoretical foundation in order to explain the fact that hypnotherapy works. Therefore, following an overview of family psychology and therapy, we present our five Master Techniques, which the experienced clinician will modify and enrich *à son goût* once the essence of these techniques is understood. Then, we take you through the three main stages of family therapy, explaining how our method works. Finally, we tackle the difficult issue of evaluation and assessment. Nothing in this field should be employed if there is no sufficient reason to believe that it will be helpful to the clients involved. Evaluation can (should?) be the meeting point of theory and practice.

Only after this foundation can we confidently present our actual work. The "facts" we offer in Part II will make sense with the explanations given in Part I. The thunder, we hope, will have only one reasonable explanation—electrical charges.

3

1

Overview:
Family Psychology
and Therapy

In a sense, family therapy cannot be understood in itself. It takes meaning within the framework of *family psychology*. One of the most outspoken authorities on family psychology is L'Abate (1983,1985a), who emphasizes the importance of prevention over intervention as far as the contribution that *psychology* can make to family functioning. To do family therapy, it is necessary to know about *healthy* family functioning.

In the field of psychology there has been an overemphasis on dysfunction or what others, more loyal to the medical model, call pathology. Courses on abnormal psychology appear in practically every graduate and undergraduate psychology program. Seldom do we find any course on "the psychology of the effective person," "the psychologically healthy individual," "issues of healthy functioning in society," or the like.

The field of family psychology (L'Abate, 1983,1985a) emphasizes prevention of problems and malfunction, although the practitioner is ready to intervene therapeutically when problems arise which interfere with healthy family functioning. Thus family psychology starts with evaluation, moving into prevention, and ending in therapeutic intervention when necessary. According to L'Abate (1985a), it takes a comprehensive approach including biological and cognitive/affective bases of behavior, child development, social psychology, and research methods (including single-case and observational methods). Although the methodical study of family psychology is recent (the American Psychological Association officially recognized family psychology in 1984), the American Association of Marriage and Family Therapy (AAMFT) has emphasized much more than just "therapy." This is a hopeful sign in view of the fact that AAMFT is the standard-setting body in the field of family therapy recognized by both professionals and the Federal government. In the six areas of training required by AAMFT for its clinical members, only two—"marital and family therapy" and "supervised clinical practice"—have a primary focus on dysfunction. The other four areas are, at least in theory, oriented toward healthy functioning. These areas are "human development," "research," "marital and family studies," and "professional studies." But in practice, many family therapists until very recently were pathology-oriented, perhaps because most family therapists came from previous training in traditional programs of a psychological nature, be it professional counseling, social work, pastoral counseling, or similar curricula. Only a small minority of those practicing family therapy came from academic programs specializing in the field of family psychology.

However, since the former Department of Health, Education and Welfare in 1978 recognized AAMFT as the accrediting body for training programs, more and more academic curricula in marital and family therapy have developed. Moreover, many general counseling programs established specialization sequences in marital and family therapy, as the survey of Hollis and Wantz (1982) indicates (see also Bloch & Weiss, 1981; Cooper, Rampage, & Soucy, 1981; Everett, 1979). Because of AAMFT's educational requirements one can hope that younger family therapists will have a healthy-functioning orientation, rather than a pathology bias.

TOTAL PICTURE OF THE FAMILY

To understand healthy functioning, the family cannot be isolated from the social realities in which it exists. Single-parent families, it was predicted by *Newsweek*, will increase dramatically by 1990 (Gelman, Finke, Greenberg, et al., 1985); sexism is still the unwritten law of the land in many areas; dual-career couples may soon become the rule; homosexual households, teenage mothers, voluntary choice against parenthood, single-parent adoption, and many more deviations from what was the norm not too long ago—the nuclear family—are to be considered when trying to understand healthy family functioning in the last part of the twentieth-century in the Western world. Added to these changes are problems that also affect healthy family functioning. Among these are the popularized use of dangerous drugs; family violence; sexual abuse; difficult economic realities victimizing the wage earners; corruption at the highest levels of government, both civil and religious, which in turn undermines respect for authority and the law, weakens traditional moral values, increases the number of homeless in rich societies like the United States, and curtails social services for those who need them the most. The family is in the midst of all this.

What then constitutes healthy family dynamics? We see family health as the coincidence of several vectors, both individual and societal. Healthy family function occurs when the individuals are able to satisfy their basic needs—physical, emotional, intellectual, social, and spiritual. Without getting into an area that would take us too far away from our main concern, we believe that there is no healthy family functioning unless the essential needs of all the family members are met in these five areas. By *spiritual* we mean the human tendency to be creative, to transcend reality through imagination manifested in any art form, in actions that transcend cold reason, logic, and calculation. This, of course, includes but is not limited to religious beliefs, prayer, and rituals.

Regarding the societal vectors, we consider such facts as the opportunity to develop one's talents without prejudice based on sex,

race, religion, physical health, formal education, or age. Another
societal vector is justice, protection from corruption and crime,
freedom to move, change careers, choose partners in business,
marriage, entertainment and religion, in intellectual interests, or
cultural pursuits.

All these variables are required for optimal family functioning.
To overlook these while doing family therapy is myopic. Why are
we meddling in other people's lives? How do we justify this intru-
sion? We can justify this only when it is *not* intrusive. And unless
we keep in view the total picture of the family (as outlined above),
family therapy easily becomes intrusive. Family therapists must
deal with the family in its sociocultural framework or else the therapists' experiences and values will interfere with their work. Since
it is impossible to assimilate another person's or family's beliefs
and culture, the therapeutic model mentioned in the Introduction
begins with *observation*. This is a respectful, value-free, and non-
judgmental acceptance of what the family members are, even of
their "rigid mind-set," as Ritterman (1983) calls it.

MIND SETS

This topic deserves attention in order to understand the mental
activities required of family therapists in the initial step of observation in our clinical paradigm, the OLD C. What follows owes
much to Ritterman (1983), to whom the credit for it should go. To
help people change, as we do in the second step of our model, we
ask people to give up their rigid mind set by enlarging it. They must
recognize new possibilities for themselves, new options—the freedom to act beyond their rigid mind sets. Through the clinical process of "leading," they realize the possibility of breaking the self-
imposed rules, interiorized from their family or societal contexts.
These rules, rigidified into private laws, make change impossible
and, as such, must be repealed. But the repeal of these private laws
in therapy must come from the clients themselves, not from the
therapist.

The rigid mind set is, then, the result of interiorized beliefs.
These can be traced to a source idea that exists outside of ordinary

awareness. From this rigid mind set follow perceptions and behaviors.

An example from clinical practice will help clarify this, adding to the three clear illustrations given by Ritterman (1983, pp. 9–15). Be and Leo requested therapy at Leo's insistence because he felt "pushed away" by Be. They were not married or living together, as reported elsewhere (Negley-Parker & Araoz, 1985b). Be's source idea was "A relationship is a threat to my identity." Before therapy she was not aware of this or of her private law that said "Thou shalt not lose your identity in a relationship as you did in your first marriage." This colored her perception of Leo's behavior and negatively energized her own behavior away from him. He wanted to see her, as a rule, one day a week, understanding her need for autonomy, independence, and solitude. Be perceived even this limited request as an imposition and a curtailment of her freedom. Her refusal to grant him one day a week came also from her source idea. Not until she repealed her "private law" in therapy was she able to change.

Going back to the total context of the family, it is not difficult to understand that the individual's mind set, originating in a source idea, is shaped by both his sociocultural context *and* his own family context. These two contexts must be considered, respected, and worked on in family therapy. Both create the beliefs, superstitions, myths, and blind faith contributing to what Watzlawick (1984) called the *invented reality* and Goleman (1985) called the *vital lies*. This self-made reality shapes our preception and our interpretation of our experiences, although we seldom are aware of it.

To some extent we all have a rigid mind set. I (DLA) was raised a Catholic. For many years I was not able to question dogmas such as transubstantiation, papal infallibility, resurrection, and virgin birth. My faith kept confirming my rigid mind set, which had originated from the source idea "My mother's faith must be mine. No questions should be asked in matters of faith." The personal law emanating from this was "Thou shalt keep your faith, even if it kills you (martyrdom)." It is important to become aware of our rigid mind set, for only then can we embrace freely whatever beliefs *we* choose.

THE RIGID MIND SET AND THERAPY

Interviewing families requires more than just family therapy skills. The needed understanding of the psychological concept of mind set is an example. We use our therapy model to evaluate the mental sets of the family members in order to identify familial sociocultural contexts. These not only produce the rigid mind set but generally affect perceptions and behaviors in both constructive and limiting ways. As was mentioned in the Introduction, we try to start from strengths and positive resources in the family and its members. However, in searching for these elements one invariably comes across the rigid mind set. This perpetuates itself through negative self-hypnosis (NSH), which, in turn, produces self-fulfilling prophecies (Araoz, 1985). These confirm the rigid mind set completing a tight cycle which repeats itself again and again, as will be explained presently.

In the case of Be, every time Leo brought up anything related to his one day a week with her, he unknowingly activated her source idea and its corresponding imperative. Her reaction was to protect herself from the supposed threat to her identity. Without realizing it, she was using typical NSH thoughts: "If I do it because he wants it, I'm putting him first and denying my identity," or "If I see him because he wants me to, I'm allowing him to dominate me." In family therapy, therefore, NSH can be seen as any thought used to reinforce one's rigid mind set. We contend that unless this negative self-hypnosis is acknowledged and recognized, we cannot help families improve. Therefore, the easiest way to the rigid mind set is by uncovering NSH. In family therapy, an effective way to do this is to ask the person, as Be was asked, to get in touch with what happens inside of her when the other person behaves in such and such a way. Since the rigid mind set needs NSH to survive, only by stopping NSH can the mind set cease to be rigid. Once the individual has recognized *NSH* he can start to challenge the *source idea* which produces the *rigid mind set* and, in so challenging, his options multiply, his perception expands, and the interpretation of his world stops being subjectively dogmatic. The individual is also able to trace the roots of the rigid mind set and recognize as fallible the family or sociocultural context in which it developed.

The chronological sequence that the therapeutic intervention of uncovering NSH reverses is

context (family/sociocultural) → source idea → rigid mind set → NSH

The last two elements in this sequence form an endless self-feeding loop. Only an external factor can stop it, such as accident or sickness; unusual insight from a powerful message; dramatic changes in status, such as in marriage or job; unexpected turns of fortune; or therapy. Otherwise, the self-feeding loop often produces self-fulfilling prophecies, as mentioned earlier. These in turn become another form of NSH. And so on and so on.

To summarize, Be found in therapy that Leo's interest in her elicited "thoughts" that took two forms: affirmations or statements ("If I say yes to this, he'll want more," "Every weekend, as he wants, doesn't give me any time for myself," etc.) and mental imagery (seeing herself unhappy with Leo as she had been with her husband, bored in the car or in the house together, enduring long silences and talking only in a negative or rough manner, mainly to complain about something). Before family therapy Be had not been aware of this mental activity of hers. Now she realized that when she refused Leo's reasonable demands she was actually following her own "hypnotic" suggestions (her own affirmations and imagery).

The therapeutic use of NSH is twofold or, rather, may go in two directions. *Symptomatically*, the client is encouraged to use different, though true, affirmations (in this case, they were statements like "He is different from my ex," "He's always treated me with respect," "He does take my feelings seriously"). The client is also taught to foster different imagery: to relive good times he or she had together with a mate on a trip, in bed, in the car, and so on. When we asked Be to relive these moments, her spontaneous comment was, "I can't think of any time with Leo that was not good."

The other therapeutic use of NSH is to trace it back to its origins. Here is where the client finds herself face to face with her rigid mind set, which says, "I can't react in any other way" or, "This is the only way to handle this situation." From her NSH, Be discovered the source idea or belief at the core of her rigid mind set, "A relationship is a threat to my identity," expressed in many different ways from day to day. She understood from this discovery that *the familial context* which had produced this belief was, in reverse order, first her former husband and second her parents, whose traditional marriage had placed her mother in a subservient and inferior role to her father. The private law emanating from the source idea was basically correct and true ("Thou shalt not lose your identity in a relationship as you did in your first marriage"), but her application of it was exaggerated. Whereas before family therapy she had been thinking in *either–or* terms ("Either I am my own person or I lose myself in a relationship"), now she was able to think in *and–also* terms. In other words, Be was able to realize that a good, positive relationship can enhance her identity and sense of selfhood.

The *sociocultural context* contributing to Be's source idea included her self-awareness as a woman, as well as her reaction against the traditional roles of women during the years of her growing up. "I hate the Mrs. John Smith" thing, she repeated, meaning the obliteration of a woman's identity and its fusion with that of the husband who ended up as the one lending his identity to the woman.

In family therapy, unlike what happens in individual counseling, the couple literally works together. This means that, after Be and Leo had gone over all the foregoing material in the therapy sessions, it was Leo's obligation to act more tactfully and, when appropriate, to remind Be in agreed-upon terms or ways of his genuine intention to respect her as an individual.

FUNCTIONAL CONTEXT

The mind-set concept leads to two other aspects of family therapy emanating directly from psychology, the *function* of behavior in its familial *context*. Because they are so intertwined, they can be considered one principle. Since *the contextual aspects of behavior* are easier to explain, we address them first. Context simply means that individual behavior can be understood only in the systemic circumstances in which it takes place. The use of a contextual view "is perhaps the single most important skill the family therapist must have," say Alexander and Parsons (1982, p.10), and we agree. Our clinical paradigm's first step—*observe*—is meaningful only in the family context. Only as each member relates to the others can behavior take on significance. This is what Ritterman (1983) has described as a type of mutual hypnosis that takes place among family members: one's behavior is elicited by the other's and so on and on. No behavioral injunction, including those of the Ten Commandments, makes any sense out of context or in and of itself. And without awareness of the context—how family members *inter*-act—no therapeutic intervention will be effective.

To become aware of the behavioral context, the family hypnotherapist must constantly ask questions such as:

1. When does this (behavior) happen?
2. What is person A trying to get from person B?
3. Who elicits this behavior?
4. What happened just before this behavior took place?

However, context in family therapy includes elements of the family's history, or of the relationship that has developed between certain family members through the years. Consequently the therapist must also ask:

1. What relationship exists between persons A and B?
2. What does A expect of B?
3. When does A overreact to B?
4. In whose presence is A sensitive to B?

Questions like these help us acquire the contextual view of family interaction. In the case of Be and Leo, she had perceived him at the beginning of their relationship as "manipulative, pushy, stubborn, and too strong." Even though Leo had effectively changed, that original perception of Be's was still coloring her view of his behavior: every time he expressed a want, she saw it as a demand. Reciprocally, each time Be refused the smallest request, Leo saw it as rejection and as an indication of her lack of commitment. Recognizing the contextual aspects of their behavior was a big step toward a more mature and satisfying relationship.

However, the other psychological element mentioned at the start of this section is intimately intermingled with that of the familial context. This is *the function of behavior* or the results that a behavior between A and B produces in C. The third party might be a family member or an outsider. By pushing Leo away, Be was "telling" her 24-year-old son, who disliked Leo intensely, not to worry and to continue liking her. Alexander and Parsons (1982) refer to "personal payoffs" for the one engaging in a particular way of acting. Be's personal payoff in rejecting Leo was to attract her son to her. It is obvious that there might be many payoffs for a person: since Leo was financially well-to-do, Be's former husband had started to be remiss in payments agreed upon in the divorce settlement. By distancing from Leo and thus befriending her son, Be was also obtaining an advocate for her cause since the only child her former husband listened to was the son.

Since the actions between family members are strongly interdependent, one positive outcome of family therapy is to untangle this complicated set of relationships. Only when this couple realizes the functions of Be's behavior toward Leo—or the results that her behavior toward Leo has on other members of the family constellation—can they produce effective change for their mutual greater benefit. Leo's reaction to Be's distancing had been to end the relationship, but when he understood the functional context of her behavior, he was able to move past his anger and find alternative ways of handling the situation. He worked on befriending Be's son; he sent business to her former husband and met him through business; and, above all, he became even less aggressive than before in requesting ("demanding" in Be's perception) more time together. A year later they were married at Be's insistence.

FAMILY PSYCHOLOGY

To return to the concept mentioned at the beginning of this chapter, the contribution of *family psychology* to therapy is threefold: theory testing, evaluation, and prevention (L'Abate, 1983), leading to mutually compatible combinations in family therapy. These combinations become practice stemming from proven theory; practice providing new data for research; and therapy that is concerned with prevention of future difficulties.

Theory Testing

Hansen and L'Abate (1982) complained of the rampant pseudo-theories and "theorettes" in the field of family therapy, which are empty, rhetorical, and sterile. The need for testable theorizing comes from the professional imperative to link methods of intervention to theories. This is an essential aspect of psychological assessment. Otherwise the field will continue to mushroom with nonsystematic and gimmicky techniques rather than developing methods that can be repeated and reproduced systematically.

The clinical example of Be and Leo is rooted in two testable theories, one relating to human change in general, the other corresponding to the method used. The latter, in turn, comprises the theory of NSH and validates the clinical procedure used—the OLD C model.

The theory of human change has been researched, explained, and tested by several of the authors from the Mental Research Institute (MRI) in Palo Alto, as well as by others influenced by the MRI such as de Shazer (1985). This theory basically states that meaningful human change (*metanoia*, or change from within) transcends reason, logic, and argument (Fisch, Weakland, & Segal, 1982: Watzlawick et al., 1974).

The second theory, regarding NSH, has been developed and tested since 1981. The good reception accorded NSH (e.g., Blumenthal, 1984; Ellis, 1985; Golden & Friedberg, 1986) further indicates its usefulness. Regarding the method or clinical procedure employed, it is based on the OLD C paradigm, fully explained elsewhere (Araoz, 1985). This method is derived from the general theory of human change and follows broadly the Ericksonian outline of therapeutic intervention, as explicated by Rossi (1980). In theoretical terms, it could be stated that to follow these steps in clinical psychological work is conducive to human change. This method has been tested with regular families (Araoz & Negley-Parker, 1985; Negley-Parker & Araoz, 1985b), with families of chronically ill children (Negley-Parker & Araoz, 1986), as well as with student nurses coping with stress (Negley-Parker & Araoz, 1985a).

We saw that Be *changed* not through reasoning but through inner awareness of her NSH and its familial and sociocultural roots. To modify her source idea, the use of imagination was effective, while other methods attempted by Leo, before requesting therapy, had failed, even though both people involved were intelligent, educated, well motivated, and sincere. Leo, on the other hand, *changed* in his interaction with Be, allowing her to change. The behavioral mutuality bears witness to the functional context of family interaction. Both changed because of a fresh perspective on their behavior and its functions.

Evaluation

This refers to the professional responsibility to make sure that what one is doing is right, indeed is *the best* one can do at this point for this client (individual or family). Evaluation is a way to objectify information about both theory and interventions (see Chapter 6). Psychology has developed methods for evaluation from the early days of Wilhelm Wundt and Francis Galton, refining them further through the work of the behaviorists. Clinical psychology differs greatly from experimental in that the former is concerned with helping the individual, whereas the latter is concerned with averages and independent variables that will prove or disprove particular hypotheses. However, clinical psychology must regard with respect the concern with evaluation that the laboratory psychologist has shown. Without it our work becomes confusing at best and chaotic at worst. If perchance we do something effective, without evaluation "we have lost it" because we have not paid close attention to the procedure used, the steps taken, the timing, and other circumstances. Evaluation is especially needed in family therapy to compensate for the quasi-religiosity of fads mentioned in the Introduction. Some brave attempts at self-criticism are welcome signs (see Salin, 1985; Schwartz & Perrotta, 1985; Walters, 1985; Wright, 1985).

The research outlined in the Preface is an example of our attempt to evaluate the work we do. We learned the most from the 10 families interviewed. As was indicated, they had responded to the written questionnaire and had been ranked on two scales, one regarding *attitude* toward therapy and the other *clarity* in expressing their reactions to their family therapy experience in the questionnaire. As mentioned, we selected two families with high scores, two with low scores, and one each with average scores for each scale. From the information thus obtained, we learned that people appreciated the fact that we encouraged them to get in touch with whatever was going on in their inner mind at the moment. "You taught me to get in touch with myself," we were told in different ways by many of the former clients. Others indicated that, after a while, they had learned this method and knew that it had to be "experience first, then talk, then experience again," the last three steps in the OLD C model. They found it useful and beneficial. In fact, even among the low-ranking families, several people mentioned spontaneously that they had used this approach in other areas of their lives since their experience of therapy. Everyone talked about the "surprises" they had when seemingly unrelated things came up and were quickly connected in their mind in some meaningful way without intellectual effort. The fact that all the 50 families in the written report and the 10 in the interviews stated that they were in agreement with this method to obtain meaningful change (either to strengthen family life or to obtain a divorce) further confirms the method.

Evaluation obviously does not always have to be positive. A negative evaluation may influence one to take an objective view of the therapy method in question.

The case thus far used for clinical illustration points to the built-in evaluation in the OLD C model (see Introduction). Every segment ends with the hypnotic practice of *checking* to evaluate the previous experience made possible through the therapist's *leading*. Thus when Leo "accepted" Be's explanation justifying less contact than he wanted, he was asked to check how his whole self (not just his "reason") was reacting to it. In the process of checking, he became aware of important feelings he had been rationalizing away. What he had accepted rationally was still far from being integrated by his innermost self. Be, on the other hand, was able to evaluate her decision, first of not seeing Leo every week and, later, of compromising with her initial position, also through the method of hypnotherapy—through an awareness of her inner experience at the moment it was taking place, not by mere reasoning. As an aside, it is very important to emphasize that this method is not "unintellectual." Rather, it integrates the inner experience with the rational mind, based on the proven fact that self-attribution is more effective in human behavior change than external influences (Kopel & Arkowitz, 1975; Olson & Dowd, 1984).

The "scientific" aspect of this work lies in the concern with research *while* family therapy is carried forward according to an established clinical paradigm. By "scientific" and "research" we, like Lieberman (1977), mean much more than the so-called scientific method, which, in clinical work, is not the best method to find the truth about the worth of our work.

Prevention

Community psychology refined the concept of prevention, distinguishing three types (Mace, 1983). There is an important point to be made in favor of applying prevention to families and their interactions. The concept will help family members view therapy as a way of preventing future recurrences of similar problems and of teaching families effective methods of interaction; it can also offer nontherapy preventive services to families who, though functional, are at risk of future breakdown. If the principal focus is on family *therapy*, one risks a skewed perception of reality (one invents his own reality?), believing that self-limiting conflicts are the rule. (Again, there is a need for evaluative studies to obtain objective information.)

Perhaps one explanation for the lack of emphasis on prevention is merely political. To obtain the respect and consideration awarded doctors in our society, we must do therapy, we must cure. Prevention is largely a teaching function. And in a young, changing society, where a 200-year history is considered tradition, teachers are not revered, as they are in ancient cultures. Among us, teachers teach skills, not wisdom. How to do it is more important than philosophy providing principles and general norms. The American Association of Marriage and Family Therapy used to have *counseling* in its name, but even this organization changed to *therapy* because of political pressures.

We see prevention both as an essential part of any good therapy and as an entity in itself. More than "a part" of psychotherapy, prevention ought to be a natural by-product of it. If therapy is effective, one of the unavoidable consequences is that the family will have learned (sorry about the connection with teaching once more) attitudes, techniques, and ways of handling conflict more productively; communication skills which are effective; mutual respect of needs, feelings, perceptions, and moods; sensitivity and consideration toward each other; and a joyful family philosophy or set of values which has become enriching of all the family members. This ideal outcome is often attained indirectly. The presenting problem solved serves as a model, in many cases, to other solutions in other areas of difficulty or dissatisfaction within the family relations.

To return to Be and Leo, she became more yielding and giving after having worked on the conflict between her needs and her responsibility toward Leo or her commitment to the relationship. Leo became more sensitive to Be's "personal" needs, related to her identity and self-definition. Both of these outcomes are preventive of future difficulties in this area. But because this one area was so basic in their relationship, the benefits derived here become easily generalized to other areas as well, enriching the relationship as a whole.

However, prevention is also an entity in its own right, separate from therapy. Thus enrichment programs and seminars such as the popularized Marriage Encounter, or Dinkmeyer's STEP (Systematic Training for Effective Parenting) (Dinkmeyer & McKay, 1976), those of the Association of Couples for Marriage Enrichment (ACME) founded by Vera Mace and David Mace (1975), and the Couples Communication Program (Miller, Wackman, & Nunnally,

1983) are all methodical programs of an educational rather than therapeutic nature.

The apparent lack of concern with therapy shared by these programs comes from a clear definition of their goals, which include enrichment of an already healthy, viable, and basically satisfying relationship. This nontherapy attitude is welcomed because it makes logical sense and keeps things clean, without the dishonesty of offering enrichment programs in order to lasso couples and families into private therapy. On the other hand, for therapists not to be concerned with prevention borders on the unethical and may betray a vested interest in having families return to therapy again and again. Preventers should avoid therapy, but therapists should be concerned with prevention. L'Abate (1985b) is not clear when he claims that *both* practices should be united synergistically. Prevention becomes contaminated by therapy.

SUMMARY

Since family therapy is the application of psychological principles to the interaction within a natural social system, it seems to be advantageous to begin at what recently has been called family psychology. The three main contributions of psychology to family functioning are theory testing, assessment and evaluation, and prevention. These call attention primarily to *healthy* family living, which is a convenient point of departure for the family psychotherapist. However, since the family is far from an isolated unit but exists within the larger system of *society with its culture*, this too has to be taken into consideration by family therapy. Moreover, because culture affects perception and behavior, the family members' *mind set* must be understood and the *rigid mind sets* made wider and open in order to change the *functions of behavior* among family members and thus improve (make more satisfying and enjoyable) the *family context*.

The running commentary on Be and Leo, a couple with problems of relating, exemplifies the clinical application of the psychological concepts underlying therapeutic interventions with a family.

2

The Five Master Techniques of Family Hypnotherapy

The master techniques are techniques that have been found useful with a great variety of problems or difficult situations. They are used typically during the middle and final stages of family hypnotherapy. De Shazer (1985) calls them "skeleton keys," consistent with the title of his book. The ideological position taken by de Shazer sounds unorthodox and almost iconoclastic:

> The therapist need not know many details of the complaint in order to at least initiate the solution of the problem. The interventions, therefore, need only prompt the initiation of some *new* behavior patterns. The exact nature of the trouble does not seem important to effectively generating solutions, because the intervention needs only to fit. Just a skeleton key is called for, not the one-and-only key designed to specifically match the specific lock. (de Shazer, 1985, p. 199)

In the New Hypnosis, as it is applied to family therapy, we have found five master techniques. These, like de Shazer's skeleton keys, can open many locks and give us access to many doors as

21

family hypnotherapists. Whereas de Shazer does not restrict himself to "hypnotic" techniques, the five we discuss in this chapter *are* hypnotic.

Of the five master techniques, one is future-oriented, *Mental Rehearsal*, which has two modalities, *Goal Attainment* and *Change Process*. Another master technique is past-oriented, *Past Accomplishments*, and related to this is *Inner Wisdom*. The last two— *Activation of Personality Parts* and *Positive Outlook*, or reframing— focus on true positive aspects of one's personality or the situation to which one is reacting. The next sections describe these techniques and explain how they can be applied in family hypnotherapy.

MENTAL REHEARSAL

Generally speaking, Mental Rehearsal is a cognitive/experiential method to prepare oneself for future situations. Athletes use this to improve their performance. Common sense moves many unsophisticated people to "prepare" themselves mentally for difficult situations. People "psyche" themselves up to face things that produce fear and panic. Hypnotically clients can learn to use this common "mental trick" in a methodical way.

Strictly speaking Mental Rehearsal has two aspects. When we visualize the attained goal we have in mind and experience ourselves already there, we call it Goal Attainment, but when we rehearse mentally the steps we need to take in order to attain our goal, we describe this technique as Change Process. Both are discussed in detail.

Goal Attainment

Zilbergeld (1986) called this "result imagery or goal imagery" (pp. 204–210). In this technique "the client in a relaxed state (hypnosis) imagines over and over again having accomplished his goals and what his life would be like given that accomplishment" and, later, "the client is instructed to imagine how he would feel, be and act in different situations, given that he has achieved his goals" (p. 206). Zilbergeld concludes that "result imagery gives a client opportunities to experiment with new self-images. In imagining himself being certain ways, he starts changing the way he looks at himself, which in turn allows him to change his behavior and to integrate those changes in a consistent and meaningful pattern" (p. 210).

The ultimate purpose of *Goal Attainment*, as a hypnotic technique, is to help people change their self-image. As long as people "see themselves" as anything (impatient, uncaring, irritable, nongiving, or any other negative self-definition) they force themselves to act that way. As Zilbergeld says, "Most clients build an identity or image based on their problem" (p. 206). Because of this, Goal Attainment uses the same mental process, reversing it by sharply focusing on the goal clients believe they can attain. It must be noticed that this method is simply a change of focus and concentration. Rather than wasting energy and time on "the problem," clients are encouraged to hypnotically imagine again and again how things will actually be when there is no problem. This "hypnotic imagination" is a detailed, prolonged, attentive, and vivid mental representation of the attainable goal, *as if it had been attained already*, while being in a relaxed, concentrated state of mind and body. Unlike a simple way of imagining, in which I quickly represent in my mind something, hypnotic imagination becomes a goal-directed daydream, "a focused state of awareness," to quote Zilbergeld (1986, p. 206) once more, in which I detach myself from my surrounding reality, thus making my inner reality my main center of attention. The family hypnotherapist must be careful to insist on staying with the attained goal, rather than with the process by which this goal can (and will) be attained.

The process of attaining a goal is what the next technique is all about, as will be explained presently. Often these two techniques can be combined, but we prefer to concentrate on Goal Attainment first. Many people become so fascinated by this mind exercise that they do not need to practice Change Process. For those who respond positively to Goal Attainment, the goal or result they are after becomes, as one father described it, a "therapeutic obsession." Once he was able to see himself clearly the way he knew he could be, once he experienced how good this felt by tasting his new state of being in his mind, he had no choice: he had to keep this goal in sight until he had reached it. This was a case of a father, married for the second time to a woman who had three children of her own from her previous marriage. The "loudness" of two of her teenaged children used to "drive him crazy." He would react to their loud music, their arguing, and their shouting by "losing his temper" and hollering himself, only adding to the already upsetting situation. By practicing Goal Attainment he resolved the problem. What he saw as his goal was to be able to completely ignore the children's loudness. He became so happy with this goal that he found the means not to pay attention to their noises and, instead, to concentrate on happy thoughts. The children's shouting itself became the trigger for his inner peace and state of contentment.

In another case, a mother who had thoughts of killing her child, a 10-year-old boy, and who had seen several psychiatrists without finding relief from different types of medication, learned to concentrate so intensely on her feelings of love for the boy that in merely a few days she was able to use any thought about her son as a stimulus for all the positive feelings she had toward him.

A third example is that of a teenager brought up in a very religious home in which sex had been considered sinful. Away in college, he had fantasies of self-mutilation, since his penis was the center of his sinful thoughts. Goal Attainment, in combination with True Statements (Araoz, 1982, p. 153), was used effectively. He accepted the statement that his body was good and holy and that sex was God's invention and consequently also good. His goal was to react to any sexual awareness with a sense of gratitude to God and peace of mind. Eventually he even learned to accept sexual pleasure as desirable, honorable, and good. This 18-year-old and the young woman he loved, who attended the same college away from home, had come to see us because of his constant worry about not sinning sexually. By helping him, with the assistance of his girlfriend, to find a true statement about sex in his inner mind, we were able to establish the goal stated. He concentrated on it, reviewing how wonderful it was to react positively to his sexual awareness, his erections, and his arousal. This exercise led him to maturely question many of the "false statements" about sex, bodily pleasure, and eroticism that he had received from his grand-mother, the woman who had raised him in lieu of his mother, who had been only 16 years old at the time he was born.

Goal Attainment is a very flexible technique. It does not imply that we, the therapists, decide what the client's goal should be. The therapists help the client identify the goal that is desirable, reasonable, and possible. Then the client is led to experience in the innermost mind all the good feelings attached to having attained that goal. This repeated exercise starts changing one's self-definition. In the preceding case, the client was defining himself as one who considers sex negatively. In the practice of Goal Attainment he found a new definition of himself as one who views sex positively, maturely, and responsibly, accepting the pleasures and joys related to it.

Rather than following Zilbergeld's (1986, p. 206) suggestion to imagine how the client "would feel, be and act in different situations given that he has achieved his goals," we proceed differently. The client is asked to visualize the goals he or she has in mind very concretely and in detail. Then we select with the client one specific goal and ask the client to place herself there, as if the goal had been reached already. It is not to feel how she "would feel," but "to be already there." This is a form of age progression. The clients are already "living" in their mind the new reality of the goal attained and enjoyed. This "previvification," as we describe it to clients (as opposed to the traditional "revivification" of past events, appropriate to another master technique, Past Accomplishments) has to become very vivid and real. Here is where hypnosis is necessary. You cannot just talk about it. You must "live" it in your mind. The story is told that Picasso used to sit and stare at the empty canvas for a long time before he started to paint. They say that he seemed to be completely absorbed in that vision of what he was going to paint on that canvas. Was he in a trance? Was he visualizing his "goal," what he intended to paint on that surface? We think so. Picasso was practicing Goal Attainment, complete with the hypnotic state of mind and all.

We insist on helping family members to get into this new reality of their possibilities: what they can accomplish and do. We don't ask them to imagine how it "would feel" to be there. We put them there, or, rather, we help them put themselves there. Once they have experienced themselves as having achieved their goal, they are "programming" themselves to achieve it in their daily reality. It is as if their whole life is moving toward that goal, once they have relished it and enjoyed it in their inner mind. This is what popular authors in management consulting (see Araoz, 1984a) describe as sharply visualizing one's goal before one starts to take any action. Goal Attainment, then, is a flexible and useful technique to help family members attain what they want. We usually emphasize the role that each person will play in the "new reality" of a more satisfying family: not what the others are supposed to do—this is what family members usually talk about at the beginning if the therapist allows it—but what "I can do to improve the situation."

Goal Attainment usually is the first master technique we employ. It serves as a diagnostic measure in the sense that we can predict where prople stand. If family members cannot visualize their goal and "see themselves" there, we may be dealing with resistance. Then we address that resistance with Activation of Personality Parts, a technique explained later in this chapter. But if the family is able to benefit from Goal Attainment, we know that we can help the family move rapidly toward their goals. We introduce this technique by using words like the following:

> Now that you are relaxed and concentrating on what is going on inside of you, make an effort to see yourselves the way you believe things could be in your family. We'll discuss all this later. Now, simply let your mind easily concentrate on what you want your family to be. See yourself in this changed family. Your parents, your children, you, enjoying things much more than ever before. Pick one situation in your family life. It may be early morning, when everybody is rushing to get to work or to school. Stay with it and make it the way you want it to be. Take your time and enjoy what you are experiencing. Look at the whole thing from this new perspective. The way it can be. The way you want it to be. The way it is *now* in your mind. Enjoy what you are experiencing right now. Put it in

> slow motion and let it run in front of your mind's eye. . . . You may now think of something different. Mealtime, perhaps. Again, stop and enjoy what you are experiencing in your mind. It can be that way. You *are* in the family that you find so enjoyable, so wonderful for yourself. Take a slow look at what you see in your mind's eye: the way everybody acts, listen to what they say, to what you say, look at their faces: everybody is happy to be part of this family; to be in this family. You listen to each other, you *care*. You love each other, effectively, really, truly. Everyone in this family is important to you and you are proud to belong to this family. Your family.

This type of hypnotic talk is continued as long as it is necessary, according to what is happening to the family members. One cannot "prepare" this type of speech; the above is merely an illustration.

Depending on the specific goal of each family, the words you use will change. It should be remembered also that often the family comes to therapy because of the problem of one of its members. Even though we know that the problem of one family member is also that of the others—much as in sex therapy, the dysfunction of one partner is also the problem of the other—we accept initially their own view of the situation but involve the whole family in Goal Attainment by saying something like the following:

> Now that you are all relaxed and concentrating on what brought you here, you may want to review the whole situation from a new perspective. Look at (Johnnie's) problem and ask yourself, Can I do something to help him? Let that question echo inside of you. Let that question reach your insides: your brain, your heart, your gut. Perhaps you have missed something before. Now that you are using self-hypnosis, you may discover something you had missed before. What can I do to help (Johnnie)? Is there anything I can do? Don't strain yourselves. Let your inner mind go to work. Let your inner mind search for the truth . . . And now see yourselves after the problem. The problem is a thing of the past. Johnnie is quite OK now. There is no problem. You can remember the difficult

times you went through. But now you can be grateful that all that is over. Forever finished. What a relief! And look at what *you* did to make it better. Look back and review what your contribution was to improve Johnnie's situation. Give yourself credit for your contribution, for what you did. Feel good about it.

Goal Attainment, then, can be used in many different ways with the family. Because of this, we designate it as one of the master techniques of family hypnotherapy.

Change Process

Mental Rehearsal may also focus on the process of change, rather than on the goal itself. It also is future-oriented. We use it when the Goal Attainment technique does not work right away. If after trying Goal Attainment once or twice, we sense that the family finds it difficult to visualize the goals they want to reach, we move on to Change Process. At times this is called mental rehearsal, although this name can refer also to Goal Attainment, but to stress the concentration on *the process* of change, we call it Change Process. Simply put, this master technique encourages family members to go over, in their inner mind, the steps they have to take to make change possible. It becomes especially useful at the discussion point. When family members exchange their ideas of what steps should be taken to attain what they want, the ground is ready for compromise, negotiation, and ultimately cooperation. But our experience is that to engage the family in such discussion without having led them through Change Process is a waste of time. People can talk profusely about the steps to be taken to attain certain goals, but unless they visualize those steps and rehearse them in their minds, the discussion becomes long and unproductive. Once they had "gone through the steps" in their inner minds, it becomes much more real and profitable to discuss concretely what each can do to improve the general situation that bothers them and brings them to therapy. As can be understood, Change Process assumes that the family has agreed on what they want. You cannot plan and visualize steps to be taken unless you know where you want to go. Consequently, before applying this master technique, the therapists have to help the family come to an agreement on what they want to attain as a unit.

Change Process then concentrates on the steps to be taken to get somewhere. We encourage the family to "prelive" the sacrifices they may have to make to improve the family situation.

For instance, a single mother of a 14-year-old girl was losing control of her daughter, who had become openly defiant, critical of her mother, and generally rebellious. The mother felt too insecure about her daughter's love to impose firm discipline on her. Change Process allowed the mother to take one step at a time, mentally role playing every detail of possible confrontations with her daughter. She would practice Change Process in her therapy session until she felt confident that she could control the daughter, although the awareness of how good she herself felt being able to fulfill her parental role was what she liked most in this mind exercise. During the week she would actually put into practice what she had rehearsed mentally in her previous therapy session. As her success increased, the mother became increasingly confident and the daughter felt more secure and protected from her own impulsive behavior; in a few weeks the two of them were able to attend family hypnotherapy sessions to start negotiating issues such as distributing the household chores or doing homework.

Since Change Process is mental rehearsal or role playing of situations that the client does not believe she can handle properly, it is important to be very patient and to move extremely slowly at first. Each small discrete action should be "practiced" repeatedly until the client is sure she can do it in the difficult situation outside of therapy. This master technique fails when the therapists try to cover too much ground. In the preceding case, the mother had to rehearse how to talk to her daughter, when to do it, in what room of the house, and so on. She had to be very clear in her mental practice about the point she wanted to bring up to her daughter. Often in postulating in her mind how the daughter would react, the mother realized that she was not focused enough on one issue and through Change Process she cleaned the one issue she was interested in of any "adhesions," as she came to call them, of other side topics. Change Process, then, often helps improve one's communication through a preview of the manner in which one comes across to the other person. One of our clients described this exercise in terms of modern typewriters which do not print directly on the paper but allow the typist to watch on a screen what has been keyed in before it is printed. Only after the "preview" shows that the typed text is correct is it transferred from the memory in the machine to the paper.

To apply Change Process, we always start with a moment of "self-centering," or "going inside of yourself." This leads to a visualization of the place where the new behavior is to take place. Any and all circumstances that make this place more vivid should be used: time of day, surrounding furniture, and so on. The client should be aware of her emotional and mental state whether it be nervousness, fear, or any other unpleasant affective state. At this point the therapist encounters negative self-hypnosis, when the client emphasizes the negative feelings rather than what she is about to learn through the practice of Change Process. If negative self-hypnosis is at work, the therapist needs to verbalize for the client such ego-strengthening statements as, "I'm about to learn a new way of handling this difficult situation. I'll finally be free of this anxiety (or whatever the negative experience has been). I know I can learn a new way of handling this (person or situation) so that I master this encounter (or situation) and I do want to do so." This way of counteracting negative self-hypnosis is necessary as a preliminary to Change Process. The therapist who misses the client's negative self-hypnosis wastes time: while the client is led through a new behavior, the client has not stopped giving himself or herself self-defeating messages.

The actual Change Process technique varies immensely with the circumstances of the situation. The following wording is given as mere illustration of it. The family was grieving over the death of a son, 34 years of age, who had taken an overdose of cocaine. They had been blaming each other: so and so had not contacted the brother in several months; the mother had lost her temper with him two days before the overdose; the father had refused to lend him some money he said he needed for his rent; another brother had actually used cocaine with him on several occasions in the past year, and so on. What happened was that every time two or more family members got together, they would start this fruitless blaming of each other, and they felt they needed help to stop doing this. After working through the anger they felt at their deceased relative for what "he had done to them," we taught them to use Change Process. The following is an excerpt of one of the sessions with the mother, a brother, and a sister. The dead man had been the oldest of the four children (three men and a woman, who was the youngest at 27). This is an example of how to use Change Process with several family members at once:

> Before you visualize yourselves with each other, get in touch with the positive feelings you have toward each other. Say to yourself, "I love my brother (children)" and let this statement become very real, very true. Allow your whole being to relish this true statement of fact. I love my (brother, sister, children). Repeat it to yourself until you feel very good about it. . . . Now see yourself together, perhaps in your parents' living room. Go slowly. Pick up good memories, good feelings attached to your parents' living room. You are there. Be clear in your mind: see yourself there, sitting or standing or reclining on the couch. Now, in your mind's eye, let another family member come into the living room. Connect again with your positive feelings about this family member. Hear yourself talking to him or her. Just regular chitchat. Notice that you are relaxed. Are you getting into this? Both of you remember Jeff (the dead brother) but you don't talk about him. You are concentrating on each other. You are genuinely interested in the other: what's in his or her mind; what has happened in his or her life in the last few days. You care and you feel good about caring about the other. Still with it? Go slowly and enjoy the good feelings between the two of you. Stay with these good feelings for a little while longer. Still OK? Notice that something has changed when you are together. You feel a new but old warmth toward the other and you feel the other's warmth to-

ward you. Enjoy this reality. The beauty of belonging to the same family. The comfort; the security. Imagine clearly the other person standing there or taking a seat. You feel relaxed with each other. You take in what the other is telling you. A very pleasant exchange.

The family practiced this type of mental rehearsal several times, mentally role playing different situations in which they were together, either with one person or with more than one. They also used Change Process to imagine a situation in which one would start blaming others about Jeff's death and how each could defuse it. The report of this family was unanimous: all had learned to avoid blaming and in so doing they had come to terms with Jeff's death. Now their grief and mourning were pure and unpolluted by blame.

Whereas Goal Attainment, as explained in the last section, is a form of age progression, Change Process is a form of mental rehearsal, both techniques used in hypnotherapy by traditional as well as New Hypnosis workers. They are considered "master techniques" because of their great applicability to many different situations. They are not restricted to specific problems and, depending on the therapist's flexibility and creativity, are almost universally useful.

PAST ACCOMPLISHMENTS

While the last two master techniques deal with the future, Past Accomplishments makes use of previous successes and accomplishments. To succeed at something we need a number of skills, both mental and physical. Among the mental skills we have used to succeed at anything in the past we can count such things as attitude and planning. The physical skills comprise a wide range also, involving many senses and motor abilities, from moving to talking to observing and so on. What we frequently need in therapy is to convince clients that they can do what they know is good for them but for whatever reasons they don't believe they are capable of doing. Rational arguments do not work to convince them. What does work is the vivid review of past accomplishments. They know that they have done those things. By reliving them, they get back in touch with their pride, well-being, joy, and other positive feelings that were real in the past. If they experienced themselves as successful then, the chances are that they can experience themselves again as successful. We build on precedent, not on possibilities.

There are several ways of using Past Accomplishments. Two of these are the reliving of any past accomplishment, no matter how unconnected it may seem from what must be done now, and the reliving of an accomplishment similar to the current issue at hand. The rationale for bringing to mind any past accomplishment is this: in doing anything successfully, a person must involve her whole personality. Some of the inner resources, talents, skills, attitudes, and values at work in that past accomplishment *may* be useful now. In this case we may say:

> Be there again. Put yourself in the place, with the people, at the time. You did this (whatever it is) well. You know you accomplished something. You are proud of yourself. Other people recognize, perhaps, that you succeeded. Be there again. Enjoy *now* the good feelings that came from your accomplishment. You are there now. Relive the whole scene. Put yourself in slow motion and enjoy every aspect of your success: what you do, how you look, who is around, how are they reacting, what you see, what you sense, and especially how you feel. Stay with your feeling of accomplishment, success, and pride.

Once the client is fully involved in her success situation, we establish the bridge to the current event:

> Now ask yourself what you can learn, from that great event from the past, for the current task you are thinking about. Some of your attitudes may be helpful now. Some of your actions, talents, skills may lend themselves to what you have to do now. Allow your inner mind to review gently but thoroughly how what you already did and enjoyed can help you now. Perhaps you don't know it yet, but perhaps your past success was a preparation, a dress rehearsal, as it were, for

your future success. You did it before. You can do it again now: succeed, accomplish what you want to accomplish, do well what you want to do now.

One case in which this master technique was beneficial was with a couple who were dealing with the fact that their daughter, 26, who had a delicate heart condition as the result of an accident a few years earlier, refused to follow doctors' orders and insisted on doing strenuous exercise, which could reactivate a dangerous malfunction. The mother had tried to persuade her to stop but her response was that she was an adult and she was going to do what she wanted regardless of what the doctors had told her. The mother worried constantly and the father did not know how to help his wife or what to do. By practicing Past Accomplishments, the mother was able to regain her peace of mind. She indexed an instance in the past in which her daughter had insisted on riding a motorcycle against her parents' wishes. The more they asked her not to do it, the more she boasted of her riding ability. The mother had learned with great effort to stop mentioning the bike to the daughter, then 20. The result was that the daughter had confessed later that she actually was very careful riding the motorcycle, never doing it in traffic and seldom riding on public streets or highways. By reliving the way she had handled the previous situation, the mother realized that she could act in a similar manner now and started rehearsing how she would respond to her daughter when the latter would bring up her exercising.

An example of a successful situation unrelated to the current event was that of a husband who started to become overly jealous about his wife's relationships at work. This was the second marriage for each, and they had a caring and mutually supportive interaction. The husband had never been jealous in the past, but when asked to identify any situation in which he had been successful he thought of a crisis he had had in his business a few years back. He had handled it "superbly," as he put it, and had saved his company a lot of aggravation and money. While reviewing this event he felt again very good about himself. However, when we discussed his mind practice he could not see any connection between that successful event and his current jealousy. Going back into self-hypnosis, ENP kept asking him to relax and trust his inner mind, repeating that something in that past event was probably related to his jealousy. Increasing his relaxation, he said that Charlie's face kept appearing in his mind. He explained that Charlie was the old man who had been security officer at his plant for the last few years. He and Charlie used to chat every day on his breaks. ENP asked him to concentrate on Charlie for a while and to allow anything to come up in his mind. At this point, he said in a sleepy voice, "Security, security. Insecure. That's how I feel. I don't believe she loves me to the point that someone else may not take her away from me."

As it turned out, Charlie had been hired by the client, as part of the "superb" job he did for his company. From here, ENP encouraged him to relive his success and helped him realize what elements of that set of circumstances he could utilize to resolve the jealousy toward his wife. The client "age regressed," as the traditional hypnotherapists would say, and found that he had not paid attention then to the possibility of failure. He had acted "as if" he was going to come up on top of the entangled confusion he had been asked to resolve. Spontaneously, he connected this mental attitude with the current jealousy. He said, "I must believe that she loves me enough not to be tempted." Since she was present during this mind work, it became easy to discuss the issue of trust afterward.

The practice of Past Accomplishments has a wide range of applications. The creative family hypnotherapist will use it smoothly when different family members focus on failures and negativism. The general message clients understand from this practice is that past successes may hide valuable information about their capabilities, inner resources, and talents to be used in the current difficulty. The therapist must be patient, first to help the client find an event in his life that he truly considers outstanding with regard to his way of having handled it. The therapist must also be patient while leading the client, as exemplified at the beginning of this section on Past Accomplishments. Before any mention is made of the current problem, the hypnotherapist must be sure that the client is, indeed, reliving the past success. Only if the client is able to internally experience that triumph anew—as if it were happening all over again in the present—will he be able to transfer elements of it to his present conflict. This has been our experience. The past success has to become real, genuine, and true again, so it can be connected in some way with the present. This, then, is one of the many "bridges" established hypnotically for therapeutic purposes. Watkins and Watkins (1979) explained initially the mechanism of their affective bridge. This is one of the many modifications of it.

The families that have benefited from this master technique have told us repeatedly that it has helped them in many circumstances to counteract negativism and self-defeating thoughts in the face of difficulties in general. By learning this technique people acquire a new method to cope with uncertainty and unwelcome situations. Past Accomplishments seems to generalize spontaneously to other areas of people's lives.

ACTIVATION OF PERSONALITY PARTS

John and Helen Watkins (1979,1981) described this technique in detail. Even though theirs is a psychoanalytical orientation, those who explain human behavior differently can still use this technique effectively. In this case, technique transcends theory. Based on what people commonly express as "part of me wants this, but another part stops me," or similar expressions, the hypnotherapist encourages clients to activate this "personality split." More intense and experiential than the Gestalt technique of assuming different aspects of one's personality and dramatically representing them by changing seats or positions, Activation of Personality Parts allows the client to become fully familiar with different aspects of his total self. More than just being in touch, the client has an opportunity to experience himself as "the other selves" in hypnosis. He becomes first one, then another "person," all true but often unacknowledged aspects of his total self. Watkins and Watkins (1979,1981) refer to ego states, meaning this full owning of different aspects of the self.

In family therapy, the Activation of Personality Parts helps people come to grips with many of the ambivalences that exist in family relations: "I hate him and I love him," "I can't stand her but I want to protect her," "She treats me like garbage but can't do anything without me," and the like. If the family hypnotherapist is observant of people's language, both verbal and somatic, it is easy to find many opportunities to use this master technique. The point of it is to give people a new sense of order and control of their lives. By recognizing different "parts" in themselves, clients find it easier to accept negative aspects of themselves! I am not lazy, but part of me is. She is not mean, but an aspect of her can be very mean. Since there are at least two "parts" in the same person, one can start to balance them and eventually decide which will be the ruler. Ultimately, as Scholastic philosophy holds, "intellectus est gubernare" (reason should be the ruler) and our process to facilitate inner experiencing ends always in the client's rational decision about his life. In the OLD C sequence, "D" is the step in which one discusses rationally what the previous inner experience has taught the individual. Inner experiencing leads to rational decision, without which the inner experience becomes inane.

We shall show practical applications of this master technique in the three case studies to be presented in Part II. However, a typical script of the way we might introduce this concept will illustrate this master technique. We usually take advantage of one of the expressions frequently used by people, as mentioned earlier, indicating at least two aspects of the self:

> It sounds to me that you are really talking about two parts or sides of yourself. You just explained how much you labor to take care of your old parent but, at the same time, you dislike intensely the fact that you are trapped: running home to provide for her and never having free time for yourself. Do you agree that there are these two sides of you, the one who does all this caring and the one that resents it?

The client, a 58-year-old divorced woman who had moved in with her mother, age 80, to take care of her, responded with great emotion, "I don't only resent it, I hate it. I am trapped. I have no life of my own.'' The therapist took advantage of her last statement to stress the Activation of Personality Parts:

> Yet, in spite of the fact that you hate it, you do it. Part of you hates it and part of you does it. Try now to visualize yourself as only one of these two parts. Start with one. Which one will it be? OK, the one who hates doing all this for your mother and hates not having a life of her own. OK, now go inside of yourself and become that side of you in your inner mind. You are that part of you who hates the current situation with your mother. Try to see yourself in that light. How do you appear in your mind's eye? How old are you? How are you dressed? Where are you? Give it time and don't rush it. You—part of you—hates this situation. You can focus on that side of you and see yourself as the one who has no use for what's happening now in your life. (This type of talk is continued until the client is able to get in touch with that part of herself. Then we proceed.)
>
> Now get in touch with all the anger you are experiencing. Let it come closer to your awareness. Yes, I *am* angry. Repeat this to yourself. I am angry at . . . You fill the blank. You are angry, you hate. You hate. . . . Fill the blank. You want to recognize what's going on inside of you. This *is* you. Not the whole of you, it's true, but still *you*. Give yourself permission, right now, to be angry, to hate, to rebel. Experience all the frustration, helplessness, discouragement that's inside of you. Feel all this as much as you can. Because it's there. It's part of you. (This is continued as long as it is necessary for the client to experience that side of herself. Then one continues.)
>
> Now into that picture of yourself hating this current situation, allow the other part of you to step in. Imagine the part that does all the work and caring to come into focus. Put the two parts of you together. Take your time. The hateful you and the devoted you. Both together, meeting, talking. Both are you. Both are right from their own points of view. But you'll start feeling which "you" you want to run your life, which "you" will make the important decisions. Let that concept ex-

pand in you. Both parts of you cannot have the same power and control over your decisions, over your life. Start feeling which part will be the boss, which part will be responsible for the weighty decisions in your life. Hold on to this until you start feeling really good. Feel at peace with yourself. Let the decision-making you talk to the other you. See the two parts together again. The one that runs your life and the other. Let them interact in a loving, respectful way. Let them interact without questions as to who the boss is. (This, again, continues as the hypnotherapist realizes it is useful. Then one concludes with something like the following.)

Now that you are truly in touch with those two parts of yourself, you may want to promise yourself to come back to them again and again, until you are absolutely sure that the one *you* want to be the boss *is* the undisputed boss in your life. (At this point it is useful to associate the experience of greater control over one's life with some external gesture or action— what the neurolinguists call "anchoring.")

We have found that the best "anchoring" is to utilize the position in which the client's hands are at the time and to associate this posture with the therapeutic experience that just occurred. Thus if her hands were gently folded on her lap, the hypnotherapist may say:

Every time your hands rest gently on your lap, the way they are lying there now, the decision-making you will take over. You'll connect again with that part of you and you'll feel great about it. Conversely, when you want to activate the part in you that you want to run your life, it can become easier by resting your hands on your lap. Feel your hands there fully now and imagine that connection between them in that position and the part of you that can take over control of your whole life.

All techniques are means toward enriching the client through a greater freedom of personal choices, especially in perception and attitude, so that the person becomes more able to manage her life with greater ease than before and with greater enjoyment and inner peace. Hypnosis is especially useful to attain this multiple goal of psychotherapy because it allows the individual to experience the self in new ways. The client discovers that she is more than she used to think she was, that she is able to do more things than she thought she could. And within hypnosis, Activation of Personality Parts provides a flexible and highly practical modality for attaining the rich goal pf psychotherapy: Because I experience myself as being able to be different, I become capable of being different, to paraphrase Virgil's "Possunt quia posse videntur," one of the truly genial summaries of the hypnotic process.

POSITIVE OUTLOOK

Reframing is another name for this master technique. Nowadays quite popular among family therapists of all persuasions, reframing is an attempt on the therapist's part to change the frame of reference of the family. In family hypnotherapy, however, this process is eminently *experiential*. Rather than explaining, as others using reframing do, we encourage clients to allow themselves to view the situation (whether behavior of another, motivation, set of circumstances, or sequence of events) differently. We are frequently surprised to discover how quickly people change their frame of reference, at least temporarily and tentatively. If they do not do it spontaneously, without our help, we suggest one new (different) possible way of viewing or understanding what is bothering them. Then, as the next step, we invite them to place themselves mentally in the new frame of reference, to mentally act "as if" the situation were different. The intense imaginative involvement in this exercise is a way of testing the old situation under a new light, as it were, or a way of trying on a new perception, interpretation, and attitude. Ulysses believed that the storms he encountered in his famous odyssey were manifestations of the anger Poseidon, the god of the sea, unleashed toward him. Had he been able to reframe the events as atmospheric manifestations, his whole attitude would have changed and we would have been deprived of the immortal description of his naval adventures. *"Opportunity is nowhere"* can be read as "no–where" or "now–here." Reframing gives clients a chance to change their frame of reference from one that produces dysfunction, creates limitations, and discourages productive human development and growth to one that does the very opposite.

In family hypnotherapy the therapist is engaged in a constant effort to provide new frames for clients. Many examples of nonhypnotic reframing have been provided recently, especially by the paradoxical therapists (L'Abate & Weeks, 1978; Sherman & Fredman, 1986) identified with strategic interventions (Haley, 1976,1980; Madanes, 1981,1984), with brief therapy (de Shazer, 1982,1985), and significantly with the Italian contributions to family therapy (Andolfi, Angelo, Menghi, & Nicolo-Corigliano, 1983; Selvini Palazzoli, Boscolo, Cecchin, & Prata, 1978). We prefer to designate *hypnotic* reframing as the master technique of Positive Outlook to differentiate it from the more prevalent left hemispheric intervention of reframing. Within the family system we encourage all our clients to experience their reactions within their own imaginations while assuming that the same behavior has a different meaning. Thus the child who complains about his mother's nagging is asked to imagine himself hearing her insistent words, looking at her intense face, and so on, but this time saying to himself, "If she didn't love me, she would not pay any attention to me," or something similar. Rather than telling the son that his mother's nagging is a sign of her love and caring, we make it possible for him to live this in his own mind. By "practicing" the new frame of reference, the son tests his reactions. Frequently there is an immediate shift, the child saying something like, "Oh, that's different. I understand that." When we obtain this agreement, we ask the person to go back to the hypnotic experience.

In hypnosis he becomes mentally used to being exposed to the same behavior but it is interpreted by him differently now. This mind exercise is repeated until he feels comfortable with the new, less upsetting reaction to his mother's behavior. Then, by rehearsing "dangerous" situations which he foresees in the fairly near future, he adds self-suggestions based on the new frame of reference which will help him react in the "new" way rather than the way he reacted before when he perceived her actions as nagging. As Sherman and Fredman state, "By reframing the purpose to something

that is positive, the climate of the (family) system is changed"
(1986, p. 198).

As in any form of reframing, hypnotic or purely logical, the therapist's problem is not to violate reality. In the case just mentioned
the mother may be a prepsychotic or otherwise a very disturbed individual whose sadism is evidenced in her nagging. The therapist
must be very discriminating in using any therapeutic intervention,
but especially the paradoxical ones. We shall always remember a
married woman in her early thirties who was having sexual difficulties with her husband. They had been to a sex therapy clinic
where one of the staff had tried to "reframe" an early period of sexual molestation by her father when she was reaching puberty. The
message that this woman received was that her father was showing
his love in a primitive and rudimentary manner, even when he
forced her to submit to sexual coitus.

In systemic thinking, the symptom exists for the self-regulation
of the system. Thus the system requires the symptom. While the
family wants to eliminate the symptom, it does not want to change
the system itself (which "creates" the symptom). Reframing, as
well as other paradoxical interventions, affects the system: it alters
its interpretative balance. Instead of accepting that A happens because of B, a new element is introduced which makes A the result
of C. Thus not only is the recipient's reaction altered, improved,
made less painful, but the elicitor is literally changed. In the case
above, the nagging mother becomes the loving mother. At this
point the symptom can cease to exist. If she is a loving mother,
she'll try to do what pleases the son without hurting him; she'll
trust him and so on. Only when the system is changed can it become functional and fulfilling for all its members. What makes a
system dysfunctional is the frame of reference in which those in the
system are operating. If B does not cause A, B's position in the system changes, and with that change the whole system is altered. But
by changing B's position and role, A's role and position are also
changed: the whole system is now different from before the paradoxical intervention.

Positive Outlook is the hypnotic manner of reframing. An example from a family therapy session may help illustrate how Posi-

tive Outlook is applied. The daughter, aged 14, lives with her mother. The father left the family and keeps minimal contact with the daughter, Marcy. The parents were divorced seven years ago and the father is remarried and he and his second wife have one child. He has not seen Marcy in more than eight years but calls her two or three times a year. Marcy expresses "hate" for her father, who has not supported her since he left her mother. What brings Marcy and her mother to family therapy is that in the last three months Marcy has been found shoplifting twice. The second time her name was placed on a special police list. If she is again found shoplifting, she will be prosecuted through the legal system. Marcy's mother's worry is that the girl does not show any compunction and has become increasingly insulting and disrespectful toward her mother in the last few months. The mother is afraid that Marcy is taking illicit drugs, although Marcy denies this vehemently. The reason her mother worries about this is the drastic change in behavior shown by Marcy lately. At one point in the first session, the following exchange took place:

Marcy: I hate my mother.
ENP: Why do you think your mother is being such a pain in the
    neck?
Marcy: I don't know (shrugging her shoulders and looking away).
ENP: I guess there is a part of you that knows very well why your
    mother is being such a pain in the neck.
Marcy: I don't know . . . I guess.
ENP: (looking at her and waiting) What about the part of you that
    does know why?
Marcy: Well, she thinks I'm being difficult.
ENP: And what else?
Marcy: What do you mean?
ENP: What else does your mother think that you are?
Mother: I can't take it any more. If she doesn't . . .
DLA: (interrupting) Mrs. B., we'll have plenty of time to talk in a
    few minutes. Watch what's happening between Marcy and
    Esther.
Marcy: She just said it, she hates me.

Mother: I don't hate you, but I can't take this any more. You are being horrible . . .

DLA: Mrs. B., let Marcy speak first. Then all of us will have a chance. OK?

Marcy: She does. She hates my guts. And I hate her. I wish I could find a place to live away from this bitch.

ENP: Marcy, one thing we have to do here is to treat each other with respect. I don't call you names. I don't want you to call me names or your mother names. OK?

Marcy: I'm sorry. OK. Now what?

ENP: Now, what if you could pretend for a moment that your mother *does not* hate you. Can you pretend that? Just pretend.

Marcy: What good will that do?

ENP: If your mother did *not* hate you, how would she be different? What would she do differently with you if she didn't hate you?

Marcy: I don't know what you mean.

ENP: Pretend that your mother loves you, instead of hates you. How would she be different now that she loves you?

Marcy: (with tears that she's trying to check) She doesn't love me. She hates me.

ENP: I'm asking you to pretend. You can do that, can't you? Pretend that your mother does love you. How is she acting toward you? Imagine it. Just imagine it.

Marcy: Oh, if she would love me . . . I don't know. I guess she would not want me to act the way I do.

ENP: You're doing OK. Keep it up. Keep pretending. If she'd love me . . .

Marcy: If she'd love me, I guess she would . . . I guess . . . I don't know.

ENP: The part of you that knows. Come on.

Marcy: You mean, how would my mother be different than now if she'd love me? (ENP nods yes.) She wouldn't be so damn angry . . . I guess . . .

ENP: Why is she angry? The part of you that knows, OK?

Marcy: I guess she does love me. In a way . . .

ENP: All right, then. Let's pretend that your mother's anger and the misery you are going through are *because* she loves you.

Stay with this for a minute. Don't look at me. Don't be distracted. Concentrate on it. Because your mother loves you, she's upset at you. Does she have reasons—any reason—to be upset at you? You can be truthful. Come on. Be honest with yourself. Your mother, who loves you, is upset at you, because . . . You fill the blank.

DLA: (In the meantime has stopped Mrs. B. several times from interrupting.)

Marcy: I don't know. I guess . . . I guess she does have some reason to be upset at me. It may be her menopause, you know.

ENP: Come on, Marcy. Stop the nonsense. Why is your mother upset *at you*?

Marcy: You know it. You're playing games with me. Of course she's upset because I shoplifted. Big deal! I got caught. Others don't. If I know I won't get caught, I'll do it again and again. What's the big deal? The stores rob you blind anyway.

ENP: I'm not playing games with you. I'm just trying to see whether you are aware of what you did. Whether the stores rob us blind or not, shoplifting can get you in trouble. I'm not arguing that shoplifting is bad or illegal. I'm just concerned with what shoplifting can do to you now and in the future. So don't tell me I'm playing games with you. Want to know a secret? I think you are playing games with yourself.

Marcy: So what?

ENP: So, your mother loves you. That's why she's upset at the way you are messing up your life. It's that simple. You agree?

Marcy: I guess so . . . I know she loves me. I don't like this any more than she does. But she still treats me like a child. And I'm not a child any more. She has to understand that.

ENP: You just said that you don't like this situation either. Think now for a minute. What can you do to improve this situation with your mother?

Marcy: I don't know . . .

ENP: Come on, Marcy. The part that does know.

Marcy: I guess I can let her know that I do love her too . . . I do. I don't know why I get so angry at her. I guess it's because I can't get angry at my dad. I say I hate him. But I guess I don't.

I wish he would show that he cares about me. So I get angry at my mom. She married the son of a bitch. It's her fault! I know it's not, but I have to blame someone. So I . . . I don't know. I know she loves me but I'm still angry at her.

ENP: Stay with that statement, "I know that she loves me." Say it to yourself, slowly, again, again, "I know that she loves me." How are you reacting to it? Check how your body feels. Don't tell me yet. Just be aware of how your body reacts to that statement, "My mother loves me."

Marcy: (More relaxed and quiet now) I guess it feels good.

ENP: Go back to what *you* can do to make this situation better. You have more power than you think. You can use it to make this situation with your mother better.

Marcy: I guess . . .

ENP: Don't guess now, Marcy. You know what you can do. Face it now. If you can do it, you might as well do it.

Marcy: I don't know what you mean.

ENP: Come on Marcy. The part of you that knows exactly what I mean. What can *you* do to improve the situation at home with your mother?

Marcy: I guess . . . I don't know.

ENP: Yes, you do know. I guess . . . what?

Marcy: I guess I can be nicer to you (looking at her mother). Yes, I can. But you, you must make me feel better. It's always what I do wrong. Never what I do right. I want you to make me feel good about the things I do right. Why can't you do that, eh?

Mother: I'm so afraid of what can happen to you. The damn drugs. Your lousy friends. I don't know what to do. I'm so afraid . . .

DLA: Can you go back to what Marcy said about your making her feel good by talking about the good things she does, not only the bad things? How can you praise Marcy more for the good things she does?

Mother: Yes, she does a lot of good things around the house. I guess I don't praise her enough. But, what the heck, I do a lot of things too. Who praises me? . . . Well, I should praise her anyway, I guess.

ENP: Can you imagine yourself telling Marcy that she is OK? See it in your mind's eye. See yourself praising Marcy.

Mother: I guess I can do that. Yes, I can.

ENP: Now promise yourself that you'll be more . . . you'll praise Marcy more. Try now to see yourself doing just that. At home. You are in the kitchen and Marcy has just been helpful to you. You feel good. You really appreciate what she's done. And you tell her so. Your nice feeling about Marcy comes out spontaneously in your words of praise.

Marcy: That'll be the day.

DLA: Get into that mental picture your mother is now watching, Marcy. Pretend, as Esther said before. Get into it for a minute. You're with mom and she's praising you. Check your feelings. You are surprised perhaps, but you also have other feelings. Check that out and stay with your feelings for a little while.

ENP: And in doing this, you may remember other good feelings you had for each other, perhaps not too long ago. Your minds can sharply focus on one single event of the past recent months when you were happy with each other, happy to be mother and daughter, happy to be with each other. Is something coming into focus? (Both indicate affirmatively.)

DLA: Take your time and review in your mind that good scene from the last few months. Then go back to now, having a good moment together at home. Feeling good toward each other.

The reason for this long excerpt is to show that these master techniques cannot be imposed on families arbitrarily, regardless of the clinical situation at hand. As is clear, the therapists took their time and, especially at the beginning of the excerpt, respected Marcy's pace without relenting and firmly guided her to change. It should be noted also that in this vignette, the five master techniques are used, though with a great amount of overlapping and without formal introduction or clear distinction of one from another. They are used naturalistically in the service of the clients. Finally, it might be helpful to note how the focus of therapeutic attention changes from one person to the other or to the system as such. A reader not yet familiar with the five master techniques described in this chapter might find it beneficial to go over the excerpt once more, identifying the different techniques even though they are not clearly differentiated.

SUMMARY

In explaining the five master techniques as they can be used in family hypnotherapy, this chapter has attempted to show their great flexibility and adaptability. Consistent with our New Hypnosis posture, we help people activate right hemispheric functioning, bypassing analysis and critical thinking, leaving this for the discussion which always follows the actual experiencing that these techniques make possible for the clients.

3

Early Stages of Family Hypnotherapy

Of the 50 families who took part in our survey, 32 had been in other types of psychotherapy before we saw them, be it family, group, or individual therapy. These people "knew" what they did wrong, why they did it, and what they should be doing differently. But they kept repeating ineffective patterns of reactions, behavior, communication, and so on, in spite of their knowledge. As mentioned elsewhere (Araoz & Negley-Parker, 1985), the conditioned talking response in therapy had been established. This is what hypnotherapy must bypass, shifting attention to inner experiencing. The therapy sessions are spent more on one's inner experiences, on getting in touch with one's inner realities, than on intellectualizing. These former patients of traditional therapies want to talk. But the more they talk, the less they change. More of the same won't do. To effectively change, they must start, in family hypnotherapy, to experience themselves in new ways, and thus to enrich their self-perception and the perception of their world. Our thinking regarding pathology as an interactive phenomenon and human change resulting mostly from inner experiencing was influenced by the group of the Mental Research Institute (Fisch et al., 1982; Watzlawick, 1978; Watzlawick, Beavin, & Jackson, 1967; Weakland, 1976; Weakland, Fisch, Watzlawick, & Bodin, 1974). The model of right hemispheric function referring to inner experiencing is used as some of these authors do, without scientific claim of its accuracy.

Family hypnotherapy therefore, means to experience oneself differently within the family and thus to find new ways of interacting in order to make the family system more beneficial to self and the others.

This chapter is devoted to the central issue of inner change within the family, which, as explained elsewhere (Araoz, 1983, 1985) we like to call *metanoia*—a total, lasting change in attitude. Having outlined the OLD C model in the Introduction, we now zoom in on its initial application to family therapy. How is the OLD C applied in the earliest contacts with the family? Much as the New Hypnosis considers induction already a part of the therapy proper, family hypnotherapy evaluates the family while starting to intervene. Induction is not separate and distinct from hypnosis, and family evaluation (taking a family history) is not done *before* therapy proper starts but while the first stages of therapy are going on. This, of course, is not new in family therapy (Haley, 1976) or in individual counseling, for that matter (Rogers, 1951). The evaluation of the family focuses mainly on the *functional* context, mentioned in Chapter 1.

A related view of behavioral function considers it that aspect of interaction with one person which serves the function of *merging with* or *distancing from* or *opposing* that person and/or another family member at the same time. Behavioral functions are usually nonconscious, which is part of the explanation for their creating problems within the family. However, this does not mean they are discovered inferentially. We do not ask, "*Why* do you do this?" but, "*What* is your typical reaction *when*. . .?" We help the family understand behavioral function from observation, first and foremost during the therapy session itself and also from what the family members tell about their interaction in other circumstances. The function of behavior is discovered in its effects, not from its conscious motivation. "But I was only trying to help," complained the husband when his wife berated him for nagging. The observable behavioral sequence was that he would ask her to do something not urgent and quite reasonable. She would agree. Then he would "remind" her more than once a day until she did it. Both their behaviors, from mere observation, not from analytical inference, are seen as functional, in the sense it is used here. The couple, in this case, has to discover what function their behavior is serving. Ultimately they concluded that his "reminding" her was an ineffective way on his part "to make her like myself." Her delaying, she realized, was her ineffective way of demanding respect and trust for her as a mature and responsible person. Both were engaged in nonproductive attempts to get closer, to be more united. But because these pieces of behavior were nonproductive—though the function was valid and meritorious—they needed to find new ways to attain their desired closeness and communion.

Finally, it should be noted that we feel very free about the external context of family therapy. We do not interview all members of the family together all the time. As a matter of fact, we believe that much research is needed in this area of the treatment of choice. Systemic family therapy cannot mean a rigid adherence to an external context for therapy. Often the parents should be seen alone for a while—or even exclusively—in order that they can work together, consistently and effectively, towards the well-being of the family. In practice, then, we never commit ourselves to seeing the whole family together all of the time. And we tell the clients so in the beginning, especially when they think that family therapy means only family sessions. Systems therapy, in our view, is an attitude more than a practice. The attitude makes us perceive the problems of the family as systemic rather than individual and intrapsychic. The practice is accommodated to many circumstances with great flexibility on our part, without altering the systemic attitude.

EARLY STAGE GOALS AND TECHNIQUES

To return to the initial hypnotherapy contact with the family, three groups of operating techniques are presented. It is stressed that these are considered *in addition to* many other, nonhypnotic techniques used very effectively by traditional family therapists.

Our *ideal* goals in the first stages of family hypnotherapy are the following:

1. To help clients understand "the problem" in systemic terms: the way we relate to each other makes the problem possible.
2. To stop blaming each other and to specify goals of what each wants within the family: the need to reframe.
3. To discover how each person's contribution to the family's well-being will benefit all: the value of trade-offs.

Consequently, the three types of hypnotic techniques to be described aim at each of these goals. It should be noted that all the techniques mentioned in this and the following chapters are presented as samples. They are merely means to an end and, thus, should be adapted, modified, and edited by the clinician. We hope that with practice all practitioners interested in using hypnosis with families will create their own techniques. As was mentioned in the Introduction, we emphasize hypnotic *principles*, not techniques as such. The latter spring forth from the former.

The Family as System

(a) *Ideal family.* One opening technique in this hypnotic category consists of asking the family members to spend some time "imagining their *ideal family*: to view a mental picture of every family member as you wish he would behave, wish he would be." We insist on going very slowly, asking family members to see themselves and the other members in the kitchen, in the living room, in the car, and so on. In hypnosis, they experience their "ideal" family and mentally try on this new model. After spending a few minutes in this silent mind exercise, we discuss each person's experience and compare notes. Then we ask them to return to their inner selves in hypnosis and to focus especially on what "I can do to improve the family situation. What change in me can make things better?" Then we discuss this until there is some agreement reached as to specific types of behavior each promises to the others. These new behaviors are to be practiced until the next family therapy session.

(b) Earlier connections. Another hypnotic technique for opening interaction in family therapy is *to lead* whomever is talking into a fuller inner experience of whatever they are expressing. Only after connecting with their inner experience and becoming aware of it are they asked to "explain" it or describe it or report about it in words. Then the other family members are asked to react and to engage in verbal exchange. A father said: "I'm fed up with her. For years we have argued about this. Why does she have to jump in in the middle when Danny [18 years old] and I are having an argument?" At this point the therapist asked the father to focus on his "I'm fed up with her" and led him to get in touch with any feelings, memories, images, or sensations while concentrating on his statement and figure of speech. This concentrating becomes the hypnotic "induction," and he is encouraged to stay in self-hypnosis for a while to give him time to encounter his subsconscious realities. Afterward he described what he had been "thinking" about: "I was getting more and more pissed. All sorts of incidents kept coming back since Danny was a little kid. She was always afraid I would hurt him. Always thinking of me as violent and cruel. Yes, I am fed up. If she doesn't know me after 20 years, forget it."

Then, instead of being asked to react to the father, the others were invited to "go inside of yourself and connect with what's going on inside you right now." The wife, after spending a couple of minutes in self-hypnotic concentration, said: "Yes, I know I'm doing the wrong thing. Even Danny said to me many times, he said, 'Mommy, stay out of it; it's between me and dad,' he said. But I just can't do it. I guess, yeah, I just remembered my own father when he shouted. The house rocked. And he did become violent, throwing things, breaking furniture, punching walls. He went crazy. I was so afraid . . . so many times. When Bob and Danny argue, I guess all that comes back to me as it did just now," (meaning during her self-hypnosis).

This hypnotic technique helps the family become aware of deeper levels of feelings at work when they interact with each other. The father, in this case, was eliciting feelings and memories from the mother's childhood and she was reacting to them more than to the current incident. The father, on the other hand, became overly defensive of his "peaceful nature" because, as he noticed in his self-hypnosis experience, he did have violent images and impulses, which he made a special effort to control and even to deny.

As can be easily understood, these hypnotic techniques are usable by family therapists of any theoretical orientation and are not suggested as overshadowing any of the nonhypnotic opening techniques proposed by different authors, such as Alexander and Parsons (1982). Hypnotic or not, opening techniques in our view should make family members aware of the interactive network in which they relate and operate.

Reframing

From the beginning of family therapy it is important to help the family view events within it differently, in a different frame. They must interpret their relationship in new ways, as was mentioned when referring to the shift from the individual to the family system. One obvious aspect in need of reframing is that of mutual blame since a family that comes for therapy is usually in a blaming frame of mind. Unless they move away from blaming each other they cannot make progress as a group, as a community—one common body. Reframing is the process by which different attributes of a situation are uncovered and used to change one's reaction to that situation (see "Positive Outlook," in Chapter 5).

(a) Personality parts. Reframing can be done hypnotically through what Watkins and Watkins (1979) called ego state therapy and Araoz, giving full credit to them, renamed *activation of personality parts* (Araoz, 1985; see also Chapter 2, this volume). The 15-year-old son who complains about the restrictions imposed on him is told,

> You are right about feeling bad. No one wants to be restricted. But that is only part of the story. Part of you hates the restrictions. But just to be fair, see if you can discover another part of you who may see these restrictions differently. Close your eyes, relax breathing slowly, letting your body feel very mellow, kind of lazy and relaxed. Now check inside of you until

you discover that part of you who sees the restrictions in a different light. To make it easier, start with the complaining part. Imagine yourself complaining, annoyed, feeling bad about your parents' restrictions. Got that? Now imagine another part in you, another *you* as it were, who views these restrictions as something other than restrictions. Stay with it and become a little curious. How can restrictions be other than restrictions? Be curious and find out what that other "you" really thinks. Give it time.

This procedure may continue for several minutes.

This technique requires a fairly healthy personality in an intelligent individual and each therapist will have to decide when to use it. It is, however, a very useful and flexible method to help someone reframe things. If he or she does not discover the new "frame" through this technique, emphasis can be placed on "a positive side and a negative side of the situation," so that the part he or she is not familiar with may focus on the positive side. A variation of this is a form of age progression, asking the patient to place himself or herself hypnotically 5 or 10 years ahead of the present and now view the current situation and react to it. All these variations have the same purpose, to enable the person to perceive the event or situation differently.

(b) Reverse hypnosis. Another hypnotic approach we find effective is reverse hypnosis. Instead of guiding patients into right hemispheric activity, we (the cotherapists) enter into a light hypnotic state and allow ourselves to imagine what the family is like and what each member in it really wants. In a light trance we carry on a conversation between the two therapists about the family. One may say: "I see Jeffrey wanting his father to pay more attention to his tennis. 'It would be so great if dad asked me once in a while about my game,' I hear him say to himself." To which the other may add: "I imagine dad feeling more and more disinterested in the whole family thing. He has worked hard. He has provided them a good life. Now he wants to be left alone or, perhaps, to be taken care of by them." We tell the family not to interrupt us while we are

"in trance" but to listen carefully so that at the end, when we are back to left hemispheric tuning, they can react to our family fantasy, correct our guesses, and tell us the truth about themselves. This technique is a powerful way to engage all the family members and to specify goals they have for family therapy. Admittedly it is a risky technique but it can get the family moving rapidly toward improvement.

Constructive Outlook

A constructive outlook, which is related to reframing, is at the core of the effective solution to human phychological problems and is indispensable for compromise and for accepting trade-offs. The 11 principles of Brief Therapy explained by Weakland et al. (1974), especially the overemphasis or underemphasis on difficulties in living, with its sociocultural ramifications, could all be repeated here. However, as stated, the purpose of this book is not to build theory but to present clinically effective family hypnotherapy techniques for change. The following are hypnotherapeutic approaches for the achievement of the last of the three initial goals of family therapy mentioned earlier. This goal is related to each person's responsibility for the well functioning of the whole family system.

(a) Inventory. In a hypnotic state of inner peace, family members are invited slowly and gently *to review all the benefits* each obtains by being in the family. Not infrequently the first session of family therapy becomes an exchange of accusations. This technique is beneficial to avoid that waste of time, energy, and results. It puts family members in a more constructive state of mind, more ready to negotiate and accede in exchange for some of the good things which are real and true in their life thanks to the presence of other family members. The trade-off concept is thus utilized hypnotically at the beginning of family therapy.

The following transcript shows the way we introduced this hypnotic technique with a family who presented the 20-year-old daughter, living at home with her parents and two younger brothers, 17 and 15, as lazy, selfish, "20 going on 13," and a few other choice descriptions. We work in such a way that either cotherapist starts and the other complements, interjects, repeats, expands, adds, and so on. The 15-year-old son was not present.

ENP: We need to change the general tone. I'm sure you have heard these accusations before you came to see us. But we want to move past them. We told you earlier that we work differently from most therapists. We try to get quickly into the things that are going on inside of your mind. To do this now will change the general tone of our conversation and will help you improve your relationship within the family. Ready?

DLA: Close your eyes for a moment. Move in your chair if you want to so that you feel comfortable. Yes, you may sit on the floor (to the 17-year-old son), even lie down if you want. Calm yourselves down by paying attention to your breathing. Very slowly . . . think of relaxation, inner peace . . . very calm . . . breathing gently . . . feeling nice and at peace . . .

ENP: Give yourselves time . . . breathing . . . calmly, relaxing, so you can . . . think better afterward and really accomplish . . . what you came here for. . .

DLA: Get even more into relaxation . . . calm, quiet, peace . . . start feeling . . . mellow . . . loose . . . relaxed . . . (Similar chatter continues for about four minutes.) . . . now think of your family in positive terms. A great many good things come to you from being in the family. Review them slowly in your own mind . . . gently . . . allowing any good things to come to mind . . .

ENP: Any good feelings, memories, recent or from way back then . . . good feelings about belonging to this family . . . fun things, good things, recent or past, that are part of this family. My family . . . I have reasons to be proud of my family . . . I have reasons to feel good about my family . . . I really want to get into this now more and more. . . (This type of hypnotic suggestion continues for a few minutes.)

After this exercise we were able to discuss, first, the good "things" that had come to mind for each of the four family members present.

This exchange creates a more unified and cooperative atmosphere. Then we focus on "the problem." After this hypnotic exercise it is possible to define it more precisely, so that previous, ineffective attempts at solution are discontinued and new behavioral tasks are agreed upon in order to attain the desired goals. It is obvious that the four points—definition of problem, awareness of past "solutions," goals, and tasks—follow the Brief Therapy model of the Mental Research Institute for producing change (Watzlawick et al., 1974).

(b) A family fun event. A similar hypnotic technique is that of asking the warring family to recall a *fun event*, preferably recent, be it a trip, a wedding, a party, or the like, and to relive it hypnotically. In hypnosis the feelings experienced there are rekindled, and details involving as many senses as possible are used to increase those positive feelings. This exercise produces the effect of placing the family members in a constructive mood to negotiate improvement and to compromise reasonably. It also gives them a true positive point of reference: if they were able to enjoy themselves as a family, then they may be able to do it again by changing certain conditions mostly within themselves.

The three general goals for the early stages of family therapy (think systemically; reframe; use trade-offs), all related to the systemic way of looking at family functioning, can be approached hypnotically, as shown.

Generational Interaction

Parents "bring" their children for family therapy, often hoping that they themselves will not have to be part of the therapeutic process. It is helpful to ask parents to allow themselves to think of the "ideal" child they would like to have. To help them focus on this issue in a right hemispheric way and to avoid idle intellectualizations, the family therapist can tell the parents something like this (an adaptation of the first opening technique listed earlier): "You are the real experts when it comes to your child. You know your child, probably better than anyone else in the whole world. So, now, sitting comfortably, close your eyes and let your mind wander. Think of what your child could be like. Both you, mom and dad, try to imagine this: your child at his best. Imagine him at home first. Place your whole fantasy in slow motion, *very slow motion*, and really get into it. Are you with it? Let the thoughts, the mental images become as real as they can become. Check how you feel with such a good kid. Stay with your good feelings for a little while. Enjoy them. And, again, pretend that this is happening. Give yourselves permission to get into this mental picture. Don't cut it short by letting your realistic attitude interrupt this fantasy."

After this introductory exercise—which becomes a way of teaching them to become right hemispheric during family therapy and checking how well they get into this type of mental activity—the therapist discusses with the parents the mental images they produced. The child, in the meantime, is there witnessing the whole procedure. This gives them, first, ground for focusing on "positives" and strengths and, second, an opportunity for exchanging impressions, hopes, and possible actions to take in order to help the child become what the parents believe he can become. Often this simple exercise is beneficial to refocus away from the negativism that motivated them to seek family therapy and starts the process in a hopeful mode. They realize on their own that there are truly good things to build on.

If the parents voice their inability to concentrate on what the child could be like (on his potential for improvement), parents are guided into a type of age regression. They are asked to go back in time to those days *before* the problem which brought them to therapy. Once they agree on some period of time when things were all right, they are encouraged to *relive* that time and to select a segment of their family life to do so. For instance, if the child is now missing school without reason, the parent can remember vividly when he was happy to go to school. The family therapist guides them by saying something like the following:

All those memories are stored in your mind. Bring them back to life now. Relax for a moment and allow yourselves to go back in time to those days. Get in touch with the feelings you had then about your child. The memory of those feelings is still in your mental files. Bring those good feelings back to life. Enjoy them now, once more. Be there, as if you had gone back in time, reliving those good days.

However, parents may respond that the child has never been "good." In this case, the family therapist may ask them to imagine how good the child *could* be. Both parents do this in silence. At the end, by comparing their imaginary mental productions, they are able to realize either that their expectations are unreal—as in the case of a child with learning disabilities—or that both of them have to cooperate more effectively to help the child become "better." In this last possibility, the child's reaction to what the parents expect of him are useful to plan concrete ways of improving the situation, involving the family in a contract with each other.

The family therapist not familiar with hypnosis has to be ready for the initial discomfort felt when one keeps interrupting the clients, inhibiting their "talk" and their need to provide details, in order to get them to "go inside of themselves" and check their images, feelings, memories, and bodily sensations. Families respond well to this approach because often they confess to being tired of talking about the problem without noticing real improvement in their family interaction.

It is also important to keep in mind that a similar approach can be used with children who complain about their parents. Rather than encouraging the child to list all the things that the parents "are doing wrong" one asks the child to use imagination "to pretend" that the parents are just right, the best parents he could have. After a few minutes of this mind exercise, the child is asked to report on the imaginary parents and to check which elements in that fantasy are possible and which are unrealistic. We are always surprised to realize that in most cases the child becomes quite realistic, recognizing his parents' limitations. At the same time the child realizes that he must contribute more effectively to a better relationship with his parents. One often hears comments like, "Yes, they could trust me more but I shouldn't have stayed away from home last weekend without letting them know where I was. I know." At that point it is easier to encourage both the child and the parents to negotiate better means to communicate and meet each others' needs.

CHANGE, INSIGHT, AND RESISTANCE

Patients who come to family therapy after having had individual psychotherapy or nonhypnotic family therapy are the most difficult to treat. As stated at the beginning of this chapter, they honestly believe that the only way to change is to talk in order to obtain insight from early events in their developmental history. They know what therapy should be: a verbal review of events and memories.

Our aim is concrete and defined. We expect change in behavior stemming from change in perception of each other and oneself, which inevitably produces change in attitudes toward each other. Because the act of relabeling or reframing their behaviors from negative to positive connotations is a powerful therapeutic maneuver, we begin by relabeling family therapy itself. It is first and foremost a new way of *experiencing oneself and the other family members*. The sessions are used as a workshop or laboratory for this new inner experiencing. From the beginning, therefore, we redefine family therapy by our actions. We thus enter into an explicit contract to have *experiencing therapy* as opposed to *talking therapies*, as they have had previously. In so doing, we imply that our method reduces the duration of family therapy to 3 to 10 sessions, typically.

When we refer to behavioral change stemming from attitudinal change, we do not claim that there is a need for intellectual insight. De Shazer (1985), for one, gave us a wealth of techniques to change perception and attitude without needing to understand the origin and the underlying causes of either the initial behavior or the change process itself.

The model of human interaction we keep in mind is Horney's (1945) elegant and practical typology of movement *toward, against*, and *away from* people. Rubin (1983) applied it to both healthy and neurotic relationships. This typology helps establish the kind of change or movement desired. To move from a "neurotic" family relationship to a healthy one is the ultimate goal of all family therapy.

Most people find it helpful to realize what type of dysfunctional interaction they are locked into, and the kind of healthy family functioning they want to attain. This typology is easily explained and understood.

The advisability of a *road map* comes from our method of working toward concrete and attainable goals in family therapy. This typology contributes to specificity. The ideal family interactional pattern has elements of cooperation (*toward*), creativity (*away from*), and friendly competition (*against*). Ineffective relationships have mostly unfriendly competition and even antagonism. When families describe their interactions, we might suggest that they could have more cooperation and friendly competition; otherwise, we clarify the goals to be attained in the language of Horney's model, without lecturing on or even explaining the typology.

Once the family has a fairly clear idea of what they want to obtain through family therapy, they are ready for our hypnotherapy. Our method, of course, is what this book presents. We have noticed that when people start with us under this agreement, by the second or third session of therapy they have been reconditioned not to talk, explain, analyze, speculate, read other people's minds, and the like. They learn quickly that "going inside of themselves" is much more helpful than all these other maneuvers in order to attain a more satisfying and enriching family interaction.

What the opening techniques actually do is start the new family therapy experience. They gently and effectively introduce the family members to a new way of perceiving change. By practicing self-hypnosis under our guidance they become convinced of its usefulness. They realize that human change comes from within, not from external circumstances. By helping them along this realization we give them the means to literally change their attitudes: they "see" more; they enlarge their perception of themselves as individuals and of the other family members as belonging to the sociopsychological system that is part of their self-definition.

This introspective approach (in the literal sense of "looking inside") makes it easier to accept the concept of functional context in a practical manner. Often family members have a sudden realization that, yes, that's what I am doing. In the case mentioned earlier,

Bob became aware of his poor timing when getting into an argument with Danny. He realized in self-hypnosis without the therapists' having to point out anything to him that "from the corner of my eye," as he put it, he was watching to see what Ann, his wife, would do. In getting into these arguments he was testing Ann, setting a trap for her. He also was indirectly criticizing her for not having settled with Danny what he felt obliged to settle now, as if that were her responsibility.

One clear advantage of these hypnotic techniques is that they diminish intellectual resistance since the person is confronted with these truths about himself experientially, bypassing intellectual evaluation. In getting in touch with his inner self, he "sees" what he is doing. In some cases we have found people who have this inner realization but then, when we talk about it, they do not mention it. It only comes out several sessions later. Even in these instances they are unable to hide the truth from themselves. They hide it from the therapists and even from the other family members, but now they know better. And sooner or later, it is admitted to the others, too. Resistance, therefore, is not a main concern for the family hypnotherapist. The application of the OLD C paradigm to working with families minimizes the obstacles to change and by applying it repeatedly the patients themselves confront the truth about themselves. At that point they are able to make decisions with a new sense of freedom and control.

The other advantage of using these opening hypnotic techniques is related to the very concept of resistance. This benefit is the shorter time hypnotherapy takes compared to "regular" family therapy. What Kempler (1981) states about experimental family therapy applies adequately to family hypnotherapy as well. Because the truth about oneself is confronted and accepted by getting in touch with one's internal dynamics (in the sense of "what is going on" inside), old, ineffective patterns of behavior are disrupted in the therapy session itself. "Symptom removal, improved family interaction, altered observable behavior in the sessions and subtle peripheral cues usually confirm the value of [this approach] and point to other progress as well" (Kempler, 1981, p. 19). Once old patterns of perception, reaction, and behavior are shattered, people cannot go back to them as before. If they do, they are aware—at least minimally—of their inefficacy, they feel bad because they go back to them, or—what constitutes another benefit of family therapy—other family members call their bluff, react angrily, or simply ignore them.

SUMMARY

From the beginning of therapy, families can be helped hypnotically, especially those who have become conditioned to the therapy = talk erroneous equation. To help families, the therapist must keep the early stage of family therapy goals clearly in mind. These goals aim at reframing perception and interpretation so that all family members see themselves as part of a system and thus become willing to *effectively* be part of it through active changes in their attitudes and behaviors.

To keep a clear view of the goals to be attained, a typology of human relations taken from Horney (1945) and expanded by Rubin (1983) is suggested as helpful.

The advantages of these opening hypnotic techniques center around brevity and effectiveness regarding resistance to change. If applied from the beginning, the family gets used to employing the family therapy sessions as a laboratory in which they "construct" new patterns of interaction and from which they get a genuine support system to make these changes last.

4

Middle Stages of Family Hypnotherapy

Many of the familial problems that motivate people to seek family therapy spring from intergenerational issues. Simply put, parents have forgotten what is was to be a child, and children have little or no sensitivity to what it means to be a parent. As a matter of fact, most of the families employed in our research presented problems with a child: rebelliousness on the child's part or loss of parental control or unmet needs on either side or any number of variations of these general themes.

The real contribution of family therapy, as was mentioned repeatedly, is to make us aware of the fact that "we are individuals in appearance only," as Kempler (1981, p. 20) so aptly put it. This means that we think in terms of family interaction rather than individual psychopathology. But the systemic view of families does not do away with individual psychodynamics: the family influences and affects each family member as an individual, or, again in Kempler's words, "The battlefields are interpersonal; the battle is intrapsychic" (1981, p. 22). Family conflicts activate internal struggles of the individual family member which are manifested in the systemic interaction.

However, this view does not mean that only by resolving intrapsychic conflict can we enrich family functioning. The contrary direction is also operative: by improving family interaction, individual psychodynamics are worked through and made more functional. Therapy, then, focuses on the *current* interaction between family members and between them and the therapists. We find ourselves placing more emphasis on the process of interaction than on the subject matter or content of it. Through the effort to stay in the present, many subconscious dynamics are spontaneously—naturalistically—elicited.

One depressed 36-year-old man, living with his brother because of his depression, became angry when we reacted with annoyance at his "I didn't have time to do it" excuse in spite of unemployment resulting from his depression. He kept smiling instead of expressing his anger. ENP asked, "Do you always smile when you are angry?" His older brother was becoming restless and moving nervously in his chair. The depressed patient said in a whisper, "Fuck you," and immediately looked away and closed his eyes as if expecting a blow. ENP said, "Something is coming up in your mind. Stay with it. Get into it. Say again, 'Fuck you' and connect with your feelings right now. What happens?" He remained quiet for a short while, turned back toward ENP with an apologetic smile just for a split second, then kept looking away but appeared less tense. ENP encouraged him further: "Stay with any memory that comes up. Check the echoes of 'Fuck you' inside of you. Any sensation when you say to me 'Fuck you'? Any memories or feelings? Let them come to you." When this exchange was over he felt less depressed and explained that in his mind he found himself bullied by his older brother, who was now so solicitous. He was only 8 or 9 and the brother was 14 or 15. While his brother was teasing him, humiliating him, abusing him verbally and physically, he said "Fuck you" and then became very frightened that his brother would have heard him. He had relived the whole scene and had become aware that his current depression was somehow connected with those years. The older brother, then, expressed very emotionally how guilty he felt now for the way he had mistreated his younger brother for many years when they were children. He had never mentioned this before to his brother.

From that day on the depression lifted and the patient was able to function more independently of his brother. The issue of the younger brother's independence was worked out during the following sessions, to the point that in a couple of months the younger brother was employed again after having been out of work for two years, and in four months, he was able to move out of his older brother's home into a small apartment of his own. Shortly thereafter he resumed dating, an activity he had interrupted when his depression started, eight months before therapy and six months after his divorce.

This clinical vignette illustrates the constant interplay between intrapsychic and interpsychic dynamics: the battlefield was the interaction between the two brothers but the real battle was intrapsychic for both brothers: the older had to resolve his guilt and his neurotic way of coping with it by now making the younger brother dependent on him; the younger had to stop his way of getting back at his brother through his depression, which had inconvenienced the former's whole household and, at the same time, had to face his dependency, which kept him depressed and unemployed.

The intergenerational dimension of family therapy includes both the inner connections we all have established with parents and other important figures of our developmental years, whether they are still alive or not, and the interaction taking place between generations or of rank distinctions, as in the case just mentioned.

MIDDLE STAGES

Once the family has understood their difficulty as "systemic," has succeeded in reframing their problem so that blame of each other or the pointing at one person as "the cause of trouble" has stopped, and once the need for personal effort in order to improve things has been accepted, the family starts moving directly toward healthy interaction. This step constitutes the middle stages of family hypnotherapy.

Most people in a family believe that they know each other like a book. But we have found that the middle stages are a wonderful opportunity for family members to really find out who they are. Inevitably people are surprised at discovering so many new things about themselves and about the other family members. In the middle stages the true *vivencias* take place. Before describing a few examples, we consider the three areas of work during the middle stages: learning what makes the other family members tick; learning what makes me tick; and getting things done in the family and as a family.

Understanding the Other Family Members

The OLD C paradigm starts with careful "observation" of language style, important statements, and somatics. *How* people express themselves is emphasized at least as much as *what* they express. We help the family become aware of the fact that people think differently or, as neurolinguistic programming puts it, have different "representational systems." This process of becoming aware of each other's thinking mode is not demonstrative, didactic, or intellectual. It is rather a way of coaching family members to approach the representational system of another family member as shown in the three areas of "observation" in OLD C.

Let's assume that the brother is saying, "I can't take it anymore. I can't stand it," and the sister responds with, "I don't see what the big fireworks are here. As if everything were so gloomy." If we notice a consistent pattern showing a possible preferred representational system (in this case, kinesthesia for the brother and visualization for the sister), we encourage one to approximate the other person's system. In this case, we might say to the boy: "Check where you see yourself in your mind's eye when you say 'I can't stand it any more.' Are you some place in particular? What comes to mind? Are you really standing? Check it." To the girl, we may suggest: "Stay with the fireworks. Can you hear them? Are they far away? Close by? When they crack, do you feel it all over you? Where are you?" In other words, we attempt to expand their own inner modality. Once they have succeeded in approaching the other person's mental system, we put them together. In this case, we would ask both brother and sister to "See yourself close to each other; feel the closeness. Where are you? Are you standing? Can you hear each other's voice? Can you see each other's face? Pay special attention to the details of the other person's face."

After they have engaged in this mind exercise, we discuss it in order to bring it to the awareness of the left hemisphere. At this point they may have the proverbial "Aha!" experience and they recognize the need to try to approach the other person's thinking style in order to really commuicate.

However, many persons take longer than those in the preceding example to expand their systems of mental representation. If we are unsuccessful in our first attempt to help one family member approximate the other person's mental representation system by attending to the "language style," as just demonstrated, we repeat our effort in more detail and with greater refinement by focusing on "somatics." To the brother we may say: "Please, say to yourself once again 'I can't take it anymore. I can't stand it.' Repeat it to yourself or out loud, . . . once again, please." This time, while he is doing this we pay special attention to his gaze or the direction in which his eyes are moving. Applying with caution, as explained below, the findings of what neurolinguistic programming discovered by studying such geniuses of communication as Erickson and Satir, we check first whether his eyes do, indeed, move downward. This movement has been found correlated with auditory (eyes down and to the left) and kinesthetic (eyes down and to the right) mental activity (see Cameron-Bandler, 1985; Grinder & Brandler, 1976; Grinder, DeLozier, & Bandler, 1977). If his eyes move downward we assume that there is congruity between his words and his inner experience in this case. This means that he is not using mental pictures or visualization and that we must help him form such inner representations if he is to approximate his sister's mental modality. This we do by asking him to listen carefully to what he is saying to himself or to the words he is hearing in his mind, or else to become more in touch with the bodily sensations elicited in him while repeating those two statements. This repetition, by the way, is done hypnotically, in a relaxed state, with eyes closed, very slowly, and under the gentle verbal prodding of the hypnotherapist.

If he reports what he is saying to himself (auditory modality), we suggest that he pay close attention to those words in order to check whether they are connected with a particular person from his past or from his current life. We might ask: "Who else might be saying this? Can you recognize the voice you are hearing as being that of someone other than you? Listen carefully." If the person makes this switch and recognizes, for instance, a teacher from grammar school, we encourage visualization by saying something like this: "Look at her carefully. Notice her facial expression. Where is she? What's she doing? Is she looking at you? Standing? Sitting? What does the room look like? Is it daylight or night time?" In this manner we help the brother construct visual images gradually in order to approximate the mental modality of the sister.

In the case that he may report bodily sensations, we encourage him to visualize by slowly enlarging his kinesthetic experience into a visual one. Thus we may say,

> While you say to yourself "I can't take it anymore. I can't stand it," become aware of what it is that you can't take any more. What comes to mind? Anything that comes to mind now is important . . . say those sentences again and check your mental screen . . . repeat once more and let whatever comes to mind become sharper and clearer . . . are you standing someplace? On the ground? Below ground level? Above it? Where? What are you facing? Are you alone? Is it dark or bright?

And, as above, from his mental activity (kinesthetic) we lead him to a new modality (visual) in order to come closer to that used by his sister. With her we would use a similar method to get her to come closer to the brother's kinesthetic mode.

This refinement of the *observation* step in our OLD C sequence of hypnotherapeutic intervention becomes especially useful in family therapy. Every family seen in family therapy has problems of communication. What our method does is refine Satir's (1972) model of communication (congruent) as opposed to her four ineffective models. Satir's paradigm is further enriched by the research of the neurolinguist programmers (see Bandler, Grinder, & Satir, 1976, and the fascinating chapter on Family Therapy in Grinder & Bandler, 1976), as noted earlier and as will become even more manifest throughout the book.

That "Aha!" experience referred to earlier is a significant step toward truly "knowing" another family member. The discovery of different modalities of experiencing events fascinates most people with whom we work. The middle stages of family hypnotherapy fulfill one of their goals (getting to know each other) through the method outlined above. The case studies in Chapters 7 to 9 offer many instances of this approach. Families exposed to this intervention learn to be much more sensitive with each other and frequently generalize this new learning to other relationships where communication can improve.

Getting to Know Myself

After the foregoing type of practice it becomes natural for the individuals in the family to recognize natural limitations in their own thinking style or mental modality. At the same time, it is easy to accept the advantages of expanding one's modality in order to have greater mental flexibility in understanding others.

Here is where the metamodel for language, in part deduced by Bandler and Grinder (1975a,b) from studying great psychotherapists at work through observation, consultation, and analysis of their writings, as they did with Erickson and with Satir, becomes especially important for family hypnotherapy. The result of using these guidelines will be more congruent communication among family members. Congruency implies agreement between one's inner experience, springing from a true perception of the outside world, and the language used to report on it. Congruency is further detected, as Satir (1972) emphasizes, in what we call *logosomatics*, the agreement between "language style" and "somatics" (to use the designations of the OLD C paradigm). The body, or, more precisely, the head and face, the arms and hands, the legs, torso, and shoulders, as well as posture, gestures, gaze, breathing, voice volume, tempo, and intonation, all are in accord with the words expressed. Or, inversely, the words confirm and validate the external demeanor of the person. There is an overall sense of balance, harmony, matching and coordination.

The neurolinguistic metamodel points out the pitfalls to avoid in order to make communication congruent, thus contributing to a refinement of Satir's (1972) model. Communication can be seen as a two-way translation: from the outside world with its events to one's inner experience of it; and again, from one's inner experience of the world to the accurate reporting on it (Sherman & Fredman, 1986). Or, in neurolinguistic terms, to move from contact with the world (experience) to deep structure (one's perception and meaning of the world) to surface structure (language and expression).

To review the metamodel for the purpose of explaining family hypnotherapy, congruent verbal communication takes place when the following four elements are *not* present in the verbal exchange: 1) generalizations, 2) deletions, 3) distortions, and 4) idealizations based on subjective expectations. We added the last category as a sensitization of the first three from neurolinguistic programming, to the degree that it becomes essentially different from each. An example of the first category is: "All men expect to be served"; the second, "He doesn't care about me" (referring to an adolescent child); the third, "This is a source of worry" (where his actual worrying is distorted into an "objective" worry); and the fourth, "He can't be that mean to me" (where her expectation—idealization— of him interferes with her recognizing what goes on in the interaction between her husband and her). The neurolinguists "challenge" the first three defects in verbal communication by appropriate questions. For instance, if a wife says, "He's constantly picking on me," they would ask, "How specifically does he pick on you?" or, "What does he say and do when he picks on you?" This is an example of "unspecified verbs." An example of "nominalizations" is when one says, "It's painful to go through this." The "challenge" lies in asking, "What sort of pain do you feel going through this?"

In working with families we find that our hypnotic method works quickly when it is meaningful to clients. Thus in the example of unspecified verbs, we would respond by saying, "Go inside of you and check what comes up. What feelings? Any words? Any mental pictures? Check your body sensations and anything that spontaneously comes up for you when you think of your husband picking on you." For the example of nominalization we would retort, "Check your pain. Where do you feel it in your body? Do any other things come up? Sounds? Pictures? Any other sensations at all? Take your time to check this thoroughly." As is obvious from the OLD C model explained in the Introduction, our response becomes the "L," or leading step, of therapy.

In the discussion ("D") that follows, the client has a good opportunity to become aware of his or her language style as a reflection of the thinking mode or representational system. Although neurolinguists refer to primary representational system (Bandler et al., 1976) or preferred representational system (Bandler & Grinder, 1975b), the findings of Coe and Sharcoff (1983) question the concept. They found that there is no evidence for the claim that people have "a primary representational system that characterizes their way of dealing with the world across different settings and varying circumstances" (p. 8). Regardless of the final outcome about the evidence of *a* preferred representational system, we are inclined to believe from our clinical experience that people tend to use one system over another depending on the circumstances and on the person(s) they are dealing with. Visualization in our culture, if not necessarily the most universal mental system used to represent one's world to oneself, is nevertheless easily accessible to most persons. It may be that in our society, because of television and movies—especially animated cartoons—we have developed a very rich collection of mental pictures and of possible mental pictures we can easily summon without much effort. This great exposure to visual stimuli may also have "trained" us for the facile use of imagery, both creatively constructed and vividly remembered. Future research will decide whether in humans to dream, fantasize, and daydream are physiological skills which, when highly stimulated, as they are in our culture, make visualization the most commonly used representational system for adults in the Western world (see Singer & Pope, 1978).

In the middle stages of family hypnotherapy the family members get to the point of becoming aware of their differences in "thinking." Frequent comments heard are: "Now I realize why we were unable to agree," or, "And all these years I thought he wasn't paying attention to me," or, again, "I never knew I was thinking in words that I could hear in my mind." At this point we are reaching the goals of the middle stages of family hypnotherapy. More specifically, each family member is getting to know himself or herself; each is becoming aware of his or her thinking modality and how it affects family communication.

People learn that communication is not merely words and content, but mainly logosomatics. Because this learning is essential for congruent communication, we spend time during the middle stages of family hypnotherapy helping people become aware of the way they speak to each other and of the many elements, other than mere words, that enter into personal interactions. Unlike the neurolinguists, we insist on getting in touch with anything and everything that emerges when clients "go inside of themselves," as mentioned earlier. Very seldom do we "challenge" the clients' language forms with the questions used by the neurolinguists. To reconnect language to the experience it represents, we apply the OLD C paradigm, as explained earlier. This method is the practical difference between our use of the neurolinguistic metamodel and *their* manner of applying it. To illustrate once more: if the wife says, "It's wrong to hurt him," we do not ask, "For whom is it wrong?" or "Who says that?" But we invite the person to get in touch with her inner experience of the moment and connect it with any and all significant elements that might emerge at the time, leading ("L" in the OLD C model) her to own completely what she is experiencing.

In this respect it is helpful to keep in mind what Bandler et al. explain: "Each communication . . . can be understood to be a comment on three areas of the ongoing experience: self . . . the other and the context" (1976, p. 58). If there is a lack of balance among these three, the communication is not congruent. Thus the "computer," or superreasonable communicator, in Satir's (1972) typology, deemphasizes the self and the other while overconcentrating on the context. The "blamer" stresses the self to the extent that the context and the other are ignored. The "placater" is so concerned about the other that the self and the context get lost. Finally, the "distracters" or irrelevant communicators are more or less detached from the whole process: their own inner experience is ignored while they are also unaware of the other person's feelings and communication as well as of the context and circumstances in which they are interacting. Only the "congruent" communicator keeps the self, the other, and the context balanced by avoiding the verbal defaults (generalizations, deletions, distortions, and idealizations) and thus succeeding at logosomatics.

In family hypnotherapy this typology is used in one of two ways, either by exaggerating one's communication style in self-hypnosis or by using self-hypnosis to help the person realize more thoroughly how much other communication types (with whom there is interaction) make congruent communication impossible. Finally, the congruent style is mentally rehearsed until the clients assimilate this effective way of relating to others. The following situations illustrate how Satir's styles are used in family hypnotherapy.

A couple made up of a distracter husband and a blamer wife is encouraged to push their communicating modality to an absurd degree. The husband may be told to keep talking about nonsense, to make jokes, to respond with some absurdity to anything that the wife says. If he cannot do it, the therapist coaches him. For example, the wife just finished saying that she is upset because the husband does not help her with the discipline of the children. The therapist, coaching the husband, may state, "Remember the time we went to Hilton Head in South Carolina?" (The children were not with the couple that time.) She responds by stating that she is talking about the children, and the therapist, prodding the husband, may say, "Yes, other people have 10 children and they manage. Isn't that funny?" And on and on, until it becomes dramatically evident to both that the "distracting" style is not effective for communication.

The same, of course, can be done with the wife, encouraging her to continue blaming the husband or his mother or his first-grade teacher until they realize how absurd this direction is. Then both are asked to go inside themselves and to imagine a conversation in which each listens to the other, each is in tune with the other—each assumes the other person's state of mind, as it were. In the hypnotic state, they are encouraged to enjoy that "mental" conversation, so that afterward, when they are back into the ordinary mental channel, they can exchange impressions of what they experienced in hypnosis. At this point, incidentally, it is helpful to point out any manifestations of their defective communication style.

The other situation in which Satir's styles can be used hypnotically is by helping the individual realize more thoroughly how much of a hindrance an ineffective communication style can be. In this case the person is asked to relax and to gently review what really bothers him or her about the communication style of the spouse or child or parent. Reviewing this in a relaxed way, without anger, produces clear insights into the minutiae of their communication, so that later they can discuss objectively what really bothers them. At the discussion point, they can compromise, give each other cues to stop doing what the other dislikes, and enter into contracts or agreements.

Thus the emphasis on communication styles contributes to a better understanding of self. "This is me, the way I communicate," is the message they obtain from this focus.

Getting Things Done as a Family

The final goal of the intermediate stage of family therapy is to learn to work as a family team, pulling together toward the same destination. The master technique of mental rehearsal (Chapter 2) is to be considered for this purpose. The family members are simply invited to "imagine yourselves acting as a cooperative family, everyone pulling together, happy to help each other." This suggestion is repeated in different ways until all of them enter this mental activity. Then the family discusses what each experienced during the exercise just completed. If there are disagreements during the discussion period, the family is encouraged to go back to self-hypnosis and rehearse the cooperative style once again. This is repeated and discussed several times so that every detail of the improved reality they are constructing is increasingly refined.

To get things done as a family, the family members must learn to communicate congruently. We use the discussion part of the OLD C model to help them become congruent, applying what we described in the previous section regarding communication styles. To encourage congruent communication or logosomatics, we must be keenly aware of the complexity of messages being given. For instance, in one of our cases, the father said to the teenager who was reluctant to talk to the therapist, "Go ahead, tell him what's in your mind. That's what we're here for," while at the same time looking out the window and leaning back, away from the others in the room. We as therapists must be aware of the somatic messages contradicting the verbal output. The way the teenager reacts will uncover how he and probably the other members of this family "read" each other's messages. If we dissect the father's messages (verbal and somatic) we find: 1) verbal encouragement to talk; 2) verbal recrimination to the son for not talking with possible implications of money spent in therapy e.g., "If it weren't for you, we wouldn't have to do this"; 3) bodily expression of indifference or boredom; 4) bodily expression of distance from the son and the other family members; and 5) voice tonality indicating impatience or annoyance. As Bandler et al., explain masterfully, we can at this point recognize "what the family members may perceive and act upon when they experience incongruent communication" (1976, p. 83). Note that the authors are talking about family rules, so that "what the family members *may* perceive, etc.," refers to the limits or range of freedom used by this family in the case of incongruent messages.

In the case mentioned earlier, the teenaged son replied, "What's the use? Nothing will change." ENP asked the son, "What did you notice when your father just spoke?" The son then explained that the father did not mean what he said. The father became angry at that remark, but we asked the father to repeat what he said, this time really meaning it and making sure that the son believed that he meant it. The father changed his body position, facing the son, leaned toward him, moved his right arm from the back of the chair where he had placed it when he was looking out the window, and said in a softer voice, "Come on son, tell him what's in your mind. I mean it." Then the son continued talking, as Chapter 8 describes in detail.

Analyzing the elements of the father's communication in the second instance, there is: 1) verbal encouragement to talk; 2) no verbal recrimination but a soft tone of voice; 3) bodily expression of interest and concern; 4) bodily expression of closeness; and 5) a relaxed, almost gentle smile, while looking the son in the eye. In both cases the son "listened" more to the nonverbal messages than to the verbal one, or content. After this exchange, we asked the family to reflect on what had just happened between father and son and they themselves recognized the importance of the nonverbal communication. This helped us generalize the pattern to all other communications within the family. In other words, from this exchange they learned a model for congruent communication.

Once they tuned up their communication, the discussion in the OLD C model becomes meaningful. However, after the discussion, we ask them to "check" hypnotically how they are *really* reacting to what they talked about or to what they agreed to do. We'll return to the final "check" later on. In the discussion, as shown in the exchange between father and son just described, we pay close attention to the total communication and the reactions of the other family members to it. This is the time for contracts and compromises, for negotiations and agreements. It is important to make sure that no one gives up more than the others and that everyone has about the same amount of "obligations" to the others.

In one family of both parents, a girl of 19, a boy of 17, and girl of 16, the issue being discussed was finances and expenses. At the discussion point, the father agreed to sit down with his wife to go over the regular expenses so that both could later bring the children into the discussion on the need to save. In spite of the fact that the parents had received increases amounting to $550 per month since the previous year, they had not saved any money during the same amount of time. Both parents agreed that they should have been able to save since one of their plans was to spend a month in Europe without the children. The wife was not content with the husband's general agreement and wanted to pinpoint a specific hour and day when they would sit down and discuss finances. The husband balked: he did not want to be pinned down. We asked him to present an alternative, to which he responded with a vague proposal to discuss the matter sometime in the next few days. Since he had repeatedly stated that he did not want his wife to be unhappy, we insisted on a more concrete plan of action. Finally he agreed to a specific day and hour when they would sit down to go over this issue. At the following session, they reported that, indeed, they had talked about it. The husband was pleased and the wife was satisfied. Neither felt that the other had gotten away with anything. They had been able to cooperate in a matter that was important to both of them.

The final point of our OLD C model is a hypnotic check. After they have agreed on something, we ask either each person individually or the whole family to go back into themselves and review gently what they have just decided or agreed upon, to see themselves acting the way they have agreed, to get in touch with any feelings that may emerge, and to check carefully whether there might be any part of them that is not comfortable with what they have decided consciously before. We keep them in this exercise for a few minutes until they have time to become aware of their inner reactions and feelings about the issue at hand. Then we suggest that they return to the ordinary mental channel and briefly discuss this last experience. If everything is fine, we dismiss the issue and summarize whatever they had agreed to do before the next session. If, however, there is some discomfort with the decision made, we direct them to connect more fully with that discomfort and to allow new images, memories, feelings, sensations, or inner reactions to emerge. In other words, we return to the "lead" step in our OLD C model, and continue from that point on.

The wording for the "check" step may be a variation of the following:

> Now that you have come to a decision regarding (X, Y, or Z), give yourselves a few moments to let that decision rest comfortably inside of you. Look forward to the greater harmony (or happiness, or peace of mind) that this decision will bring. Relax. Consider yourself in greater control of your life because of this decision. You had to compromise, give in to, but you had good reasons to do so. The trade-off makes sense. Does it? Check how your whole being reacts to it. Memories, bodily sensations, feelings, mental images. Check them while you re-

lax. Gently get into them, into any of these inner experiences. Don't talk now. Just stay with whatever is coming up for you while you think of the decision you just made, of the compromises you made. How are you reacting? Don't tell us but be aware of it. Is your body accepting it thoroughly? Is there any tension when you focus on your decision? Where is the tension? Notice it first; then point to the area of your body, so we know what's happening. No tension? Then continue relaxing while you rehearse now how you will enact your decision. Watch the movie in your mind. Feel proud of yourself while you review your decision in action, translated into your actions. Connect with the feelings. You had good reasons for making this decision. Let your reasons and your feelings come together. Perhaps you can enjoy this compromise once more in your mind.

The wording changes, but we hope that this example gives an idea of what this last step is all about: an integration of left and right hemispheric activity, a unification between reason and inner experience.

In the subsequent sessions, the family reports on the way in which they did what they had resolved to do. They also discuss problems or difficulties they might have encountered. When things go well in the area that they were working on, it is time to move on to other areas or to terminate family hypnotherapy, depending on the case.

SUMMARY

The middle stages of family hypnotherapy, as the three case studies presented in Part 2 will demonstrate, concentrate on working through the new attitudes, perceptions, and actions that the family has decided will be more beneficial for their functioning as a healthy system. These are the sessions in which the family learns to work as a unit and enjoys the benefits it brings to each member individually. During these sessions, and while they are reviewing their progress or lack of progress as a family unit, they are refining their communication skills, weakening their unproductive and ineffective relational styles, and reinforcing the new behavior they are practicing in daily living. Throughout these middle stages, the hypnotic method of checking things inside one's inner self by the use of the five master techniques (as explained in Chapter 2) allows family members to integrate reason and emotion. They become comfortable utilizing the process of checking rational decisions with inner reactions and integrating the latter with reason.

By going through this process hypnotically rather than "rationally," families benefit in several ways. They learn to trust their inner perceptions and feelings; they move faster toward a resolution or the point at which they feel comfortable, at peace, with their decision; they operate in an environment of cooperation rather than competition (using "reason" allows for the smart ones to win over the less smart members of the family). In our approach, there is no right or wrong answer. All inner experiences are valid and to be accepted by all family members. This method tends to generalize so that from the experience of family hypnotherapy they learn to trust their inner experiences; to utilize these inner experiences; and to cooperate with others, making acceptable compromises, yielding to others for the common goal to be attained, and so on. (See Kohn's review of research showing that "despite our cherished belief in the virtues of competition, study after study shows that nothing succeeds like cooperation"; 1986, p. 22).

The final stages of family hypnotherapy, as described in Chapter 5, are sessions in which the gains attained are tested, reinforced, and validated while, at the same time, difficulties or unexpected surprises encountered in the practice of new attitudes and behavior are resolved. It often happens that the final stages of family hypnotherapy do not take place "on schedule." Even though the family and the therapists believe that they are entering the final stages, new problems may arise which bring them back to the middle stages. Illustrations of this process will appear in Chapter 9, describing the family hypnotherapy journey of the Vesuvius family.

5

Final Stages of Family Hypnotherapy

Experienced therapists know that the stages of family therapy in general (and of family hypnotherapy in particular) are not distinct. They overlap. Because of the systemic thinking in family therapy, the focus of therapeutic intervention is concrete, aimed at eliminating specific symptoms or at improving areas of discomfort. Unlike vaguer therapeutic aims of other approaches, such as personality restructuring, family therapy acknowledges the presenting symptom seriously and helps family members deal more effectively with each other and with diverse circumstances of their living. In practice, this means that the family learns new skills, coping mechanisms, and forms of communication which make their lives less painful and stressful. Families know when they have reached their therapeutic goals and family therapists generally do not interpret the family's desire to terminate as a manifestation of resistance.

GAINS MADE

The final stages of family hynotherapy start when the family has assimilated the techniques of right hemispheric activation and applies them to the improvement of their family living and when they have moved from individualistic thinking about family problems to systemic thinking, thanks to the application of hypnotic methods in their lives. The final stages may take from one to five or six sessions, although usually we prefer to start separating sessions of the final stage of family hypnotherapy by more than one week. When we realize that the family has made progress in dealing with problems and with each other, we review what they are doing right (and different from what they were doing before therapy). Then we suggest that they continue to practice what they have learned during the two or three weeks between the counseling sessions. At the same time we encourage each member to keep a private written record of highs and lows of family interaction. This written record is not to be shared with other family members until we meet again in the therapy session.

Araoz (1985) has referred to the New Hypnosis method as the quintessence of client-centeredness because it reaches more directly the inner mind experiences of people, unlike the approach to therapy that relies mainly on words and self-description to reach the person's current feelings. The first goal of the final stages of family hypnotherapy is just this: to have learned to respect one's inner experiences and to use them for the enrichment of self and family. The constant repetition of this method during the family therapy sessions is in itself a training that gradually becomes part of the new perspective on family difficulties our clients develop. Thus the therapy sessions themselves are a laboratory where people learn that this method is productive and has good results for their family well-being. When we hear comments about their using this approach on their own, we know that we are reaching the final stages of family hypnotherapy. People say such things as, "I was getting more and more annoyed at my son on the way home, going over in my mind the things I was going to tell him. Then I started to listen to myself and realized how angry I was and how demeaning to him I could become. So I changed my mental movie and started to run the film of my talking to him, reasoning with him, and not saying anything that would be demeaning to him. By the time I got home I was calm and when I talked to my son I did it just right. I felt very proud of myself." This was a situation in which the

20-year-old son owed the father some money and had not paid him on time, as promised. Events like these, reported to us when we ask the family members for signs of improvement, are the proof—both for us and for the clients—that they have learned new and effective ways of resolving difficulties and dealing with each other. This same family entered family hypnotherapy complaining about constant fighting, especially between father and son. Each used to become abusive towards the other, and then both would feel depressed and withdrawn. The above comment was made by the father during the ninth session of family hypnotherapy. The son had reported earlier on similar coping reactions to situations that otherwise could have become very negative, as in the past.

EFFECTIVE CHANGE

At our presentations to professionals, we frequently hear the objection that our method is simplistic, that change seems to happen too quickly. We do not believe in apparent change, as expressed initially when we lead people into the experiential centeredness of the New Hypnosis. We must believe them when they recount incidents like the preceding one. Once they start paying attention to their reactions and recording an increasing number of effective coping maneuvers, we have the proof that we need to justify our method. After a couple of months of improvement, family hypnotherapy is finished. It seems that our culture has accepted as valid the twofold belief that effective change requires understanding of all the forces involved in the formation and maintenance of the problem and that change is a prolonged and tedious process. To realize thoroughly the fallacy of this twofold belief, one needs to understand the complexities of human change.

Since its inception more than a quarter of a century ago, the Mental Research Institute (Fisch et al., 1982; Watzlawick et al., 1974) has been studying this issue systematically. It is impossible to summarize their scholarly work in a few paragraphs. However, for our purposes, two concepts developed by them must be mentioned. One of the basic principles needed to understand how problems develop and stay is that of the "more of the same" syndrome. In many human conditions this becomes an important contributor to the very problems the "more of the same" solution is trying to resolve. The abuse of alcohol is not addressed adequately by restrictions culminating in prohibition, as history has shown. Government opposition is not stopped by increasing limitations to freedom for the dissenters. More of the wrong solution, in both cases, exacerbates the problem.

This concept is intimately related to the distinction between *first-order change* and *second-order change*. The first takes place within the system without altering it, whereas second-order change is a drastic alteration of the system itself. An example from family therapy is our initial attempt at improving the interactions between family members (first-order change). If this does not succeed, the family may have to change drastically through divorce or the separation of a child from the household (second-order change). The same distinction applies to change in external behavior without change in one's self-perception and attitude toward one's life, purpose, meaning, and values (first-order change) and, on the other hand, the *internal* change we help people achieve through right hemispheric activation: the second-order change of self-perception and world-perception. When I see myself and experience myself differently from before, I change my internal system. This second-order change was described as "self-transformation, or metanoia" by Araoz (1985).

Therefore, the apparently superficial changes that take place thanks to the use of hypnotic methods and techniques occur at the level of self-perception. They are, indeed, a change in one's existential reality. Because clients have an opportunity to experience *themselves* differently by means of the hypnotic methods used in family hypnotherapy, they modify spontaneously the way they perceive and interpret the world and its events around them. As we said earlier, the final test of the success of this approach lies in the clients themselves. More so than in individual psychotherapy, in our case we have the whole family to confirm and validate the assertions of one family member claiming that there is improvement. The whole family atmosphere tells of the genuineness of the improvement.

These issues, perhaps verging on philosophy rather than mere statistical assessment, are relevant especially during the final stages of family hypnotherapy. The therapist as an individual has to be clear in his or her mind regarding what change is all about. At what point can we truly state that the family has changed for the better? Pragmatically and existentially we must assess the postintervention family style as compared with the preintervention way of relating and the effects it had on the individual family members. If before family hypnotherapy one or more individuals felt nonvalidated by other family members and now they feel comfortable in the family constellation, we know that "change for the better" has taken place. This instance is representative of what many families report, frequently adding that they do not know exactly how much our interventions are directly responsible for the improvement. One father believed that the fairly long car trip of the family to our office was in itself therapeutic, acting as an "induction" into the hypnotherapy "mood." This is a reminder of the difficulty encountered when trying to measure exactly what the change of family hypnotherapy is about.

MULTIMODAL ASSESSMENT

The two main parameters mentioned at the beginning of this chapter—use of right hemispheric activation to facilitate interaction and a systemic attitude toward family issues—also comprise improved communication, as discussed in Chapter 4. With this in mind we use an adaptation of Lazarus's (1976) convenient multimodal BASIC I.D. as a checklist for family interaction progress. An example of a couple who were on the brink of separation illustrates the multimodal assessment. Before family hypnotherapy, the BASIC I.D. for the husband who did not feel validated by his family looked like this:

Behaviors: "Whenever I talk about anything that interests me, my wife and children say that I am lecturing or show distinct disinterest in what I am talking about. I then become annoyed and tell them off. We end up in a fight."

Affect: "They seem to dislike me; not to care about the things that I care about. I feel tense when with my family. I have to watch everything I say. Often I end up feeling down and depressed. And even then, I don't feel I can talk to my wife about it because I have tried to do it in the past and all I get is 'You take everything so seriously.' "

Sensations: "I sense their tension when I start talking and I become all tensed up myself."

Imagery: "They seem to have a made-up picture of me as a bore and I keep thinking of a pleasant family in which we are interested in each other, listen to each other, etc."

Cognitions: "I keep thinking, 'I'm just the breadwinner. They don't give a damn about me otherwise.' "

Interpersonal: (See above: each one of the BASIC entries is in this case "interpersonal.")

Diet: He had mentioned several times that because of "A" and "S" he often lost appetite or ended up having a drink instead of eating with the family.

We decided that family hypnotherapy was coming to an end after 11 sessions (three with the couple and their two children and eight with the couple alone) when the BASIC I.D. had changed as follows:

Behaviors: "Now we can talk without fighting. Family meals are a joy. None of the fights we had before."

Affect: "Oh, I feel much happier. I know now that Ruth cares, she's interested in what makes me tick. And everybody seems happier. There is more humor and joking around. It's really nice now."

Sensations: "I don't have any of the old tension I used to have every time we were together. And they are much more relaxed with me in general. I like it."

Imagery: "The early picture of a nice family has become a reality. And I have to thank the children and especially Ruth for that. I wanted family therapy. They first laughed at me and now, look at them. They are all better off for it."

Cognitions: "As I say, I am grateful for my family and, you know
    what? I think they are happy with me too. I keep saying to my-
    self that I had come to believe that things were never going to
    be better but I was wrong."
Interpersonal: "Because I am in a better mood, I don't mind helping
    the kids and helping around the house. I have more energy
    and seeing the family happier keeps my energy flowing. I get
    less angry when things don't go the way I want them, etc."
Diet: "No problems with appetite now. In fact I have to watch my
    weight now. I went back to jogging, I smoke less, I drink less.
    I feel pretty good about myself."

The preceding example of how we use the modified BASIC I.D.
belongs to the father who had the initial complaints that brought
the family to therapy. The same checklist, based on Lazarus's
model, is also applied to the other members of the family. This we
do while the session is going on, not as a specific assessment interview. When we have gathered the "evidence" from all family members that there has been a change for the better, we can conclude
that family hypnotherapy has come to an end.

Of the hypnotic techniques that we stress more emphatically
during the final stages of therapy, we select those that the family
has found especially helpful. As Chapter 2 described in detail, we
keep in mind the five master techniques. In general we have found
Mental Rehearsal and Activation of Personality Parts especially
helpful, with Positive Outlook coming next in usefulness for the
future.

The final stages of family hypnotherapy are really the training
needed to continue in the future (without therapy) benefiting from
what was learned during the therapy sessions. As mentioned earlier, we purposely stage the last therapy meetings farther apart to
make clear to the clients that they *have changed*, that they are reacting and behaving in ways that are more satisfying and enriching to
them. After the last *session* with the family, (see Part II) we still keep
in contact as a follow-up.

FOLLOW-UP

The follow-up questionnaire consists of a series of questions, as indicated in the Preface. The five questions are open ended and allow the family to express freely what the experience of family therapy meant to them. Since we completed the research mentioned in the Introduction, we now give these questions to the family in the last (follow-up) session, as it is shown in the discussion of the Cronans (Chapter 7). The family stays alone for a while in our office and discusses the questions. One family member is assigned to write down the answers and when the therapists return, we try not to discuss what they have written. If they have comments or questions, we address them. If they do not have anything to say, we end family therapy. However, we tell them that we shall call them on the telephone in about a month.

About four weeks later, one of the therapists calls the family to find out how they are doing and asks them if anything new has happened during that time. If we sense a loss of therapeutic gains, we suggest the possibililty of another session to review what has been going on and to reinforce the gains made during family hypnotherapy. About half of the people we perceive to be in need of this extra session accept our offer. This constitutes about 20 percent of the families we see in family hypnotherapy.

Finally, about three to four months later, we make the last telephone call and proceed as we did during the first call. If everything reported is positive in a general sense, we consider the case closed. If at this point, however, there are new or renewed old difficulties with the family, we invite them for another session. It should be clarified that these "invitations" are regular sessions for which the family pays the regular therapy fee.

We believe that a family hypnotherapy case starts with the first communication, usually a telephone call from one of the parents requesting our consultation, and ends only after the three-point follow-up has been conducted, as just explained. As a matter of fact, follow-up, in our view, is an essential part of the final stages of family therapy. Families seem to like this show of concern, as many letters spontaneously written to us at one point or another during the follow-up months testify. In the cases presented in Part 2 of this book, we indicate in detail the final follow-up *session*, which takes place before our phone calls.

SUMMARY

Even though we have discussed the three stages of family hypnotherapy, the division of the therapeutic process is artificial. Often the family goes through stages with each of several problems they present. Much overlapping takes place and, as will be detailed in the case of the Vesuvius family, the movement from "final" to middle stages is frequent. In other words, once the first presenting problem is solved, the family moves on to a new problem which was uncovered while dealing with the first issue. Thus, as often happens, a behavioral problem of a child leads to the issue of different values held by each parent regarding child rearing, discipline or family loyalty. In this case, the family in therapy moves from "final" stage back to a "middle" stage, even though the issue or problem has changed.

A more realistic conceptualization of the family therapy process is the OLD C paradigm, explained in the Introduction and elsewhere (Araoz & Negley-Parker, 1985; Negley-Parker & Araoz, 1985b). Throughout the therapeutic process we keep proceeding from "observation" to "leading," which is the essence of the change process. Again, the case studies of Part II will help make this evident. Based on what the family—each member individually and in the interaction with the others—presents, either consciously or, especially, nonconsciously (important statements, somatics, and language style), we lead them to an awareness and recognition of their true feelings, their perceptions, interpretations, and behaviors resulting from these. This honest recognition provides them with new possibilities of choice both of attitude and of behavior.

6

Evaluation and Assessment in Family Hypnotherapy

The evidence of psychotherapy outcome research is growing. Forsyth and Strong (1986) wrote an intelligent and detailed summary of what research in individual therapy has offered so far. Levant (1984) presented a comprehensive study of the evidence in family therapy outcome research building on the first landmark review of family therapy research by Wells, Dilkes, and Trivelli (1972). Stiles, Shapiro, and Elliott (1986) addressed themselves to the intriguing question regarding the equivalency of different psychotherapeutic approaches, while Howard, Kopta, Krause, and Orlinsky (1986) studied the correlation between length of therapy and effectiveness.

Our goal in this chapter is modest. We do not intend to prove that family hypnotherapy is *the best* clinical tool for working with families. We simply propose to point out the advantages of knowing how to apply this method, the cases and circumstances in which it is reasonable to expect it to produce beneficial effects, and to clarify effectiveness in terms of the family therapy goals at hand.

Forsyth and Strong (1986), although carefully and rightly qualifying the question "Does it work?," still seem to accept it as essentially valid. We believe it to be the wrong question and consequently bound to always yield wrong answers. The right question, we submit, is "When can we reasonably expect family hypnotherapy to be effective?" Our reasoning and evidence, we hope, will demonstrate that family hypnotherapy, under the right circumstances, is first not harmful ("Primum non nocere") and, second, therapeutically beneficial. The right circumstances, obviously, will be specified. Further, we hope to show that the skills necessary for using our method are valuable for the family therapist interested in helping families change.

As mentioned in Chapter 1, the clinician is concerned with doing what is *best* for the family at a particular point in the interaction and development of the family as a system. In one's attempt to help the family, the wider the range of interventions, the easier it is for the clinician to find the one that fits the concrete circumstances of the case (Sherman & Fredman, 1986). This range of interventions must consist of techniques and methods that are proportionate to achieving the goals of therapy. These goals are ultimately to help the family improve their situation (resolve their problem) so that they can live life more fully, according to their values and reality. In other words, the goal is always *to change something in the system*: situations or attitudes, external circumstances, internal perceptions, outward behavior, or all of these elements.

Family therapy outcome research is obviously based on what clinicians do or on the method and techniques employed by them to help families change. The goals of family therapy outcome research are scientific: to find the facts that allow for replication of results. This means that this type of research will help organize data into laws that establish what must be done to replicate the desired outcome. This research investigates what *has been done* in order to determine what *must be done* to attain desired outcomes and to avoid undesired ones. More concretely, it asks, "What makes certain therapeutic interventions effective?" "What thwarts the intended results?" and, most important, "What are the laws that regulate the attainment of desired effects?" Once these laws are discovered, we can apply definite methods to attain the desired outcomes and to avoid their opposites. This is the scientific nature of therapy, the point at which we reach generalization through replication of procedures and outcomes.

The exactitude of the physical sciences cannot be expected in family therapy. This platitude needs to be emphasized in view of recent attempts to make therapy scientific. For example, the efforts of Roy and Sawyers (1986) and of Shields (1986a,b) are valiant beginnings in this direction. However, as long as the model for being scientific is still that of the experimental method, the very essence of family therapy is distorted because the unpredictable variables of human interaction (at the essence of family therapy) cannot be quantified and isolated as easily as in the physical sciences. In this respect, Tomm's (1986) sober presentation is refreshing. Relying on Bateson's (1979) and Maturana and Varela's (1980) research, Tomm proposes a fresh view of "objectivity," which is hopeful and challenging from a scientific viewpoint. On the other hand, Shields' "demonstrated [evidence] that new methods exist that can be used for the empirical analysis of family therapy interaction" (1986b, p. 379) is far from conclusive.

What Lieberman wisely remarked about hypnosis applies as well to psychotherapy in general and to family therapy in particular: "The experimental factor (therapeutic technique) may indeed not be the cause of the result, but the experimental factor *interacting with something in the situation, as part of the ongoing system*, may be causing the effect" (1977, p. 65; emphasis added). Relying on Kuhn, he concludes that "in the behavioral sciences experiments are used mostly for political reasons" (1962, p. 66).

Consequently, the best we can do is to discover laws that regulate, not the inevitability of particular results as in the physical sciences, but *the reasonable expectation* that certain operations (therapeutic techniques), under certain circumstances, will produce certain results. In our case, as stated earlier in this chapter, we hope to show that family hypnotherapy allows the clinician *to expect* beneficial outcomes for family change when certain conditions are present.

First we review the two main characteristics of the New Hypnosis as applied to family therapy: it is family-centered and it is experiential. Later we address the questions posed earlier: When can family hypnotherapy be expected to be beneficial? Beneficial for what? Why is this method better than others? Finally, we enumerate some laws governing family hypnotherapy, as they are derived from our experience and research.

Araoz (1985) commented on the quintessence of client-centeredness of the New Hypnosis. This means that we use verbal communication together with body awareness to help clients get to the meanings underlying their verbal output. We do not ask them to expand on what they say but on what is going on nonconsciously while they speak. This means that talk is not the main element of therapy; inner experiencing is, as we explained in the Introduction. We use the clients' words to lead them to inner awareness and experiencing. We use inner associations to exhaust the meaning of what they are currently experiencing, even though at the initial talking level they are not conscious of that inner meaning. Anything said by clients that can be "translated" into mental images can serve as a point of therapeutic entry. If one spouse states that the other is "driving her crazy," we do not ask her to expand on that by requesting more information: "What does he do?," "How long has he been doing this?," and so forth. We invite her to stay with her statement and, in a relaxed state of mind, allow any and all associations that spontaneously come up in her mind. "He's driving me crazy" may thus elicit memories of a relative whose spouse was blamed when she had to be hospitalized for a mental breakdown. It may also bring up a cartoonlike fantasy of a person dressed like a clown going raving mad. The same statement repeated to herself may also produce a mental scene in which her husband is yelling at her, ranting and raving while she stands helpless before him. Of course, the possibilities are probably infinite.

The therapeutic paradigm for this method is summarized in the Introduction and explained more thoroughly elsewhere (Araoz, 1985). The complete and respectful client-centeredness which spontaneously leads to inner experiencing is thus essential to enlarge one's perception of self and one's world, which naturally leads to a change in reactions, attitudes, and behavior.

Total client-centeredness, well beyond the Rogerian concept, and its consequence, inner experiencing within the enlarged range of one's inner perception, constitute the two essential characteristics of the New Hypnosis approach.

Safe and Beneficial

The corollary of the last statement is that this method is safe for most people encountered in the practice of counseling and psychotherapy. Psychotics, whose delusions and hallucinations may make it difficult for them to distinguish between mental productions and external reality, form the broad category for whom this approach is not advisable.

For other clients, our method of hypnotherapy is not harmful. Our research, and that of seven former students now in the practice of family hypnotherapy, consistently shows that no deleterious consequences follow the application of this method (Araoz, 1979,1984c). This has been consistent through six years of data collecting, regardless of therapist's sex or age and irrespective of whether the family was seen by cotherapists or by a single clinician. The most negative outcome of this method was that it did not work with some families. In that case, the therapists switched to more traditional therapeutic techniques. But no damage came from using this approach.

Our interpretation is that clients accept readily the invitation to delve into *their own* mental productions. This method does not introduce any *new* elements, ideas, or images that are not first reported by the clients. The care and respect for the clients, implicit in this method, avoids resistance on their part and makes them curious to pursue what is perceived as a possible lead into one's own (unknown) secrets. Because the therapists use any of the nonconscious elements that language style, important statements, and somatics (see Introduction) may elicit, the clients are always focusing on their own inner activity. The four-step paradigm (OLD C) makes this method additionally safe. The therapists do not encourage clients to report and talk about what is happening at the moment. The discussion is left for the third step and, even there, clients are reminded that they do not have to talk about anything they do not want to talk about. The emphasis is on their inner experiencing, not on their reporting to us what they experience.

With the same "naturalness" with which this method leads clients into their nonconscious associations, the process can be stopped or interrupted at any time. This flexibility adds to the sense of safety clients experience when working hypnotically according to our approach.

A brief clinical vignette may illustrate and justify our interpretation of why this approach is not harmful. The family had practiced hypnotherapy several times before, during the first three sessions. Now at the fourth session, the son, 17, said about his mother, "She makes me sick." The transcript follows.

Therapist: Wait, Walt. Check this out. Where do you feel that your mother makes you sick? Where in your body?

Walt: I don't know . . . I mean . . . I guess in my stomach.

Therapist: Close your eyes for a moment. Put your hand on your stomach and keep saying, "Mom makes me sick." Say it slowly, again and again, and pay attention to any memories, any new feelings, and mental pictures. Just take your time until you learn a little more about yourself, your mom making you sick, you and your mom. "She makes me sick to my stomach. . . ."

Walt stayed with his own "thoughts" for a few minutes. Later he reported two main things. First, he told of memories from childhood when he was sick (he had had a "weak stomach" when he was between 7 and 10 years old). These memories included his mother taking care of him when he was sick in bed. Then earlier memories, not too clear, of someone rubbing his "tummy" as a little child. Second, he reported feeling like a baby and realizing that perhaps his mother reacted to him the same way. This feeling was mixed with guilt and a desire to do something for his mother. The following conversation between parents and son touched on issues they considered important. Some of these were a power struggle for the mother's attention that went on between father and son and the son's nonconscious desire to be sick.

The point of this excerpt from a clinical case is that our hypnotherapeutic method works with families by allowing them to move speedily into meaningful issues. We offer respectful attention to everything that clients bring up spontaneously; thus we do not use formalized inductions but naturalistically "induce" the hypnotic mental mode, based on what they have presented without being aware of what they have said—as in the foregoing case—or of what they do, as when we use somatics to lead them into right hemispheric activity.

The mother, while saying to her husband, "Tommy is the way he is because *you* are so irresponsible. When are *you* going to grow up?" had her right leg crossed over her left and was moving her right leg back and forth. The therapist asked her to keep the leg movement and repeat to herself, "When are you going to grow up?" When the mother did this, the therapist suggested that she pay attention to any feeling, sensation, or internal awareness that might come up. The result was predictable. The woman, after merely a couple of minutes, burst out, "Yes, I'd like to kick him. I'd like to kill you, you immature, irresponsible bastard. You don't pay the bills. Our telephone has been cut off. You keep those stupid investments that never turn out right and then you want me to be understanding. No! I hate you when you do that and, yes, I'd like to kick you all over. That's my feeling, if you want to know." From that instance on, the whole family was able to communicate more effectively, whereas before they had tended to intellectualize.

Through the use of somatics, we were able to help the mother get in touch with inner experiences, which she had detached herself from through intellectualizations. The fact that this intervention was a turning point in this family's mode of communicating allows us to judge this method beneficial. By collecting many instances like this, we can reach some general conclusions, as we explain toward the end of this chapter. Before doing this, we concentrate on the circumstances and situations in which hypnotherapy is effective. This discussion will naturally lead us to the advantages for the family therapist of learning this method. Then we list the general conclusions mentioned.

The Right Circumstances

T. X. Barber's (1969) findings were too carefully gathered, ana-
lyzed, and interpreted to be dismissed almost two decades later.
His conclusions refer to the interaction that takes place between
clients and professionals during hypnosis. He found that hypnosis
"works" when clients trust the procedure, have the right expectations (not magical hopes), and have a cooperative attitude (a desire
to learn about themselves) coupled with the motivation to benefit
from hypnosis (see Introduction).

What T. X. Barber discovered in individual clients, we have confirmed in families. When these conditions are present, the family
therapist can use hypnosis safely and with the reasonable expectation of benefiting the family interaction.

Besides these general conditions, however, there are special circumstances in family therapy in which hypnotherapy becomes the
treatment of choice. Sherman and Fredman, in their chapter on
fantasy and imagery, list the "powerful advantages available to
those therapists who use the techniques of imagery and metaphor"
(1986, p. 14). These are what we call "hypnotic." The six "advantages" that constitute the circumstances in which hypnotherapy
may be used advantageously follow:

1. The family is rigidly bound by the family members' own habitual patterns of thinking, which limit their possibilities (see Third
   and Sixth Laws, below). In this case, it is helpful to encourage
   them "to try on" new possibilities, behaviors, and the like. Under the same category, we have situations where feelings relating to past events need to be resolved, such as things one might
   have said to a deceased relative.
2. Family members need encouragement to expand their focus of
   perception, to become more creative, or to find further possibilities or options (see Fourth Law, below).
3. The family needs new models of behavior (see Fifth and Sixth
   Laws, below). In Sherman and Fredman's words, "The family
   envisions a scene that represents the best of all marriages, families or worlds. They describe the scene. They are asked to enact

the scene together or in imagination. The therapist assists them to restructure the scene in a way that includes new constructive relationships in the family" (1986, p. 15).

4. Families are afraid of change (see Second and Fourth Laws, below). Hypnosis, building on what comes from them, not from the therapist, becomes a safe experience. By using their own inner productions, the therapist can tactfully enlarge the family's experience. For instance, if a family is imaging the best possible relationship among its members, the therapist may add some elements they may have omitted, such as distribution of household chores or respecting each other's points of view. Because people "think" about things, they may feel comfortable facing in their own minds difficult situations that produce discomfort when discussed.

5. Families have feelings of powerlessness (see Fourth Law, below). Hypnosis allows people to rehearse situations in more positive terms than what they experience in reality, empowering them and leading to greater self-control.

6. A family's perception of their problems needs reframing and creative solutions are lacking. As Sherman and Fredman put it, "It is better to hear that you have a creative mind than that you are sick or disturbed" (1986, p. 15).

Besides these six situations, it is obvious that hypnotherapy is preferable to verbal exchange in families that are overly intellectual and rational, as well as with families that are obviously involved in negative self-hypnosis. This is what Sherman and Fredman call the family mythology:

> Many of these myths take the form of assumptive, unquestioned values and expectations that cannot be realized in the real world or with one's real partner or family. These myths may contribute to a severe narrowing of options and flexibility in the dysfunctional family. The therapist's pointing out of the rigidity or indicating new options may not be sufficient for the family to overcome the power of such myths which are deeper than digital logic and more compelling. (1986, p. 12)

To take advantage of the value we have found in activating right hemispheric activity, we tend to use the hypnotic method as our preferred therapeutic language. For the therapist who is beginning to learn this approach, the preceding list of situations or circumstances in which hypnosis can reasonably be expected to be effective may act as a practical guide. This introduces us to the benefits for the family therapist of learning this method.

Useful to Learn

To make the unconscious conscious, as Freudians say; to increase awareness, as Gestaltists state; to potentiate right hemispheric functioning, in the language of Ericksonians; or simply to get clients in touch with their true feelings, as most nonbehavioral therapists would agree, is one of the important means used by psychotherapy to help people lead more satisfying lives. Family hypnotherapy, centering totally on the system and its constituent parts and encouraging inner (personal) experiencing, provides a naturalistic means of helping families get in touch with their true feelings, become aware of inner processes and dynamics, potentiate right hemispheric function and thus to make nonconscious realities conscious. Bandler et al. (1976) studied in detail the patterns of effective family therapy. By direct, left hemispheric interaction it is difficult to help families understand the patterns they presently acknowledge and use and the expectations that they have (1976, p. 19). However, as Bandler et al. state, "By systematically connecting words with specific experiences with each of the family members" the family can discover the experiences that will be satisfying to them (1976, p. 32). Once the level of inner experiencing is reached, it is easier and more natural (less forced and artificial) to identify the processes by which the family perceives reality. Because "the unconscious choices we make are systematic and reveal a great deal about the ways in which we organize our experience, grow and change" (p. 54), a method that reaches securely, though naturalistically, to that nonconscious level is worth considering. The three basic defects in perception—generalization, deletion, and distortion (see Bandler & Grinder, 1975a,b)—by which experience is distorted (or rather, external reality is modified) can be detected more directly and easily hypnotically than by mere conversation (see Chapter 3).

Finally, since most humans' thinking is imaginative rather than abstract, as Singer and McCraven (1961) found out when studying daydreams, a method that reaches directly that modality of thinking saves steps and energy and shortens the process of change. For family therapists, particularly, hypnotic techniques do not need to be foreign. We are familiar with metaphors, reframing, and paradoxes. Papp (1984) believes that the family dysfunction itself is a symbol of the family needs. The symptom keeps the system in balance, as many strategic family therapists see it (e.g., Andolfi & Zwerling, 1980; de Shazer, 1982; Duhl, 1982; Haley, 1980,1984; L'Abate, 1984; Madanes, 1981,1984; Selvini Palazzoli et al., 1978). But this conceptualization obviously goes beyond logic and reason, thus entering the domain of alteration of external reality and inner experiencing. Hypnosis is the tool to deal with these subjective realities.

The usefulness of knowing hypnosis for the family therapist is presented by Dammann (1982) as a summary of Milton H. Erickson's contributions: the therapist's responsibility for creating a context for change; the need to assess the resistances for change in the system; and, finally, the acceptance of the fact that change is discontinuous and that strategic methods to make it happen are more effective than attempts at restructuring personalities. All three Ericksonian elements of family therapy focus on current experience, existentially respecting whatever reality clients are living in the present. The method we present in this book is both strategic and existential.

Calof (1985) points to the advantages of hypnosis to deal simultaneously with conscious and nonconscious processes. Ritterman (1983,1985) shows the flexibility and marvelous creative potential of hypnosis with families. Lankton and Lankton (1986) have shown new vistas, standing on the shoulders of their master, Erickson (if the old analogy may be used in this case). They must be given credit for building theory upon Ericksonian principles and practice, both enriching the field of family therapy and teaching new ways of applying hypnosis in systemic work.

At this point, there are too many published reports on the effectiveness of hypnotic techniques in family therapy to ignore the consistent conclusion of clinicians from many different persuasions. The following is merely a random sample. Braun (1984), rooted in psychoanalytical principles, finds profitable ways of helping families by means of hypnosis. Lange (1985) finds hypnosis useful within structural family therapy concepts. Loriedo (1985) employs hypnotic suggestion to improve the family system. Sargent (1986), in a structural–strategic mode, applies therapeutic rituals with hypnosis. Stone (1985) utilizes the metaphors of family interaction, alliances, and other structural dynamics in hypnotic ways. It is interesting to note that the work of all these authors and those cited earlier in this chapter is fairly recent. Given the current concerns with assessment and validation of therapeutic interventions prevalent in the American society, it is not unreasonable to assume that most, if not all, of these reports have paid more attention to the validation of data than other anecdotal accounts of previous times.

In conclusion, the family therapist concerned with effectiveness can no longer ignore hypnotherapy—a method that is coming into its own, not as a new school of thought or theoretical orientation, but as a *method* out of which can emerge many techniques and interventions to help families change.

GENERAL CONCLUSIONS

The following could be considered laws of family hypnotherapy. If one of the definitions of law is a generalization formulated from empirical data, we are now in a position to establish definite laws governing family hypnotherapy. Six laws may be enunciated and each will be explained in detail.

First Law: Hypnosis Is Useful When Family Communication Needs Improvement

Diamond (1986) in a comprehensive article explains the nine factors by which hypnosis enhances traditional psychotherapy. He mentions a focus on communication as the first enriching factor. In family functioning, communication is even more crucial than in individual therapy. The hypnotically trained family therapist will be more sensitive to patterns of communication, both verbal and somatic, as explained in Chapter 4. But this sensitivity will extend to specific details, such as words used (figures of speech, analogies, etc.), intonation, body language while talking and listening to another family member talk. Family hypnotherapists are concerned with and facilitate conditions which make the exchange of information smooth, and unambiguous. The observational task of the therapists (see OLD C model in the Introduction) is directed at every statement in its form and style, even more than in its content. This is so because the content is usually conscious, censored, whereas the form and style are in most cases nonconscious. By attending to them, the family hypnotherapists help the family become aware of the total meaning of the information exchange. The family therapy session thus becomes a living laboratory in which the family learns to refine its messages. This refinement involves both what the person wants to convey and the best way to convey it so that the recipient accepts the message. Awareness of the other person's state of mind, mood, degrees of receptivity, and so on, becomes habitual. Thus communication is made more effective. Chapters 3 to 5 give examples of communication modalities and nuances so that there is no need to illustrate this law any further. We shall, however, list a few types of families that benefit from this law.

In cases where the therapists notice irrelevance, there is obvious need to improve communication. This lack of congruity appears frequently in different degrees. We have noticed that therapists who allow free talking without paying enough attention to the process of communication (see Chapter 4) tend to miss irrelevance. The therapists involved in this survey were advanced graduate students specializing in family therapy and, consequently, novice therapists without solo work experience. However, it is important to notice a tendency toward a correlation between amount of free talk and irrelevance: the more people talk, the less sense they make to each other, seems to be the correlational tendency.

Another family type in need of improvement in communication is the chaotic family where everybody talks at the same time and nobody seems to pay close attention to the others' verbal output. In these families, one often finds people who ask questions and, before anyone else has a chance to respond, the same person answers the question. Finally, in families where one person takes over and "lectures" or makes speeches, effective communication is lacking.

In these cases and in many more, hypnotherapeutic techniques are beneficial. Different approaches can be taken. The family member who talks excessively or is incongruent is asked to stop and go inside of himself, to first hear himself expressing what he wants the others to know or understand. The others are asked to relax and to make themselves receptive to the first person's communication. They are warned against assumptions, mind reading, "knowing the other like an open book," and the like. In some cases, before the verbal exchange is resumed, the whole family is encouraged to imagine themselves communicating effectively. Only then are they asked to speak.

Another intervention is to interrupt the flow of words and to ask everyone in the room to examine how their bodies are reacting to the others' voice, sound, content, meanings, and so forth. Thus a subjective biofeedback (Araoz, 1984a) is established. Before the conversation is continued, time is spent reporting on each person's subjective awareness of the communication process. Frequently the original "conversation" is never resumed because in the exchange of subjective reactions, the family finds more meaning and relevance than in the original "topic of conversation."

Thus the First Law of family hypnotherapy refers to the advisability of employing this method when communication is faulty. Usually families do not become resistant to this kind of intervention. Through hypnosis we invite them to become aware, to listen to themselves. We do not explain, correct, or teach them how to communicate. We encourage them to notice their nonfunctional ways of relating to each other and then we guide them to find more relevant ways of doing it.

Second Law: Hypnosis Is Useful When the Family Is Ambivalent About Change (Improvement)

Personal experience alone teaches us that ambivalence about emotionally laden issues is not resolved rationally. Its resolution depends on the law of dominant effect, as enunciated by Coué (1922) and confirmed by subsequent research. This law states that only a stronger emotion will take precedence over another emotion. Through hypnosis, it is easy to define ambivalence emotionally rather than intellectually (reasons for and against changing) so that the family members are led to experience themselves internally in different changed situations. They are also taught to compare themselves mentally—experientially, or having a *vivencia*, is more accurate—in one situation first and then in a different one. The suggestion to "pretend" that things are different, or that "you react in a new way to the same old situation," can easily be built up hypnotically so that the person is able to have the *vivencia* (see Introduction, p. xx) that will allow him to decide what he wants.

Another hypnotic technique ready-made for ambivalence is Activation of Personality Parts (see Ch. 2), by which the client is helped to come in contact with diverse "parts" of the personality.

Often, of course, one or two family members, rather than the whole family, are ambivalent about changing. The foregoing hypnotic maneuvers are then directed to the ambivalent family members while the others join in the relaxation and are encouraged to start living in their minds what life will be like after things are changed. In this manner, the nonambivalent family members rehearse the new situations and the ambivalent member is given indirect suggestions (while talking to the others about the desired change) which contribute to the resolution of the ambivalence. A transcript from such a case follows:

Father: I don't want her to work. I can provide for her and don't need her income.

Mother: I know that. It makes me happy that you can. But, as I told you, working is good for me. It's not the money. It's that I feel

I'm not just a housewife. I feel I can contribute, you know, with my work as a professional, even though we don't need the money.

Father: I guess I know that but I still don't want you to work.

Daughter: Dad, you *are* old-fashioned. Mom likes to work because it makes her feel like a total person. Don't you understand that? Times have changed . . .

Father: I know, I know. But still . . .

Therapist: John, it sounds as if you are of two minds in this matter. Can you pretend that you feel good about your wife going back to teaching in the school of nursing? Can you pretend that you don't mind it? That you even like it?

Father: Oh, I can pretend anything. But that's not the point.

Therapist: One side of you realizes that it's good *for her* to work. But the other side still feels uncomfortable with it. Is that it?

Father: Yeah. I . . .that's a fair assessment.

Therapist: OK, then. Go inside of yourself and try to connect with those two sides in your inner mind. As we did before. Relax. Close your eyes and think of those two sides in you. Take a minute to concentrate on that. OK? Which side comes up first? The one that does not want your wife to work? Yes? Stay with it for a moment. Listen to that side of you. Look at you when that side is on, as it were. How do you look? What are you wearing? Where are you? You are saying that . . . listen carefully . . . And check your feelings. How are you reacting to this? Do you feel relaxed and good about yourself? And while you are in touch with this side of yourself, your wife and daughter can imagine what it would be like for your wife to go back to work, how happy she'll be. You two, Fanny and Kim, can enjoy the movie in your mind of Fanny going to work, teaching the way she likes to do. And you, Kim, love to see your mother happy, fulfilled as a woman. You know that modern women find fulfillment in work, like men do. And you'll do the same in a few years . . . . What about you, John? Let the other side of you come up now. Do the same as before: Listen to yourself saying that it's OK for Fanny to work. Pretend that you love to see her so happy. Enjoy the way she feels. Feel proud of your wife. She's a professional too. She's respected. You're married to a woman people look up to . . . .

This kind of hypnotic technique, repeated in different ways, places the ambivalence away from pseudo-intellectualizations and at the level of emotional reactions. In the discussion that ensues, it is easier to separate the good reasons (for and against) from the false ones. The initial ambivalence, incidentally, often turns into other issues, previously disregarded or not acknowledged, such as, in the above case, the man's threat to his perceived masculine role. These hidden issues come up spontaneously rather than being forced and thus can be dealt with—also hypnotically—when they make their appearance. Ambivalence, then, leads to further exploration of the family dynamics.

Third Law: Hypnosis Is Useful When the Family Is "Stuck"

Whether the lack of progress and therapeutic movement is due to resistance, boredom, or more positive causes such as the need to take a break, to recuperate, or to recapitulate and assimilate gains previously made, hypnotherapeutic interventions are, at this time, useful. The alternative is often intellectualizations which stop inner experiencing.

In the case of resistance or boredom, the family therapist may either help the family "materialize" the resistance or establish an affect bridge (Watkins, 1971) or an emotional bridge, as Araoz (1985) has called it, deemphasizing the psychoanalytic elements of it. When the reasons for the lack of movement are positive, relaxation, mental rehearsal (future-oriented), and hypnotic review (past-oriented) fit naturalistically into the mood of the family.

To materialize the resistance is a dissociative hypnotic technique, explained elsewhere (Araoz, 1985). The family can be asked if they agree that progress has been made. When they respond affirmatively, they are asked to consider how they could imagine their progress symbolically. Some families see it as a trip, or as the growth of a plant, or as the progressive building of a house or castle. Then they are directed to hypnotically watch that symbol, to allow it to come as alive as it might, to experience themselves somehow connected with this process. Finally, they should somehow witness the interruption or stopping of the progress. The most important aspect of this exercise is for them to become aware of their feelings, their reactions to this event. At this point they often visualize the interruption of progress as something material—perhaps a block, a door, a wall, the end of a road overlooking a precipice. Subsequent discussion leads either to active interaction, thus renewing the progress that the family had been focusing on, or to a decision to interrupt or end family therapy.

In the case of boredom the emotional bridge helps the family connect their current experience with previous ones of a similar nature. When introduced to this possibility, a family started to discuss the advantages and disadvantages of practicing their religion, which, two of the children agreed, would give meaning to their lives. They had interpreted their feeling of boredom as a lack of meaning. Another family associated their current feeling of boredom with an exaggerated sense of security that they had striven to achieve in the previous years. This led them to plan more adventuresome activities such as foreign travel and more vacations. The husband expressed it colorfully: "We are like our stock. Doing well but always more of the same."

When the reasons for having reached a plateau are positive, the family can be invited to relax hypnotically and to let anything come into their minds. Like Sacerdote's (1978) induced dreams, this technique can help the family solidify the gains previously made, feel good about new decisions reached during the previous family therapy sessions, and, in general, feel better about themselves. In Part II, we offer several instances of hypnotic review as a therapeutic intervention.

Fourth Law: Hypnosis Is Useful When There Is a Need to Increase the Family's Expectation of Success

Considered by Diamond one of the factors contributed by hypnotherapy to regular (nonhypnotic) psychotherapy, expectation of success, based on the belief that change for the better is desirable and possible, "plays a major role in facilitating successful treatment" (1986, p. 241). This is a crucial point of distinction between trained psychotherapists using hypnosis and "hypnotists" without specialized clinical preparation. It is very easy to foster magical fantasies already present in many clients, if one is not careful to emphasize the "facilitative" role of hypnosis and to deemphasize the popular myths that hinder the client's autonomy and reality-testing.

The delicate balance between magical fantasies and expectation of success working with families should be a concern of the family therapist (Smith, 1981,1984). Many families arrive at our offices with a sense of frustration and failure. Reason alone is not enough "to convince" them to be hopeful. One of the five master techniques described in Chapter 2 is Past Accomplishments. This intervention, reaching one's experiential level, allows for a time regression in which the family relives previous successes and moments of pride and accomplishment.

It should be remembered that the law of increased expectations applies even in families who deny ever having been successful, effective, or happy. In this case, we resort once more to the practice of hypnotically pretending, which becomes effectively a form of mental rehearsal, as described in Chapter 2. By pretending that they had a successful event in the past, these family members are put in touch with their fantasies and projections, which they themselves then can evaluate and use to take constructive action toward improvement.

The insistence on going through this process right hemispherically avoids resistance, intellectualizations, and excuses. Hypnotically they can experientially taste, as it were, how it feels to be different than they are in the present. Mere talk about it, no matter how prolonged, misses the inner experience. Without an increase in the family's expectation of success, we often find a mood that can be described as family depression. The family as a system is down, functioning below its own capacity and depriving itself of much enjoyment of life.

*Fifth Law: Hypnosis Is Useful When the Family Needs a Holistic
Emphasis*

By holistic emphasis we mean a reconnection between mind
and body, an experiential awareness of how one influences the
other, both positively and negatively. This may refer in some families to issues of health, nutrition, exercise or lack of it, substance
abuse, be it alcohol, caffeine, sugar, or any other substance, legal
or illegal. At the same time, a holistic emphasis, as Lazarus (1976)
points out explaining multimodal psychotherapy, is more directed
toward health and healthy functioning than most traditional psychotherapies. Hypnosis has historically been used both to influence bodily functioning through mind processes and to uncover
and understand the psychological components of bodily manifestations. A perusal of traditional hypnosis texts (for example,
Weitzenhoffer, 1957), or current ones (for example, Wester, 1987)
offers innumerable and documented examples of these two processes.

With families, the group use of three hypnotic techniques brings
the holistic emphasis home to them. These techniques are *the doctor
within* (Araoz, 1984b), *somatic bridge*, and *subjective biofeedback* (Araoz, 1985). The first makes the family aware of the health forces at
work in their bodies, leading naturalistically to a greater respect for
the body's laws and requirements. It is a hypnotic method to take
the side of health and of life. Somatic bridge starts with the body
and helps the family members become aware of inner mental associations that each individual, and often the family as a group, has
established between bodily organs and personal history. Finally,
subjective biofeedback makes the family aware of how the body
reacts to certain thoughts, memories, or beliefs.

To those who practice them, these three hypnotic techniques are
more convincing of the intimate and constant interconnection between body and mind than are reasoning and arguments. The family therapist enriches his possibilities of helping families in this
area if he can use these techniques when the family needs a holistic
emphasis.

Sixth Law: Hypnosis Is Useful When the Family Needs to Examine New Possibilities or Choices

Hilgard's (1977) research culminated the historical tradition started with Janet (1889) and Baudouin (1922) of emphasizing the ego-adaptive functions of the personality in hypnotherapy. Unlike classical Freudian models of the unconscious (Freud, 1915), the nonconscious aspects of human thought have been viewed as creative, artistic, idiosyncratic, playful, and, in general, nonpathological. Erickson (e.g., see Zeig, 1980) appealed frequently to this aspect of mental activity. The beneficial results of this focus have become well-known (Haley, 1973; Zeig, 1982).

New possibilities or choices for a family cover a wide spectrum, from moving to changing jobs, from monetary investments to adopting children, and much more. We have found that to highlight the creative in a playful and humorous way allows the family to come up with many more possibilities than when they go over pros and cons in a solemn, intellectual, coldly objective manner. Each time family members bring up a new possibility that the others are willing to accept as such, we encourage them "to try it on for size" in their mind, to place themselves in that situation and to check how they react to it. Then they discuss it and reject it, modify it, or adopt the new possibility. As can be understood, this Sixth Law overlaps with that of ambivalence (Second Law), with the "stuckness" law (Third), and with the Fourth Law regarding expectations of success. As a matter of fact, humor, playfulness, imagination, and creativity—we believe—are healthier and more effective moods in therapy than their opposites. Family therapists familiar with paradoxical interventions (Weeks & L'Abate, 1982) are probably more receptive to the benign aspects of nonconscious processes than others in the mental health field. However, it should be remembered that respected psychoanalysts have long held the belief that playfulness and creativity have significant therapeutic value (Hartmann, 1939; Kris, 1952; Winnicott, 1971).

Since most people are uncomfortable with the unfamiliar and unknown, the family finds it less threatening to consider new possibilities and choices by employing this method of make-believe and pretend, of playfully imagining themselves in those new situations. Like children frightened by their own fantasies bring themselves back to reality by reminding themselves, "It's just make-believe," families in hypnotherapy can always "try on" new possibilities, behaviors, or changes without committing themselves to anything yet because it is still at this point "just make-believe." Then, in the discussion stage following the hypnotic practice, they can exchange impressions of their own reactions to the hypnotic practice and eventually make satisfactory decisions. Because the whole family is encouraged to participate in these activities, the final decisions are truly family decisions, arrived at by the input of all family members for the benefit of the whole family system.

These six laws or general conclusions flow from our own clinical experience coupled with the published reports, as listed in the first part of this chapter. As we stated at the beginning, our intention was to point out the family therapy situations in which hypnotherapeutic interventions are useful and consequently to argue in favor of the advisability for the family therapist to learn this method. Rather than asserting that this method works, we can state without hesitation that in the conditions enumerated above, *there is reasonable expectation* for it to be of benefit to the families we work with in therapy.

Our evaluation and assessment of family hypnotherapy are pragmatic. Agreeing with Zilbergeld (1983) on the danger of making problems out of ordinary difficulties of normal living and thus selling therapy as a necessary commodity, we still believe that normal difficulties can be minimized with external professional help. This is particularly so in the case of difficulties of couples and families where several people are usually involved, and the "normal difficulties" become complicated because of the complexity of the personalities making up the family system. The normal difficulties of living produce in some families "problems." But, as Fisch et al. (1982) carefully explained, what people call problems are, more accurately, complaints. And our concern, like theirs, is how the situation persists so that the people continue to have the same complaint about it. Their basic viewpoint, with which we agree in theory and in clinical practice, is that problems are essentially behavioral, including in this term cognitions, beliefs, perceptions, and other *mental behaviors*. Clients, therefore, realizing it or not, keep repeating behaviors which sustain the "problem." The other element of this viewpoint is that families with problems find themselves making efforts to end them, although the very efforts perpetuate the problems. In the words of Fisch et al.: "The specific locus of problem-maintaining behaviors regularly lies in those very behaviors which the patient and any others concerned are performing in their attempts to control or resolve the problem" (1982, p. 286).

These self-defeating behaviors are usually learned early in life and thus are not seen as illogical. As a matter of fact, often they are logical. Because people and families are caught up in this cycle, they benefit from external (professional) help. As long as family therapists help families simplify their problems and recognize their component parts, responsible for the problems' persistence— rather than joining their "catastrophizing" and reinforcing their cultural beliefs about deep and obscure personality causes to explain their problems—our interventions will continue to enrich the quality of living for many families.

SUMMARY

The clinician has an obligation to be scientific by finding out what types of interventions work under particular circumstances to obtain predictable results. The New Hypnosis, as a method to utilize one's inner or mental experiences, is safe for nonpsychotic clients, as research has shown.

There are six situations when family hypnotherapy is advantageous: 1) when families are rigidly bound by their own habitual patterns of thinking; 2) when families need to perceive new possibilities; 3) when families need new models of behavior; 4) when families are afraid of change; 5) when families feel helpless to improve; and 6) when families need to reframe the understanding of their problem. Using hypnosis in these situations makes it possible for family members to get in touch with what they truly feel, bypassing language and intellectualizations.

The situations in which family hypnotherapy is effective, as reported by practitioners of diverse theoretical orientations, elicit six laws of family hypnotherapy: 1) Hypnosis helps family communication; 2) hypnosis facilitates the attainment of family goals; 3) hypnosis helps families move out of "plateaus"; 4) hypnosis increases families' expectations of success; 5) hypnosis facilitates a holistic emphasis; and 6) hypnosis uncovers new possibilities or choices.

From all of the above, there is objective justification to employ hypnosis in family therapy under specific circumstances.

PART II

Case Studies

We selected three families to represent our entire therapeutic contact, from the first call for an appointment to follow-up. Each case is introduced with general information that, it is hoped, will facilitate the understanding of that family. The case is then unfolded by following each session in detail. We transcribed as much material as is relevant, in some cases the whole session from beginning to end. However, rather than comment on each session at its conclusion, in some cases we interrupt the session to interject our comments before continuing the same session. At the end of each session, we add our own thinking on what happened during the time we spent with the family, as well as our projections for the forthcoming sessions.

The candor with which we expose ourselves is a sincere attempt at "showing" the reader our method of family hypnotherapy or the way we do family hypnotherapy. As an attempt at providing meaningful learning of this method, we present our mistakes together with our successful interventions. The fact that this material is in writing has the advantage over videotapes in that the reader can go back and forth from section to section, almost putting two sections together for comparison or analysis. The disadvantage is that our written descriptions of physical reactions to the ongoing process in the sessions always fall short of the actual viewing of those reactions, which is possible with videotapes.

If the first part of the book was rather didactic, this part is eminently practical. It must be read more like a play than an essay. We suggest that each therapy session be read as a whole, preferably in one sitting.

The three families were selected on pragmatic issues, such as continuity of sessions, complete recording of each session, and general participation of its members. We believe that this threefold "sample" of our work may be helpful in illustrating family hypnotherapy.

7

The Family That Knew Too Much

Mrs. Cronan (all names are fictitious, as is customary in published reports, in order to protect the privacy of clients) called on the telephone to make an appointment for family therapy. She wanted to explain many details about herself, her husband, her 10-year-old daughter, and her 8-year-old son. DLA discouraged her from talking over the phone but learned, nevertheless, that all of them had been in individual therapy until two months earlier. Because she felt that "all that therapy was getting nowhere," she had convinced her husband to try family therapy. She had been reading meaningful material on family therapy and decided that it would make more sense than having the four family members going to three different therapists (the two children were seen by the same child psychologist). As it turned out, she, Nancy, age 33, had been in therapy since the age of 8—for 25 years with the same therapist, in both individual and group sessions. The husband, Peter, 34, whom she had met in one of the groups, had changed to another therapist and had accumulated 22 years "in treatment." The daughter, Annie, had started individual therapy at the age of 5 and the son, Rusty, at the age of 6. All together, this family had had 54 years of individual or group therapy!

We felt that this would be an interesting case and a challenge to our hypnotherapeutic approach. The first appointment was set for a week after the initial phone call and two hours were reserved for this first visit.

FIRST SESSION

The family arrived on time. They looked like the ideal middle-class American family: well dressed and groomed, youthful and friendly, ready to get going without any sign of resistance or discomfort about coming for family therapy. The office, arranged as a living room, had one couch for three people, one loveseat, one reclining chair, another easy chair, and a straight-back chair. The father sat first on the love seat and the mother sat with the daughter on the couch. The son hesitated first, started to move toward the father, and then turned around and sat on the reclining chair. Even before the son had sat down, the father started the session.

Pete: I guess Nancy spoke to—may I call you, what?

DLA: Daniel is OK.

Pete: I guess she spoke to Dan.

DLA: Pete, I prefer Daniel.

Pete: Sorry, I guess, Daniel, and you know everything about us. But I want to give you my view of the picture and so . . .

ENP: (1)* (interrupting) Pete, my name is Esther. Let me stop you so we understand each other from the beginning. Nancy talked to Daniel and he talked to me afterward. I don't know "everything about your family," as you put it.

DLA: Right.

ENP: We only know that all of you have been in individual therapy and that both you and Nancy have decided to give family therapy a chance.

Pete: Yeah, that's what we are here for. But let me tell you . . .

---

*The numbers in parentheses throughout the recorded dialogues are mere "landmarks," as it were. We use them every time one of the therapists speaks. They may be helpful in finding a specific intervention.

DLA: (2) Pete, I prefer if you would hold what you have in mind for a little while. Could you? And let me first get a feel of you as a family. OK with you?

Pete: Well, I guess. You're the doctor. (Rusty gets up and picks up an art book from a side table but stays looking at it, giving his back to all of us.) Rusty, what the hell do you think you're doing? Sit down and be patient. (Rusty does as ordered without a sound.) OK, Danny, now you take over. What do you want us to do? We're ready. (The last three sentences were said very rapidly, in one breath.)

DLA: (3) (looking at Pete) You asked me how to call me; I said Daniel. Then you called me Dan and now Danny. (with a smile) First thing I want you to do is to get my name straight.

Pete: OK. I'm sorry. Let's get going.

DLA: The second thing I'm interested in is this: Why are you here? Who wants to start?

Rusty: I don't want to be here. I want to go back to see Bill (the children's therapist).

Annie: (almost inaudibly) Yeah, me too.

ENP: But why do you think you are here?

Rusty: I don't know. I guess . . . no, forget it.

Nancy: Come on Rusty, tell us what you think.

Rusty: Ah, well. I guess we're here, I guess, to talk about us (looking at mother), right?

ENP: (4) And you Annie, what do you think?

Annie: Yeah, we have to talk. Yeah, Rusty is right (looking at mother).

ENP: (5) What about you, Nancy? Why are you here?

Nancy: What I think? Well, Pete knows this. That's why he agreed to try family therapy and quit individual for a while at least. I think we have too many problems we can't handle alone. (*ENP:* Such as?) I know, the moment I said it, I knew you were going to ask me that. Well, Pete and I can't agree on many things about the children. They are afraid of him and he blames me.

Pete: I don't blame you. It's a fact.

Nancy: You see? It's all my fault anyway.

ENP: (6) All right, Nancy. Let's hear what Pete has to say.

Pete: That's about it. We have a lot, I mean a lot, of trouble handling the children. We just don't agree and we end up first fighting and then not talking to each other.

DLA: (7) (to the children) What do you think now? Anything to add to what your parents just said?

Annie: (shrugs shoulders)

Rusty: I guess so. I don't know.

Pete: Come on Rusty. Don't act dumb. What do you think? Speak up.

Nancy: You see it now. Pete comes on strong and intimidates the children. Then he complains because they don't want to be near him. And he blames me for it.

DLA: (8) I think you are defining the reasons you have to seek family therapy. So, before we go any further, please, try this. Imagine for a moment what your family would be like if you did not have this problem. Put yourself into a make-believe time machine and step into the future, a few months from now, when the problem does not exist any more. Take your time and try to pretend you are already there. Use your imagination. Close your eyes and picture your family without this problem. Everything going on smoothly and nice. Yes, close your eyes and get into your mental picture of your family without the problem.

Pete: You mean, we should imagine that everything is OK, no problem with the children and that?

DLA: Yes, exactly. Close your eyes, Pete, so you can concentrate better and let the mental movie start in your mind.

ENP: (9) Take your time, feel comfortable and relaxed, and see yourself with your family. Perhaps you are at home, perhaps in the car, perhaps at some family event with other relatives. Zero in on the scene, be there with the others. Enjoy what is happening. Everything is OK. No problems. Just having a good time. Feeling very comfortable, very happy, very relaxed.

Pete: I've thought of this many times but . . .

ENP: Wait a little while, Pete. We'll talk later. Now stay with the movie in your mind.

Pete: (sitting up and interrupting) Wait, wait, wait. What's this? Are you telling me I can't talk when I want to? (The others stop their attempt at imaginative involvement and concentrate on what the father says.)

ENP: (10) Pete, you came to us because, after finding out who we are and what we do, you decided we might be able to help you. You can choose to play tennis or checkers but once you choose the game you *must*, yes, you *must*, play by the rules of that game. You hired us as guides and, yes, we are guiding you.

DLA: (11) Should we try again? (Pete, initially annoyed at Esther, had looked at DLA, as if asking for help. Now he shrugged his shoulders and said, "OK, let's give it a try. You're right. I'm paying you good money to help us. OK.")

ENP: (12) Again, move in the chair to feel as comfortable as you can. Keep your eyes closed while you breathe slowly, calmly. You'll know you are relaxed when the eyes feel very comfortable closed. Take your time, feeling better with every breath. Your eyelids very relaxed and comfortable.

DLA: (13) And again, put yourself into your family in the near future, without the present problem. You are with the other family members but the problem is a thing of the past. You feel just right in your family, with the other people in your family. Zero in on one single situation; at home, or at a family affair, or in the car. Focus on that one situation. Watch it in your mind's eye as if it were a very clear movie. Take your time and pick up all the details. You and your family, talking, feeling good, no tension, good feelings about yourself and good feelings about the others. Are you getting into it? (Pete opened his eyes and emphatically nodded his head; closed his eyes and went back to the relaxed pose he had acquired while we were talking. The others continued their relaxation, Rusty smiling while he nodded slightly and Nancy saying almost inaudibly, "Yeah, yeah," while Annie just sat there looking very content and relaxed.) Stay with that one situation in which you are and become aware of all your good feelings, how wonderful you feel.

ENP: (14) Without missing any of the good feelings you're having

right now being with your family. You trust them, you love
them, you like them, you feel comfortable, at ease, with them.
And they love you, like you, trust you, feel great being with
you. You still there? (Again, affirmative nods from all.)

DLA: (15) Stay with this for a while and slowly get yourself ready to
return to the ordinary way of using your mind. No rush,
though. Take your time and very slowly let yourself turn to the
ordinary mental channel. So that when your eyes open, you
feel great, relaxed, rested, and all the ordinary sensations
come back to every part of your body. (Pete was the first to
open his eyes. He stretched, as if he had awakened from a
nap, and looked around his family before directing his gaze to
us with a smile of approval and making the gesture of success
with his right fist and thumb up.)

ENP: (16) You may take your time to return to the ordinary thinking. Go slowly now ready to come back to this room, today,
with Daniel and myself and the rest of the family in the same
office (Rusty and Nancy opened their eyes and smiled. Rusty
started to say something and Esther interjected.) and if you
want to stay with your eyes closed for a while, it's OK. We'll
go on talking and when you're ready you can join us feeling
very good about yourself and ready to talk about this whole
thing. (Annie stayed with her eyes closed and a faint smile,
looking very relaxed.)

Nancy: (looking around) I feel great. That was nice. How are you
doing, Rusty? You look so relaxed.

Rusty: Yeah, that was nice. Want me to tell you what I was thinking?

ENP: (17) Yes, Rusty, go ahead, tell us.

Rusty: Well, see? I remembered my last birthday, four months ago.
(Annie opens her eyes and smiles to her mother, then to the
rest of us and says, "I liked that. I also thought of Rusty's
birthday.") Yeah, it was a great party. We had zillions of people
and a magician and prizes and Dad was there all the time. And
Mom and Dad seemed to be so happy. They even danced with
each other. It was great.

Annie: Yeah, I also remembered all that. And I felt terrific. Daddy
even danced with me and the magician was great. I got that

big stuffed lion. I thought I didn't like stuffed animals any more until I saw Lee the lion. I liked him right away. It was the best party ever. I ate so much ice cream I almost got sick.

Nancy: It's funny. For a while I also thought of that party. It was great. We did it for Rusty but also for my mother's sake. She loves Rusty, you know, her only grandson among eight girls. And it was also her own sixtieth birthday. Rusty was born on her birthday, you know. But then I switched to another scene. It was before the birthday party, the night Pete and I finally agreed to have it this way. It was late at night, the children were asleep, and Pete and I were in the den. I felt so warm and comfortable with him. I felt so relaxed, remember, Pete? you felt the same. That was a beautiful moment. We really felt together. I trusted you completely and I felt you did too.

Pete: I said before that I was going to get into this and I did. But I don't see the value of this. It's all sweet superficial nonsense. What about Nancy's overidentification with the children? What about Annie's Electra stuff, you know, with me? What about Nancy's projections on me? Are we going to get into this or not? We came here to be helped, not to play little games of show and tell nice and sweet things from the past. You know what I think? . . .

ENP: (18) Pete, you didn't tell us what you were thinking about when everybody else was quiet and getting into (with a smile and leaning toward Pete) that "sweet superficial show and tell of the past." Would you, please, tell us before we go any further?

Pete: What is there to tell? I thought of that night in the den Nancy mentioned; I also remembered Rusty's birthday party and I also thought of last winter when we went skiing in Vermont; the fun time I had in the snowmobile with each one. Well Nancy was too afraid. But still and all, that was a pleasant memory. But what about . . .

DLA: (19) Wait, Pete. At this point we can use the things you brought to mind or we can get into a big discussion on the merits of the things you mentioned before—Electra, overidentification, and projections. I for one prefer to work with your own mental images. You know that's the way we work.

Nancy: Yeah, Pete, I'm interested in this and you agreed to try this method. We knew it was not going to be like the therapy we're used to. I thought we wanted a change, Pete.

Pete: I guess you're right. But, you know, what about all the other stuff? It's important, isn't it? Nancy sees her father in me and she was always afraid of the old man. If we don't work this crap through, we'll never improve. You understand? I know what the problem is, the dynamics of it, but we need help to resolve it. That's all.

DLA: (20) Pete, are we going to give this a chance or not? You just went through an important mind exercise. You were into it too. And I want to use it now to help you, as you keep putting it. (Pete is ready to say something.) Wait, please, Pete. Before, you referred to the money you are paying us to help you according to our method, remember? I'm still curious about your mental images during the exercise we did. Did you spend most of the time having fun in the snowmobile?

Pete: Yeah, it was sort of funny. I felt the cold in my face, the excitement of going fast. I could hear Nancy yelling at me to slow down. Yes, it was fun, but so what?

ENP: (21) So you were getting into that inner reality . . .

Pete: What do you mean "reality"? That's all make-believe, fantasy, crap. That has nothing to do with reality.

ENP: (22) So you were really getting into that fantasy, were you not? As if you were there again?

Pete: Yeah, I guess so.

ENP: (23) Try to remember for a minute. How did you feel while you were into that fantasy? Check inside you.

Pete: I felt great, having fun, you know. Just great.

ENP: (24) Did you feel any different when you were with Nancy in the snowmobile than when you were with the children? The snowmobile has room for only two people, correct?

Pete: Yeah, for two. I don't know, I guess I felt good with Nancy and with the children, the same.

ENP: (25) Check it now, will you? Go back to that mental scene and put yourself with Nancy there and then with the children. And check your feelings.

Pete: It's about the same, I guess.

ENP: (26) Check it, will you? Close your eyes once more. Be once more in the snowmobile. Who is with you?

Pete: I'm alone now.

ENP: (27) OK, enjoy that, the cold wind, the speed, the snow sprinkling on your face. Stay with it for a little while. Then, put one of the children or Nancy in the snowmobile with you. Go slowly . . .

Pete: (obviously relaxing and concentrating on his mental pictures) Yeah, it's great. Nancy is behind me, clutching at me, pulling on my jacket, screaming. But I know she's OK. This thing is safe. I love it.

ENP: (28) Check how you feel, really . . . then place one of the children behind you in the snowmobile . . . and check your feelings once more. Go slowly and have fun . . . (The others are watching quietly. Rusty seems to want to say something but Nancy with the gesture of silence—her index finger crossing her lips—tells him to be quiet.) And when you have checked your feelings you may want to come back to the conversation we were having before . . . but, no rush at all. (Pete takes about half a minute to open his eyes. He looks relaxed and really smiles spontaneously for the first time.) Slowly getting ready to talk about it.

DLA: (29) What you just did, Pete, answered your questions about how we can help you. Now we can analyze. What made you relaxed in the snowmobile with Nancy? (Pete is thinking in silence.)

Nancy: Can I speak?

ENP: Go ahead, Nancy.

Nancy: You see, we have a good time together, we like each other. The problem is when we argue about the children. Everything else is good, but not our looking at child rearing.

Pete: Yeah, Nancy is right. The problems start when we argue about the children. Other than that . . .

DLA: (30) Both, please, get into the fantasy of a situation where you

are talking about the children without disagreement. Wait.
Can you think of something that you have to decide about the
children in the next few days or weeks? Decide first what the
issue could be and then you'll rehearse it in your imagination.
Any issue that comes up?

Nancy: Yes, definitely. The whole thing about Annie's camp. You
see . . .

DLA: (31) No, Nancy, we don't have to know the details yet. (to
Pete) You know what Nancy is talking about, yes?

Pete: Do I know? Yes, of course, I know.

DLA: OK. Think about that issue and go over it in your mind as if
you were discussing it intelligently, without any tension.
Close your eyes and get into it. Pretend it is happening. You
are having the ideal discussion of your life. Talking rationally,
respectfully, listening to each other's reasons and arguments.
Really listening. Both relaxed.

Pete: (opens his eyes)

DLA: Keep your eyes closed to avoid distractions. Get really into it.
You are alone, perhaps in the den again. You're not distracted
with other things. You're really talking. Feeling good about
being able to discuss this issue. (In the meantime *ENP* gives
the art book to Rusty and asks Annie very quietly whether she
wants a book. Annie says no and continues watching her parents, while Rusty turns the pages of the art book without paying too much attention to it, mostly looking at the adults.) Give
yourselves permission to really get into this conversation. Listen to the other's voice, look at the facial expressions, at the
body positions. Allow yourself to be objective, realistic, rational about the issue of Annie's camp . . . take your time . . .
and slowly, get yourself ready to return to the ordinary mental
state . . . very slowly . . . feeling good and relaxed . . . just
like that . . . coming back to the ordinary mental channel.

Pete: (to the children) Boy, you two were so quiet. I can't believe it.
Like two little puppies looking at me . . . . That was OK. Yes,
I imagined a discussion with agreement and I gave in; Nancy
gave in. It was too good to be true.

ENP: (32) But possible?

Nancy: Yes it was very possible in my head.

Pete: I guess it was possible. Yes, definitely.

Nancy: I liked this. I realized that I have to let Pete finish, that I have to listen better.

Pete: Finally! I'm glad you agree. I've been telling you this forever.

Nancy: I was amazed in a sense. You know, I realized that we can talk like this. We can listen to each other. We don't have to fight when we talk about the children. It was amazing.

ENP: (33) Did you learn anything from that mental rehearsal, Pete?

Pete: Yes, to be honest, I also realized that my listening was . . . I guess it can be, much better. I felt good going over this in my mind. It looked, it felt, real, at least possible.

DLA: (34) So now you see a bit of how our approach works. And I'm glad you turned out to be such a clever user of imagination.

Pete: Flattery will get you nowhere, Doc. But regardless, I'm willing to go along with you and Esther. But now what? I followed your instructions, I felt good thinking about all this. How's this going to change things between Nancy and me?

DLA: (35) What do you think about all this, kids? How's this going to improve things when your parents argue about you?

Annie: I think they can be nicer to each other if they try.

DLA: (36) That's it. If they try. What you did today can serve you as a model of what can happen. The more you focus on the way you can relate to each other, the closer you bring it to reality, to actually doing it. So, to answer your question, Pete, I suggest that you go back to this type of mental rehearsal. Rehearse in your mind how things can be with Nancy when it comes to the children. Go over it again and again and wait for the good results.

Pete: Sounds like a crock to me but I'll try it. I will.

Nancy: I'll rehearse this, too. In fact, can we agree that we're *not* going to talk about Annie's camp until we have rehearsed this in our minds a few times? What do you think?

ENP: (37) That's a wonderful idea. You agree to do that, Pete?

Pete: OK, I'll do it, but I still have many questions.

The rest of the session was spent giving Pete an opportunity to

have his questions answered and explaining the theoretical rationale for our therapeutic approach. We also decided not to see the
children for the time being and made an appointment in 10 days for
the couple alone.

The last few exchanges of the session follow.

DLA: (38) Pete, give me back your understanding of our method of
working, will you?

Pete: Well, as I understand it, you go first to change and then to find
out what caused the problem. Do you?

DLA: (39) Basically, yes. You hired us because you felt you had a
problem. Therefore, we feel that our first obligation is to help
you resolve the problem, not understand the problem. And, as
we just discussed, we have factual evidence on our side. So,
from that point of view, let's review our session once more.
(Pete and Nancy look, waiting and agreeing.) Do you agree
that if you could discuss things the way you imagined it earlier, things about the children, I mean, you would not have a
problem? (Both agree.) All right, then, close your eyes once
more today, and go back to that discussion scene. This time
pay close attention to your body. What sensations do you perceive? How is your physical self reacting to this type of discussion? Does your body have anything to say about it? Is your
body tense or relaxed, comfortable or tense? . . . Go over the
discussion scene again. You can quickly pick up all the details
that are important. But, at the same time, check how your
body is reacting to it. Take a moment more to be sure of what's
happening . . . . Now, slowly, you may reorient yourselves to
the office, right here, once more. (Both, looking relaxed, open
their eyes slowly and look around.) What happened?

Pete: I feel great. I felt no tension. On the contrary. I was saying to
myself, I wish it were like that in real life.

Nancy: Me too. It felt good to rehearse that. You know I like that
word, I like to think of rehearsing. After all, this is important
to us.

ENP: (40) So, to make it happen in reality according to our method,
what do you have to do? (Silence from the couple. Annie said,

"You have to practice this, like memorizing a poem, over and over again.") Great, Annie, you got the idea. (to the parents) You agree?

Nancy: Yeah, Annie is right and I feel now that we both will do it to prepare ourselves for doing it in reality.

DLA: (41) All right, so everything is taken care of. We'll let the children stay home and the four of us will meet again on the twenty-first. See you then.

Comments

This being the first session, we wanted to give a general impression without interrupting the flow with our comments. The main tasks accomplished were to deal with Pete's resistance, to define the problem to be worked on as the couple's inability to discuss issues related to the children rationally and objectively, to introduce them to hypnotherapy, to give them a task to do by teaching them mental rehearsal, and to decide how to proceed with the therapy sessions in the future, that is, temporarily without the children.

Pete's resistance appeared repeatedly (1–3, 8, 9, 17–19, 21, 34, 36, 37) and in these cases it was not confronted but used within the hypnotherapeutic context. Only in exchange #20 was there some confrontation. After the session DLA realized that his initial reaction to Pete had been negative, disliking his general attitude and feeling antagonistic, even bellicose, toward him. Near the end of the session, however, DLA had felt a bit more positive toward Pete, as #29 and 34 show. In #10, ENP clarified, with a smile and in a friendly manner, what our role as family hypnotherapists is all about. The fact that she did not respond with anger, as Pete probably expected her to do because of his show of anger ("Wait . . . Are you telling me I can't talk when I want to?") made him receptive to ENP's explanation of our "guiding" role in the therapy session. In #18, after Pete asked about psychoanalytic concepts, ENP simply ignored his questions and reoriented him to his previous experience. This maneuver brought him back to his previous imaginative involvement and stirred his interest in the winter scene he had recalled. This scene was utilized again in #20, 24, and for the rest of the session.

Pete's resistance was utilized as much as possible (#21, 22, 34–36). His questions were answered rationally toward the end of the session and an agreement was elicited about giving family hypnotherapy a fair chance. Pete showed more acquiescence in #38.

The definition of the problem was attempted in #8 and was assumed in #30, after the couple agreed that they found it difficult to discuss their children satisfactorily (#29, especially Nancy's comment with which Pete agreed). Because of this agreement on what the problem was, we suggested (and the couple accepted our suggestion) that the children should be kept away from the therapy sessions for the time being.

The hypnotherapy techniques were introduced naturally, without contrived "inductions," in #8. After Pete's attempted sabotage, DLA made a new trial in #11 and Pete used the financial reason to accede. Pete's resistance was weakened by the hypnotic experience itself in #15. After this sequence of O-L-D (see Introduction), the final "C" or body check started in #25 in a naturalistic manner and ended in #28.

In the following discussion of the inner "check," the opportunity of shifting back to hypnotic thinking was seized again, quite naturally, in #30. However, when Nancy volunteered to provide details of Annie's camp—the issue that they had difficulty discussing by themselves—DLA avoided a detour into facts and simply ascertained that Pete knew what Nancy was referring to. Once the therapists were sure that the couple were paying attention to the same topic, the mental rehearsal was encouraged in #31, followed by the discussion in #32–37.

By the end of the session, the problem to work on had been identified as the couple's dissatisfaction with their communication regarding the children. They also had tasted what hypnotherapy is and had found it useful. Because of this experience of our method during the session, it was possible to suggest in #38–40 that they practice on their own the type of mental rehearsal done with us in the first session.

The rationale for concentrating on the parents without the children, as we planned to do in the following sessions, is rooted in a systemic conceptualization of this family's problem. As long as the parents are not in agreement about child rearing, the children will react predictably. They will be confused and in their attempt at coping with this confusion will become problematic in their behavior. Therefore, we prefer to concentrate on the couple. As long as the couple is not united on an important issue, as in this case, the presence of the children in the therapy sessions will detract from the concentration required to help the couple become one regarding that issue.

Many comments could be made regarding our "style." Three characteristics are worth noticing. #8 is a clear example of our future orientation, a constant effort to envision what can improve rather than what went wrong. #31 dramatizes our reluctance to obtain more facts than are necessary to induce inner experiences in clients. Instead of allowing Nancy to explain and provide more details, we led her and Pete to a mental rehearsal of a constructive discussion between them. Finally, #39 illustrates the last of our four-step OLD C sequence. The body check is our way to ascertain that whatever they worked on has become—or, at least, is becoming—part of their existential selves.

Before the next session, we went over our notes on the previous encounter and decided to keep in mind the task of mental rehearsal that both had agreed on practicing. If they had repeated this mind exercise privately, they probably would be ready for more serious hypnotic work. We also agreed on discussing in front of the couple some of the observations we had made about them during the first session. This practice can help to model a positive, mature discussion and also to share with them how we felt about the first encounter and what expectations we have developed for them.

SECOND SESSION

DLA: (1) Welcome. Come in. The tape recorder is on already.
Nancy: I see we won't waste any time, eh? Where is Esther?
DLA: (2) She's delayed but she'll be here in a little while.

Pete: What happened? She forgot about our appointment (sitting next to his wife on the couch)?

DLA: (3) While Esther makes her way here, tell me how the mental rehearsal went. How many times did you practice?

Pete: We were just talking about it on the way over. I was telling Nancy that I did it so many times that I got bored with it at the end. I haven't done it in the last three days.

DLA: (4) What about you Nancy?

Nancy: Well, I feel . . . I guess, I don't like to hear Pete, I mean what Pete just said. He gets bored. (*Pete*: [with a smile] There you go again sounding like my mother.) Let me finish, Pete, OK? I don't like your emphasis on getting bored. Did you get anything out of doing this thing?

Pete: Yes, I did, mother. Why don't you answer the doctor what he asked you?

Nancy: What did you ask me?

Pete: Talk about yourself, not about me. (to DLA) You see why we can't discuss anything really?

DLA: (5) (to Nancy with a smile) I'm still waiting.

Nancy: I guess you wanted to know if I practiced or something like that? (*DLA* nods.) Well, *I* did. Every day and I thought I had made progress. But you see what happens when we *are* together.

DLA: (6) Tell me briefly how you practiced. What did you do? Start at the very beginning.

Pete: The first few days . . .

Nancy: I thought you asked me . . .

Pete: I sat in the den late at night . . .

Nancy: Pete, you are being rude, you know?

Pete: . . . and just did it.

DLA: (7) I'm interested in more details than that, Pete. But before you go on, can you respond to Nancy and decide who is going to report first?

Pete: I, of course. No, I'm just kidding. I'm sorry, Nancy. I thought Daniel was asking both of us in general. When you interrupted I got pissed. You are so compulsive. Everything has to be done just right. So if I started talking, you couldn't wait?

Why make a big issue about it? We still have almost an hour here. So what's the big deal? You want to talk? Or can I finish?

Nancy: You piss me off when you talk to me in that tone of voice. And you know it. I guess you are right about my being compulsive and all that. But can't you stop talking to me that way? You go ahead. Finish your story.

Pete: You see what happens, Doc. It's very frustrating. But she's right. I know it. When I get annoyed, I raise my voice and sound angry and she don't like it. I should know better. But she could also try not to be so damn compulsive.

DLA: (8) You are agreeing with each other. So, what about the mental rehearsal? You sat in the den; did you close your eyes? Did you use a specific mental image? Go over it briefly so we can reinforce whatever was helpful.

Pete: Yeah. I imagined ourselves in bed. Mellowing out, relaxed, and talking. Sort of feeling good about each other. You know? Close, touching, feeling each other's body next to us . . . it made me feel good . . . . As a matter of fact, just telling you about it, I feel good. But, then, I don't remember what happened. One night I just didn't feel like doing it and didn't do it the last three days.

DLA: (9) Nancy, Pete gave us a pretty nice scene. Would you join him? Go back, both of you, to the scene Pete just described. Close your eyes, now, and see yourselves in bed, mellow, talking quietly. Very aware of each other's physical presence. Take your time and be there. You getting into it? (Both nod gently.) You may say to yourself, "This is good. I feel great together, talking, touching, relaxed with each other. I want to enjoy this moment to the fullest. I'm aware of my good feelings and I want to use these good feelings to communicate better with each other. So we can talk constructively, like now, in an atmosphere of good feelings for each other. Not letting anything rob me of these good feelings. I want to listen to her, to him; really listen and understand what he means, what she means, always feeling good about our relationship, valuing what we have, what I want to keep and protect . . . (At this point ENP opens the door quietly and tiptoes into the office.) I really want to capture the reality of this moment together, to learn from it, to help me in the future." Take your time without any rush so you can let all this sink deeply in your inner mind. And when you are ready you'll bring yourself back to the ordinary way of using your mind. Slowly and relaxed. No rush. (to ENP, out loud) Good to see you. Pete said that he had benefited from this mental scene but that then he stopped practicing it. So now they went back to it to see if they can still use it to improve their communication about the children.

ENP: (10) They seemed to be really into it. I guess now they know that this scene is useful (Pete opens his eyes and smiles at us, mouthing a silent hello to ENP, who smiles in return.) and they can go back to it to learn how to relate constructively about the children. (Nancy looks at us: "Oh, hi, Esther. I didn't hear you come in and when I heard your voice, for a minute I thought it was part of the hypnosis." She stretches and adds, "That was great! I'm really ready to sleep, I'm so relaxed.") (Both of us wait in silence, feeling relaxed.)

Pete: I still don't know what happened. Why did I stop practicing it? I suppose there was some resistance. I do this, you know? When something . . . I mean when I enjoy something, I stop it. It's the same as with . . .

DLA: (11) Hold that for a while, Pete. Go back to the experience you just had. You too, Nancy. Was it real, possible, I mean? Can you use it as a model for your discussions?

Pete: Oh, I know what you mean. The here and now. No questions why and all that. I still don't see it, but I said I'd give this a try. So, forget why I didn't practice this. What we just did, eh. How did you feel, Nancy?

Nancy: Great. I got into it right away. It's funny. First I was very aware of your smell. Nice. The perfume I like. You were just telling me about some silly thing from work. You were funny and did your characterizations and I loved to hear your voice. I loved your voice for some reason. We even got to talk about the children and you were really listening to my point of view.

Pete: I always do.

Nancy: Baloney you do. But the point is that it felt very good to be in bed with no worries and just talking without any rush. I loved it. What about you, Pete?

Pete: Well, I started the whole thing, didn't I? So I was really there. I was caressing you very gently. Not sexually but your belly, your thighs, your arms, and was feeling really mellow. Yes, I was listening to you and feeling good about it. You were talking calmly, making sense, the way I like it, the way you do once in a while, in a great while.

Nancy: He's such a bastard! Even in hypnosis, he's blaming me. If I only would talk logically, we, he and I, would not have a problem communicating.

Pete: Well, I can't help it. That's the way I see it. Yes.

Nancy: What he forgets is what he actually does when I am trying to talk calmly.

Pete: What do I do? You're full of it but can't recognize that it is your fault.

Nancy: He interrupts or goes into tangents. And he calls this to talk rationally.

ENP: (12) (to DLA) First I thought that they were making progress but now I don't know. They frustrate me. She has to learn to ignore his irrelevant comments or, I guess, childish comments. And he has to learn to respect her as an equal.

DLA: (13) I agree. If we get involved in this tit-for-tat nonsense, we'll get bogged down in an endless argument. Let's steer them back to the positive images they do have and see what they can learn from them.

Comments

The second session started without niceties or polite preliminaries, with matter-of-fact indications of the presence of the tape recorder and the absence of ENP. The task or home assignment agreed upon during the previous session was used to connect the two meetings. The possible distraction (#4) was avoided by merely ignoring the germinal argument. The couple tried again in #5 and #7 to argue, but DLA kept the center of attention on the mental rehearsal they were supposed to practice (#8). When Pete finally reported on his practice, his own mental scene was used to get into hypnosis—another way of establishing continuity between the previous session and this one. The ease with which they entered this inner experience was an indication that they had practiced during the last few days. Because this practice at the beginning of a session was to set the mood, it did not have to be prolonged. DLA's #9 was said very slowly, with many pauses and in a very relaxed tone of voice. It took almost six minutes. Several sentences were repeated at least once in a different tone of voice than the first time.

The comments of DLA to ENP also had the function of suggestions to the couple, as did ENP's response in #10. Nancy's comment (#10) was typical of people returning to left hemispheric function after hypnosis. Pete, in spite of his positive hypnotic experience, found it difficult to stay away from what for him had been psychotherapy for 22 years but made a valiant effort in #11 to believe that our approach was worth trying.

In the next exchange, when Nancy reported on her hypnotic experience, Pete again reacted childishly. His continuing to do so prompted the aside between the two therapists. When we comment, as we did, we are communicating with each other but we are also telling the family something. A confrontation which otherwise would elicit denial or other defensive maneuvers is thus avoided while the message is still conveyed to the interested parties.

CONTINUATION OF THE SECOND SESSION

Nancy: You know, I also feel childish when we get into this bickering. Pete, can you look at this objectively for a moment?

Pete: I told you this before, Nancy. I hate myself for doing it most of the time. They are right. We do sound like children. But I have a question for you, Esther. What do you mean by my not respecting Nancy as an equal? That's absolute idiocy.

ENP: (14) Pete, we could argue about this for a long time. But not to waste time, ask yourself that question, "Do I respect Nancy as an equal? Do I truly believe she is my equal?"

Pete: Boy! If that's not a cop-out. You're a sneak, Esther.

ENP: Come on, Pete. Go inside of you and try to be completely honest with yourself.

Nancy: You need any help, Pete? I can refresh your memory.

ENP: Nancy, you sound sarcastic now. What do you want to tell Pete?

Nancy: That he really does not respect me. My opinions don't count. Often he shouts me down . . .

ENP: (15) This is an important turning point. You can get into a heated argument and gain nothing. Or you can use this to really communicate. Nancy, tell Pete how *you* react when you feel he doesn't respect you. Start with "I feel . . ."

Nancy: He knows how I feel.

ENP: No, try to tell him now from your point of view, not accusing him, but telling him how *you* feel.

Nancy: OK. Pete, you make me feel rotten.

ENP: (16) I feel rotten, Nancy. Get in touch with the real feeling behind the word rotten.

Nancy: OK, OK. I feel humiliated. I feel hurt. I feel frightened. I feel unloved (crying now). I feel rotten (yelling)!

ENP: (17) Now, Pete, are you ready to ask yourself truly if you respect Nancy as an equal? Go ahead, ask yourself.

Pete: What do you want me to do?

ENP: Close your eyes. Get in touch with the most honest side of you and ask yourself the question you asked me: Do I respect Nancy as an equal? (Pete does not close his eyes.) Pete, your outward self and your inner self may not be in total agreement about Nancy and women in general. You seem to be saying that you respect Nancy and consider her your equal. But Nancy is picking up another message. Just to check where she's getting these vibes from, you can now get in touch with your inner self, your truthful self and ask yourself the question, Do I believe that Nancy is my equal? Ready?

Pete: All right, I'll try (closing his eyes), but I think this is idiotic. (*Nancy:* There goes that word again. I asked you not to use it.) Yes, OK, I'm sorry but I think this is stupid.

ENP: (18) Connect with your inner self, your truthful self. Relax. Give yourself some time. In some corner of your being you will

find your utterly honest self. We all have a truthful self. You
may see yourself as utterly truthful and honest. You may appear different than you are now; dressed differently; looking
differently. Relax and try to connect with that aspect of your
self. If you give yourself permission, you'll make contact.

Pete: (smiling but with closed eyes and almost whispering) I'm an
old man . . .

ENP: (19) Stay with the old man now. Listen to him, to you. And
get into this reality as much as you can. This fantasy is your
reality now. You can learn from it. You can discover something
new about yourself. Get into it, fully. You *are* the old man. Let
the old man, your . . . that part of you, answer that question,
what you believe about Nancy. Listen to what you, the old
man, is saying. He speaks the truth. The truth about you. Be
there. Listen . . . feeling relaxed. The truth will free you from
all the energy needed to hide the truth from ourselves. Rejoice
now that you have met the old man in you. Listen carefully to
him. Watch him. Is he looking at you? (Pete nods.) Is he sitting? Standing? You and him? Or you as the old man alone?
Whatever, be there fully, body and mind and soul. The answer
will come. You will recognize the truth and accept it. Only
then can you do something about it, if you want to . . . (In the
meantime, Nancy is watching her husband while becoming
more relaxed as the minutes go by. At this point she has her
eyes closed.) And this utterly truthful and honest part of you
will free you to really be yourself and to make whatever
choices you decide to make . . . Enjoy the relaxation while you
may want to tell this old man–you that you want to meet with
him again real soon . . . to learn more about yourself . . . to
really be you . . . slowly now, returning to the ordinary way of
using your mind . . . very slowly and relaxed . . . so that when
your eyes open you feel great and all the ordinary sensations
are back in every part of your body.

Pete: (is slowly coming back to ordinary consciousness)

Nancy: Boy, that was different! I got into it too. I was so relaxed, I
didn't even hear what Esther was saying but, somehow, I was
benefiting from it too. Weird! How are you doing, Pete?

Pete: (stretching his whole body while standing up) I feel great but I still don't understand what's going on. So, big deal, I saw this old man; I knew it was me. It was like a dream. I was the old man but I also was there. It was very clear and very confusing too. But it was OK, not disturbing—confusing, you know. Just . . . I guess Nancy is right . . . sort of weird (sitting down again).

DLA: (20) What did the old man say?

Pete: I can't believe I'm doing this. But, what the heck! I said I'd give your method a chance. Well, I've talked about dreams. So here it goes. It was like a dream. The old man was me, but I was looking at him, too. When you first started talking about my truthful self, I thought of an innocent little baby. But then I saw, like in a dream, this old man. And I knew it was me, at perhaps 75 or 90 years of age. But I had a long beard and loose clothing, like a guru. First the old man smiled and I knew what he meant. I didn't respect Nancy as an equal. But he said nothing. Just smiled. And the more he kept smiling, the more I knew I was full of shit. I had to improve many things to treat her as my equal. You kept saying, listen to him. All I heard, you know what I mean, was "I know the truth." No explanations, no bullshit. Just that. You kept talking but I wasn't paying attention to you any more. I sort of connected this about respecting Nancy with our arguments about the children.

ENP: (21) Tell us. How did you connect it?

Pete: Everything fell into place. I knew, as I say, that I was full of it. All my talk about Nancy reacting to me the way she reacted to her father is bull. The old man, I guess my truthful self, looked right through my lies. But, again, all this might be the greatest illusion yet—this whole dream and this supernatural message from that guru.

ENP: Go back to your lies, Pete.

Pete: Well, you see, I always blame Nancy. I've believed that if she discussed things differently, if she changed, we wouldn't have any problems talking. In this dream . . . I . . . well, I guess I saw the truth. I'm as much to blame as she is. In fact . . . I hate to admit this, this whole thing about the old man made me realize that it's mostly my fault. What the heck! If I've learned something in all these years of therapy it is that I have to be honest with myself. So don't you throw this back at me, Nancy. We are here. We might as well stop wasting time. Let's work on it.

Nancy: I can't believe my ears. I love you for it! You don't know how happy I am that you say that.

Comments

Pete continued resisting hypnotherapy even after having had a constructive experience of it. But we refused to argue with him and encouraged him to make some sense of what he had done. This rapid acceptance of his responsibility in the difficulties he and Nancy have when discussing different issues, especially related to the children, might be a "flight into health." It was still too early to conclude that Pete had "changed." On the other hand, his reaction is fairly typical in hypnotherapy. In the rest of the session and in the following meetings we would be building on Pete's hypnotic experience.

In #17, ENP mentioned "women in general." This could have led to further arguments on Pete's part, though he ignored that remark. Looking back, we realized that that comment could have been avoided. Again, in #19, the statement, "the fantasy is your reality," was not advisable in light of Pete's reaction during the first session (#21).

If Pete had not spontaneously connected his hypnotic experience with the issue of our concern regarding the couple's inability to discuss things constructively, we would have brought it up. However, this is another example of the wisdom of people when we make it possible for them to use their inner resources. We trust the nonconscious mental processes, as Erickson (in Rossi, 1980) suggested. ENP showed this by turning Pete's question regarding his respect for Nancy back to him and, incidentally, by refusing to get into an argument about it. She guided him and he cooperated, probably half consciously recognizing that what she was helping him to experience was important to him. His report, after the mind exercise, is indicative of hypnotic work. First he thought of a baby in relation to truthfulness but then he "saw" an old man and somehow knew that he was the old man in the mental symbol. His experience was meaningful, as #19–21 indicate. But his doubts lingered (#21), even when he was reporting the benefits of this exercise.

The conclusion of the second session was intended, first, to address Pete's doubts based on previous experience of therapy, in order to help him accept *our* approach as valid therapy and, second, to give the couple clear directions for working together, until our next session, on maintaining and enhancing the gains made in this session.

CONCLUSION OF THE SECOND SESSION

ENP: (22) Take a moment to stay with your thoughts. You, Pete, assimilating what you did just now. And you, Nancy, trying to feel good about what you just heard. Take your time. Go slowly and feel relaxed and at peace with yourself.

Nancy: Yeah, I am very happy. You don't know what this means. Pete very seldom volunteers that there is anything less than super with him. Now he did it all by himself. I still can't believe it.

Pete: You can believe it, Nancy. You know I am basically honest and truthful. I guess, when Esther started with that thing about connecting with my true self, I mean, my truthful self, something inside of me really wanted to do it . . . I suppose, to prove you wrong, Esther, but also, really, to find out the truth. I felt scared, sort of scared, and excited at the same time.

DLA: (23) So now that you experienced hypnosis . . .

Pete: That wasn't hypnosis, what do you mean?

DLA: Yes, we mean that what you did was hypnosis. But call it what you want. The name is not important. (Pete looks annoyed.) Pete, I'm not fighting with you. What you did was a way of getting in touch with unconscious things that were important to you, that were you. You agree? (Pete nods and shrugs.) So with this experience behind, I'd like to suggest that you tell us what issue, specifically, about the children creates the most problem between the two of you.

Nancy: I can tell you that—Annie's camp. That's still not resolved. But that's only one little corner of Pete's constant criticism of me as a mother. (*Pete:* Not as a mother. The way you raise them. Inconsistent. Too lenient or too strict. And also . . .) There you go. Give me your old lecture again. I'm listening, professor.

Pete: Cut the crap, Nancy. You know I'm right and you have a closed mind on this. That's all there is to it. The children are selfish little monsters.

Nancy: Stop it, Pete. You are ridiculous and you know it.

Pete: Yes, you made them into little monsters.

DLA: (24) Great performance, folks. Bravo! You're good at this and that's why I, for one, don't want to waste therapy time encouraging you to do in front of us what you do so well alone. You still have not told me concretely, specifically, what is the raw nerve in this general issue about the children's upbringing. Can you think of it and come to an agreement?

Pete: I don't know. I guess I want the children to be one way and Nancy, you have other ideas.

DLA: (25) Get into that for a minute, the two of you. Concentrate on the image that comes to mind when you think of the children. Like we did before: close your eyes and let the image of your children appear. The way you want them to be. Look at them in your mind's eye in the house or in the car or when a relative is visiting. Allow yourselves to have a clear, sharp image of the children in action. Are you into it? (Pete nods. Nancy smiles.) Stay with that image for a little while longer. Get in touch with your feelings . . . your reaction to the children. These are your children and you feel proud of them. You like them. They are behaving just the way you like it. Feel it. All the way. Glad to be the parent of these children . . . take your time. Stay with it for a moment . . . and now we can discuss what came to your minds.

Nancy: I was laughing all the time because I saw Rusty and Annie just the way they are. I think they are great kids. But I knew that Pete would never want them this way. He always wants them to be different, better—whatever that means . . .

DLA: (26) Let Pete tell us what came to his mind.

Pete: Yeah, Nancy is right. An image, a picture I guess, came to me of the children in the car going up to the mountains. They were pleasant. No fighting. They were talking to us. It was enjoyable. When you said to feel proud, I really did. I guess because I know they can be that way if Nancy would only help me discipline them better, more consistently.

ENP: (27)Obviously different. As long as you keep these images, you'll have difficulties talking about them. For the next time, I'd suggest that both of you write out a list of things that you believe *could* reasonably be expected to change in the children. Be specific. For instance, "After dinner, Annie could . . . or Rusty could . . . ." Am I clear? (Both parents nod.) Write it out and go over it, so you can be very exact. Stick to three or four instances. No more.

DLA: (28) Then, next time we meet with the children. You agree, Esther? (*ENP.* Yes, definitely. We need them here next time.) And we'll discuss the precise, specific areas in which there can be improvement. I must stress that you have to do this if we want the next session to be productive. Give it some thought. Spend some time at it. And you may resolve important differences and come closer to each other in the process . . . I need your agreement.

Nancy: Yes, I'll do it. When I said that I see the children just as they are, I didn't mean that there is no room for improvement. I'll do it. Definitely.

Pete: You mean that we should discuss this with ourselves and then write what we want . . . I mean, in regards to the children?

DLA: (29) No, no. I'm glad you asked. What we suggest is that you *don't* discuss, don't talk about this at all. Just think seriously what could reasonably be expected to change in the children's behavior. Then, that you write it out and, finally, that you review what you wrote so that by next session we have the final

version of what you believe could improve. Does that make
sense? (Both agree.)

The session ends with arrangements for our next appointment, a
week later.

Comments

Our rationale for seeing the couple without the children was our
perception of the problem as being one of disagreement between
the parents reflected in the behavior of the children. Once we
helped the parents to agree, it would be easier and more effective
to deal with the whole family system.

In general, the session accomplished one important task, that of
attaining the husband's cooperation. After resisting hypnotherapy
in the first session and during the early and middle parts of this
meeting, he finally (#21 and again #23) went along with us. As we
did during the first session, we carefully avoided arguing with him
about the merits of hypnotherapy. DLA showed his annoyance at
Pete in the first session (#20) but handled him in a less confronta-
tional manner during this whole session. His liking for Pete had become clear but there was also a personal need to succeed with this
man who had had so many years of traditional psychotherapy.
DLA's comment in #24 was not sarcastic but friendly and used for
his explanation of why fighting is not encouraged in the session.

The final part of this session accomplished the functional task of
making the issue concrete. The written assignment given was pragmatic and had to be explained further (#29). The decision to meet
next time with the children brought the family therapy focus back
to the presenting problem. By having them present, they could become part of the plans to improve their behavior. At this point, we
were still not sure whether the issue *was* the children's behavior in
reality or if they were nonconsciously "used" by the parents to deal
with other issues not yet acknowledged by the family. Pete hinted
at this in Session One (#17 and #19). To probe in this direction
could take much time. To ignore the possibility for the time being
and to bring in the children may go to the core of the problem and

resolve it, period. Agreeing with the Mental Research Institute Brief Therapy model (Watzlawick et al., 1974), we believe that the purpose of therapy is to find solutions to problems—healthy, self-enhancing, wholesome solutions. We do not believe that therapy needs to address all the issues that might be connected with the problem. Only when a "good" solution is not found in a reasonably short time do we believe that we need to point to the advisability of exploring and uncovering nonconscious dynamics (also hypnotically, as we shall show in Chapter 8). Therefore, we kept in mind the four steps outlined by Watzlawick et al.: "1) A clear definition of the problem in concrete terms, 2) An investigation of the solutions attempted so far, 3) A clear definition of the concrete change to be achieved and 4) the formulation and implementation of a plan to produce this change" (1974, p. 110), and we decided to proceed with the presenting problem.

From what we could perceive so far, the attempted solutions to the couple's inability to agree on the upbringing of the children were ineffective communication, use of blame, and use of psychodynamic concepts to understand the reasons for such difficulty. Therefore, our task was to help this family communicate effectively, stop using blame, and find other concepts acceptable to them in order to explain the difficulty. In the process of reaching these goals, we would be able to check more carefully if other issues were at work in a relevant manner in the maintenance of the problem. (We know that there are always "other issues," but many are not relevant enough to justify our attention to them.)

Only after this process would we be able to get to the third step mentioned above regarding the concrete change to be achieved. Our plan, then, was to take advantage of the children's presence in the next session to help this family achieve the three goals: to communicate effectively, to stop using blame, and to find new ways of conceptualizing the problem.

THIRD SESSION

ENP: (1) Hi, kids. I'm sure you missed coming here last week, eh? (Both children smile. *Annie.* I sort of did. *Rusty.* Yeah, you must have been talking a lot about juicy things.) What juicy things, Rusty?

Rusty: I don't know. I was thinking about it. I'm sure you didn't waste time talking about us. I guess you talked about their fights and things. (*ENP.* What fights? You tell me.) Oh, you know, they didn't . . . it didn't happen this week, but boy, can they yell. I don't even get upset any more. But not this week . . .

Annie: Yeah, Rusty is right. They were much better this week and I loved it. You were good, Daddy. You too, Mom.

Nancy: We don't waste any time here, huh? But at least it's good to hear that the children give us good grades for our behavior. What do you think of that, Pete?

Pete: I don't feel too good today. This damn cold I can't get rid of. So don't mind me today. But I'm surprised that the kids noticed it. I'm pleased, yeah. And they should know . . . you should know that I kept thinking of how our discussions could be, truly! I guess that made some difference. In fact . . . I may be sticking my foot in my mouth, but I think we resolved that whole thing about Annie's camp . . . did we?

Nancy: Yeah, as far as I'm concerned. I understood Pete's worries . . .

Annie: What worries?

Nancy: Well, Annie, Dad can tell you. But the way I saw it is that he was concerned about the liberal philosophy of this camp and I only thought that he was just stubborn. I did listen to him in a fresh . . . you know, I mean new, way.

Pete: Yes, Annie, I was concerned. I'm still worried to some extent. But your mother and I decided that you'll go to that camp. We'll try to see how good it is . . . my concern is with the permissive attitude. They sort of believe in John Dewey's permissive education thing. But I did read the brochure and had a good talk with the director, who is a very interesting woman. She was friendly and answered all my questions. I feel much more comfortable about letting Annie go after that talk.

DLA: (2) I guess the fact that we had to miss our appointment last week was a blessing in disguise. It gave you time to settle this issue. When did you see the camp director?

Pete: Oh, about five days ago, I guess. I should have done it before and we would have avoided many weeks of arguments.

DLA: So you did learn some good things about yourself, eh Pete? Out of this, you two may come up with some guidelines for future disagreements. You may want to do this at home for our next meeting. Then we can go over your guidelines together. What do you think?

Pete: Sounds like a good idea. I can't think too good now with this damn cold.

DLA: OK. So, this is what I suggest you do. From the way you handled this issue, you can list the things that you did right, the things that helped to discuss this issue and to come to a satisfactory resolution. Write these out without consulting with each other and next time we are together, we'll go over them. OK? Anything you want to add, Esther?

ENP: No, that about covers everything.

DLA: So now, let's move on.

Nancy: I think that'll be a good idea . . . (laughing) to write it out and to move on. Yeah . . .

ENP: (3) Now to you, Rusty and Annie. Both of you seemed to be pleased that your parents didn't fight last week. Rusty, you said that your parents' fighting did not upset you but still you felt good that they didn't fight. Right?

Rusty: Sort of, I guess . . . Yeah, I like it when they don't fight. I know . . . I mean, I know when it's coming, sort of. So I say to myself, there they go at it again . . . I turn the TV up or I close the door of my room and wait till they are finished.

ENP: (4) What do you do, Annie?

Annie: I do get upset. I don't like all the screaming and yelling . . . I don't know . . . I keep hoping that they finish once and for all . . . . That's why last week was sort of nice . . . although I kept waiting for them to start another fight . . .

Pete: Look, kids, I told you many times that fighting is OK. You only fight with people you . . . people who are important to you. You know that I love your mother and she loves me . . .

Rusty: But if you love each other, why do you have to scream so loud? Why get so angry?

Nancy: Dad is right. I don't think that fighting is enjoyable but it can't be helped. We let it all out and then we feel right about each other again.

Pete: (assents with nods and looks)

DLA: (5) But last week you handled disagreement without yelling and screaming. Perhaps you are finding another method to settle arguments and frustrations. It doesn't *have to be* angry fighting.

Comments

When ENP (#3) tried to get the children involved, the parents seized the opportunity to convey their belief about anger and fighting. We could have stepped into a long intellectual discussion on the merits or liabilities of expressing anger. DLA (#5) simply noted that perhaps the expression of anger in yelling and fighting is not necessary. We use many of Weisinger's (1985) cognitive methods to tame anger and correct distorted thinking. As a matter of fact, DLA's statement falls into his "counterpunch" statement category, presented by Weisinger. Weisinger's book draws on the research reviewed by Tavris (1982), which effectively demolished the popular myth about "letting it all hang out," without differentiating between useful, moral anger and mere uncivilized and immature adult temper tantrums. "Counterpunch" is a mental technique to quickly match one's own distorted thinking with rational, true, and objective statements. The types of distorted thinking that make us angry, according to Weisinger, are 1) destructive labeling or negative generalization ("He's a jerk"); 2) mindreading or attributing motives to others ("She's trying to hurt him"); 3) magnification of negative events ("This is terrible; I can't take it!"); 4) imperatives or the use of *must*, *should*, and *ought* in thinking of oneself and others.

Our goal during the therapy session is to help the family find better ways to deal with each other so that each one can be his or her own self within the family system. Because of this pragmatic goal, we did not further discuss the topic.

In the next segment of this session we return to the main goal that brought the family to us. We try to help the parents understand whether they use the children in their arguments and whether there are other issues at work that may need resolution. But at every step, we are ready to facilitate experiential activation and hypnotic activity, or, we try to help the family members to switch from left to right hemispheric thinking.

CONTINUATION OF THIRD SESSION

Pete: I guess it doesn't *have to be* fighting but that's the way it seems to end most of the time . . . I mean when this issue of the children comes up.

ENP: (6) Other issues you handle better?

Nancy: Oh, yes. No question about it . . . (Pete nods in agreement).

ENP: Can you, then—all of you—do this? Imagine all your memories like a picture album in your mind. Now, without talking to each other—as we did the first time, remember?—concentrate on one instance of a good fight. Mom and dad start talking about something—other than you two, kids—and they get into a disagreement. They start arguing. But it is a good argument. They may raise their voices but they are not ready (with a smile) to kill each other. Close your eyes and try to concentrate on that memory. But our memory album in the mind is almost magical. Once we find one of these memories, it can become very real, as if you were right there. Watch what's happening . . . listen to what's going on . . . hear the sound of voices . . . check where you are . . . sitting . . . standing . . . right there or in another room . . . take your time . . . really get into it . . . It's happening right now . . . in your mind . . . and now check your feelings . . . realize how you feel . . . what you feel . . . . How is my body reacting to all this? Some people feel things in their stomach . . . or in their head . . . or someplace else . . . . Check where *you* feel what's going on . . . the argument . . . the loud voices . . . . Take it easy and be there . . . fully . . . aware of what's going on outside of you . . . and how it makes you feel inside . . . . The

mental picture from your memory album can be very real . . .
very lively . . . happening now . . . . Stay there for a little
while longer . . . take your time . . . pay attention to everything around you . . . be there . . . and now watch how the
argument ends . . . . What happens? . . . Who says
what? . . . Who does what? . . . And slowly, you start getting
ready to come back to this room, today, with all of us, to discuss and talk about the memory you were paying attention
to . . . . (Slowly, the father first, then the daughter and
mother, start reorienting themselves to the current circumstances. Rusty stays with his eyes closed for a minute or so
into the next interaction.)

Pete: What were you thinking about, Nancy?

Nancy: The thing that came to mind was last Thanksgiving, when
you had invited Bruce (his brother) to stay with us. Remember? You invited him and *then* told me? I got furious, but somehow, we discussed it and you told Bruce not to be such a slob
and so on. Yeah, everything came back to mind and I feel good
about it. We were mad at each other but we solved the whole
thing quite well . . . . What did you remember?

Pete: (laughing) The time you crashed the new car.

Nancy: I didn't crash it! I . . . some idiot *scratched* a fender. But you
reacted as if I had totaled the damn car . . .

Pete: All right, all right (still laughing), I went tapioca. But we did
talk it over and you offered to take the car for an estimate . . .
remember? It ended up costing over $800. Ridiculous!

Annie: How come I don't remember those two things?

Rusty: Yeah. I don't remember that also.

Pete: You know, that is interesting. It's true. The two instances you
and I remembered were when the children were not around.

DLA: (7) What does that mean to you?

Pete: Well, I'm sure I'm denying something about the children. Perhaps my anger . . .

DLA: (8) Wait, wait, wait, wait. Remember, Pete, we go first inside,
experiential; then to the head, intellectual. So, go inside. Review the two incidents . . . you too, Nancy. And you, children,
relax while you enjoy watching your parents not fighting . . .

dealing with things without yelling. Relax now. While you review those two incidents, allow yourself to feel good about the way you handled it. Feel proud of yourself . . . take your time . . . go slowly . . . you are there again, in your mind's reality . . . be there 100 percent . . . and still there, ask yourself the question you asked before: Any reason why I remembered an instance without the children? Go slowly . . . allow your inner mind to capture that curiosity you have, and trust your inner mind. Let it come up with the answer. (*Pete.* It's uncanny. I think I've got it!) Wait, Pete, give it a little more time. We'll talk about it in a moment. Stay with it for a little longer . . . feel relaxed and gently ask yourself that question . . . to be sure . . . to find out something new, perhaps, about yourself . . .

Nancy: (opening her eyes and smiling) Sorry to interrupt. But this *is* uncanny, as Pete said. I'm sure I'm right. I didn't trust my father. His life was a mess. I always felt uneasy, squeamish around him. I never wanted to be alone with him. And, whether you like it or not, Daniel, I believe—I know now— that I'm transferring some of my fears from my father to Pete. That piece just fell into place. After all these years of therapy . . . how come I never realized it before?

Pete: I'm so happy to hear you say that, Nancy (almost in tears). I can't believe my ears . . . I won't say I was right . . . I just want to say that I love you.

ENP: (9) (to *DLA*) What do you think? We might stay with this, but we might also leave it for later if it's necessary.

DLA: (10) I like the way Nancy and Pete are doing. I still feel, though, that they all have to check the role the children play in all this . . . (*ENP.* Yes, let's go that way.)

Annie: I know where we fit in. It's very easy! If mom does not trust dad, that's why she's always trying to . . . you know . . . to sort of protect us . . . or to . . . you know what I mean . . . be the boss when it comes to us kids.

Pete: That's great, Annie. You are right. And the more mom tries to take over the more nervous I get and want to butt my way in. (looking at us) This kid is smart (then turning to his son), and so is this kid, too.

ENP: (11) So, what have you learned from all this? . . . Let's see, who wants to tell us?

Nancy: I suppose we need some way to correct my tendency to see my dad in Pete. Maybe you could all remind me when I do it. I'll try to remember but if I don't, you can remind me.

Rusty: How?

Nancy: You can just tell me, "Mom, you're doing it again." That'll help me to stop. You think that's a good idea?

Pete: Yeah. I think it's an excellent idea. But if I tell you, you'll get mad at me . . .

Nancy: I hope not. Just to have talked about it here can make a difference, don't you think (looking at the therapists)?

DLA: (12) Well, try it in your imagination first. Imagine that you are at home. The children come up with something they want to do. Pete says something and Nancy takes over. Start the mental movie there. Pretend it's happening now. See it clearly, with all the details . . . in your mind you are there. Check the faces, the gestures, the voices . . . look clearly to see where everybody is . . . standing? sitting? Watch the movie . . . . You now remind Nancy that she's doing it again . . . how does she react? What does she say? . . . Go over the whole thing slowly . . . in slow motion . . . then we can talk about it . . . (Everybody is quiet for about a minute.)

Rusty: I told mom to stop it.

ENP: (13) How did she react? What did she say?

Rusty: Oh, she just smiled and said . . . she said, "I know, I know. I'm glad you told me . . ."

ENP: (14) What did you see, Annie?

Annie: I reminded mom that she was not keeping her promise. (*ENP.* And? What did your mom say?) First she got mad, but then she smiled and said, "Yeah, that's why we went to therapy, isn't it?"

ENP: (15) What about you, mom and dad?

Nancy: You know? I got a kick out of this. I started being bossy and in my stuff . . . What do you call it? . . . mental stuff, you know?, the three of them stopped me. They had a singsong saying, "Mother, there you go again . . ."

ENP: How did you react?

Nancy: It felt good. I really felt grateful or something like that . . . it was a good feeling. It flashed through my mind that Pete is OK. He's not my father. I can trust him and I do.

Pete: Boy, are you saying all these nice things because I have a cold? That's great! I can't complain . . . Though, you know, when we did this thing just now, I saw Nancy getting angry first when I reminded her. But then she smiled and remembered her agreement here in the session.

DLA: (16) So, Nancy, you got the answer to your request, eh? (*Nancy.* Yeah, I guess we must try it during the week and then let you know, eh?) Yes, that's exactly it. Now, since time is running short, let's focus on dad for a while . . . I know you don't feel good today . . . but Annie gave an explanation that you liked, remember?

Pete: How can I forget? Of course I remember.

DLA: So, what about it?

Pete: What about it? I don't understand.

DLA: You said something along the lines of getting nervous when Nancy wants to take over and because of it, you push harder and Nancy gets more stubborn and the merry-go-round is on.

Pete: Oh yeah, I know.

DLA: Can you now go over this in your mind, but using what you have learned now to help you *not* get nervous?

Pete: I don't know what you're talking about.

DLA: Using self-hypnosis, as you did before, you can run one of those scenes, but this time, instead of getting nervous, you can say to yourself something like, "She is reacting to her father. It's not me," and so on. Do I make myself clear?

Pete: You mean, I should run this through my mind, as we did before, sort of . . . and not get nervous?

DLA: Yeah, try it now, if you want, Pete. The same thing is happening (he closes his eyes) and you start saying to yourself something reassuring to you . . . Listen to yourself . . . your reassuring words . . . and you feel good . . . you feel calm and relaxed . . . you *know* what's really going on between Nancy and you. Now you know and you don't have to react as you did before . . . when you didn't know what was going on . . . feel good about it . . . because now you know . . . and you love Nancy and she really trusts you and loves you . . . you're reacting very differently now . . . and you're proud of yourself. You feel very good about it. Now you handle it right . . .

Pete: You know, I'm starting to like this. It became very real in my mind. Now that I really know what's going on, as you said, I can't take it personally any more . . . it makes sense. A great deal of sense . . . amazing!

ENP: (17) What about you, Nancy? Want to go over one of those situations but now saying to yourself the right thing about Pete and your father? You know, what you learned today. (*Nancy:* Yes, I guess I should . . .) All right, then. Do the same thing Pete just did. Imagine a scene in which Pete starts to take over and you start to become anxious . . . OK? Take it from there. And you too, Pete, and the kids too, join Nancy and enjoy the relaxation. While Nancy is reprogramming her mind with what she knows now, you can feel good about your family . . . that's it, with your eyes closed and feeling very comfortable . . . and Nancy is rehearsing in her mind how she handles herself now . . . and Nancy feels so good about herself now . . . and you Pete can enjoy the relaxation, remembering that relaxing is good for the body. So you think of your health forces at work this very minute, while you relax . . . your body healing itself, getting rid of the cold while you relax and feel good about yourself. And by now Nancy knows—or will very soon know—that in your mind, Nancy, your father and Pete are separated. You have now pulled those two images apart. They are not together any more. And that feels good and you feel proud of yourself . . . a sense of liberation and freedom . . . to deal with Pete in a fresh way . . . . Stay with all this for a little while now, while you enjoy the general body relaxation . . . a few more moments, enjoying what you are doing and feeling good about yourself . . . very easy, very calm . . . peace, relaxation . . .

Pete: You know, I'm really starting to like this.

Nancy: (smiling) You just said that before . . .

Pete: No, I mean it. I even feel better. My head is less stuffed than before.

Rusty: It's nice to be quiet like this, all of us.

Annie: Yeah, I like it too. We are all together and . . . well, it's nice. Yeah.

Pete: I think we really made progress today. So what do we have to do for the next time? Will the children be here next time also? What do you think, Nancy?

Nancy: I don't know. Whatever is better. What do you think, Esther?

DLA: (18) You want to go over the things to do . . .

ENP: (interrupting) Daniel, may I answer Nancy's question?

DLA: Sorry. I am sorry. I stepped in. I wasn't thinking. Please, go ahead.

ENP: (19) No, I think it's better to go over the things to do first, Nancy. Then we'll decide about the children. Who wants to go over the things to do for next time?

Nancy: I suppose I can do it because it relates to me. Pete and the children are supposed to remind me when I start fighting with him.

ENP: (20) That's one thing. There was something else. Do you remember, Pete?

Pete: I feel a little better but I'm not completely well yet. No, I don't remember.

Nancy: Oh, I seem to recall something about writing something down. What was it?

DLA: (21) I'll help. We suggested that you write your own guidelines for future discussions, so that when you do disagree you get to a satisfactory solution more quickly. Does that make sense?

Pete: Yeah. If I recall correctly, we were supposed to write what we did right last time so we can learn from it for the future. Correct?

DLA: That's exactly it.

Nancy: So what about the children? Should we bring them next time?

DLA: (22) All depends on what our agenda for next time will be.

What do you think, Esther? (*ENP* gestures with face, shoulders, and arms to express "I'm not sure.") In some ways we could say that they have attained what they came here for. Now we have to help them maintain what they have accomplished. On the other hand, though, I have a feeling that this is far from finished . . .

ENP: (23) I agree. I can't put my finger on it, but I still feel unfinished. Let's check it out, will you all? Let's spend a moment reflecting, thinking, quietly: Where is the family now? Do we have to stop here or must we go into other areas? I'm closing my eyes and you may want to do the same . . . reviewing gently, quietly, what we have done together in the last three sessions we had . . . . Our inner mind can help us see things more clearly. I want to let my inner mind give me a true feeling about these people I met less than . . . a few weeks ago. I don't remember well how long ago it was. I like them. I feel in some ways part of their struggle to be a great family . . . I hope you two are getting into this, reviewing what we did and what is still to be done . . .

Nancy: I got into something important, I think. We don't need the children. The problem was really between Pete and me. I believe that, yes, we have corrected the problem, we have made progress, but I feel insecure. Frightened? I think we need more coaching to be sure we don't backslide . . .

ENP: Any other reactions?

Annie: I like coming here together. It's better than staying home with grandma. But now that they are not fighting, I don't think we should come back.

Rusty: Yeah. Me, too.

Pete: Annie is right. I also think that we two should see you a couple more times to check on how we are doing. That's all. The kids don't have to be here now . . . I mean from now on. If we can handle our discussions about them in the right way, I guess . . .

DLA: (24) I tend to agree. What about you, Esther?

ENP: (25) I see it this way. The couple were having difficulties dealing with one issue. They came for help and found a better way to handle it. They learned a few self-hypnotic techniques to handle their discussion about the children better. We are still in the learning process and they need practice. We can coach them, as Nancy put it, until they feel they have acquired the new skills and they use them sort of spontaneously.

DLA: (26) I also . . . I agree. We have to be sure they have learned a new way. And by "we," I mean first Nancy and Pete have to feel comfortable with what they are doing right, as opposed to the behavior that frustrated them before and brought them to us. (to the couple) What do you think?

Pete: Oh, I'm with you. Yes, we'll be back to check things out.

The last minutes of the session were used to discuss the next appointment, which, because of schedule conflicts, was made for two weeks later.

Comments

Doggedly staying with the issue that brought this family to us, we focused on their way of discussing issues related to the children. DLA's early assignment of a task to do for the next session (#2) was at best premature. The fact that it had to be repeated toward the end of the session (#19–21) indicates that it was useless to bring it up earlier. However, the theme of finding new and better ways of disagreeing and arguing was kept constant throughout the entire session, especially in #5 and 6. ENP's mention of a "fight" (#6) could have been a mistake since we were trying to emphasize that disagreement does not mean heated fighting.

An important development occurred in #8 when Nancy reported her realization regarding her father. If she perceived this type of psychological reality, we did not question it but tried to use it, as DLA did with Pete (#16) and ENP with Nancy (#17).

Pete seemed to become more comfortable with the experiential rather than intellectual approach (#7, 8). It would have been very easy to enter into an analytical discussion, both when the couple realized that they had spontaneously brought up two instances in which the children were not involved, and again, when Nancy obtained her "insight" (#8). Hypnotherapy means to trust the sub-conscious thinking processes, at least as much as the conscious ones. By leading the couple to subconscious activation, we helped them find answers (#8 and later #10 regarding a solution to Nan-cy's old reaction to Pete).

Number 10 is a good illustration of the real contributions often made by young children. Both Annie and Rusty were highly artic-ulate children with rich vocabularies. Using Annie's explanation, ENP helped the family summarize what they had learned so far but—we emphasize the point—this recapitulation was done hyp-notically (#12).

Number 17 is an example of what could be labeled multiple hyp-nosis. While ostensibly concentrating on Nancy, ENP involved the whole family in the experience, which, incidentally, seemed to give the children a calm sense of family closeness, probably helpful to counteract the negative feelings reported by them earlier (#1) dur-ing their parents' fights. Annie's comment in #17 seemed to justify our impression.

The fourth session took place two weeks later without the chil-dren. We had planned to pay special attention to the way they dis-cussed issues now, which we hoped would be more productively than before.

FOURTH SESSION

DLA: (1) How are you doing?

ENP: Hi, Nancy. Hi, Pete.

DLA: Where are you sitting today? That's a great shirt you have on today, Pete.

Pete: Thanks. Nancy's gift . . . one of her gifts for my birthday last week. I had a great day, thanks to Nancy.

DLA: I forgot. I'm sorry. Happy birthday.

ENP: Me, too. Happy birthday, Pete.

Pete: You know, it's good to be here. But everything went fine, as far as I'm concerned. So I don't know what we are going to do today.

Nancy: Yeah. I also feel good. We had no problems (taking a paper out of her purse) and here are those guidelines you wanted us to write. (Pete digs into his back pocket and hands a paper to ENP with a smile.) I think we resolved what we came to see you for. We're ready to graduate.

DLA: (2) The guidelines you wrote are not for us. Were they helpful to you? I mean, was it helpful to write them down? (Both Nancy and Pete say yes.) Did you talk about what you wrote?

Pete: Yes. That's part of it. We had a very good conversation and we found out a lot of good things about . . . (Nancy agrees.)

ENP: (3) Since everything seems to be going well, I'd like to review the whole thing hypnotically. Daniel and I call this Subjective Biofeedback. Want to do it?

Pete: I'm game. (Nancy nods assent.)

ENP: All right, make yourselves comfortable.

DLA: I'm joining you too. I also want to review what we did . . . in my inner mind, I mean.

ENP: Pay attention to your breathing . . . allow your body to pick up its own natural breathing tempo. No need to force deep breaths. Just gentle, natural, regular, peaceful breathing. Connect the breathing with relaxation . . . breathing-in calm, relaxation, good feelings; and breathing-out any unnecessary tensions. Breathing-out any discomfort or negative feelings. Stay with your breathing for a little while . . . then, when you are ready, remember what took place since we met . . . the things you learned . . . the way you can communicate better, more effectively. Let your inner mind do the work. You just feel relaxed and comfortable. Your inner mind can bring back to your conscious mind anything and everything that you learned . . . and while this is happening, notice how your body is reacting . . . . Where do you feel more comfort? More relaxation? Some people notice a sense of calm in their head, or in their abdomen, or in their shoulders. Take your time and notice where you feel more at peace. When you're ready, you may want to tell us . . .

DLA: My chest feels very relaxed.

ENP: Fine, enjoy the good feeling.

Pete: (very slowly and low) Feel good all over.

Nancy: My hands feel light.

ENP: That's fine. Just give yourself permission to enjoy any good feeling in your body that you are aware of. Just enjoy it, while your inner mind reviews the useful things you learned about yourself . . . about more effective communication . . . about discussing things productively. Feel good about each other. How much you care for each other. Your inner mind is reviewing, slowly, so that everything you learned becomes part of you . . . so that you assimilate completely whatever is useful for you, for the relationship, for the marriage . . . very relaxed while you are absorbing everything you learned. Now move to the future and watch yourself in your mind's eye, putting into practice all these things. Focus on an imaginary situation. Let it unfold in your mental screen. Watch yourself acting in accordance with what you learned for your benefit. And feel good about it. Now you're handling things better, more effectively, with greater inner peace, with more comfort and peace. Let the whole scene develop and come to an end. And keep feeling good about it. Are you with it? (Pete and Nancy make sounds of assent.) Let the whole scene come to its natural conclusion, while you feel very good about it . . .

Pete: That was good. Amazing how the mind works . . .

Nancy: Yeah. I felt bad when you said to end the scene. I was having a good time. It felt great . . .

DLA: (4) We may talk about what you experienced just now or we may let your inner mind keep it and use it again and again when you need it. Anything you want to say?

Pete: I kept reassuring myself that when Nancy irritates me, she's still dealing with her old man, I mean her dad. He was a clown! God! Strange guy! But it felt good to keep that in mind. As if everything had fallen into place now.

Nancy: Yeah. I feel the same.

DLA: (5) I found myself being sure that Pete and Nancy will be all right. My body felt very relaxed and good. What about you? Did you notice the connection between what you were thinking and the way your body was reacting to it?

Nancy: Yeah. It was like a confirmation . . . I don't know. It felt right. I felt good and when Esther said something about loving each other, it was as if I were in love with Pete for the first time. I guess my body was telling me that we are on the right track. D'you think? What do you call this, anyway?

ENP: (6) Subjective Biofeedback? You use your body as a biofeedback apparatus, as it were. And it's exactly as you said, Nancy. Your body tells you with its tension or lack of it.

Nancy: I felt no tension at all. On the contrary . . .

Pete: You know, I was almost telling myself that all that yelling and anger is bull. I felt grown up, in control, going over this sort of new process: anger, craziness, and then constructive action, intelligent explanation. It felt new to me and I still don't know whether the yelling is all that bad. But I felt good realizing that I can detour the yelling or bypass the craziness and get right to the other stuff, you know, the talk stage as it were. It was different, that's all.

ENP: (7) One thing you may want to remember is to try to do this practice on your own. After a few times, you *will* know which is the best way for you. And by practicing it in your mind, you'll find it easier, more natural, to do what's right for you. It's the type of mental rehearsal we've done before.

DLA: (8) You were right when you said that you're ready to graduate, Nancy. That's why Esther is telling you . . . reminding you of the different practices we used. I agree with you about "graduating." But we like to have a follow-up visit in six or eight weeks. We'll speak about it in a minute. But before, I want to go back to Pete. You said, after the mind exercise we just did, that the mind works in amazing ways or something like that. Want to get into that a bit?

Pete: I don't know. There is nothing to say other than . . . well I was surprised, that's all, that I was so calm, feeling so happy. I couldn't understand why. But then a soft voice in me said, "You dummy! Just enjoy what you . . . I mean, How I feel. Stop analyzing." Mr. Spock's face appeared and was mocking me while saying, "Perfectly logical, Mr. Cronan. You are human, Mr. Cronan. You can't, repeat, can *not*, be perfectly logical. You have feelings. Enjoy them!" That's why I was laughing. Then I felt that strange sense of peace and calm. It was weird . . .

ENP: (9) You also said that you kept thinking that Nancy reacts to her father through you, remember?

Pete: Yeah, yes, I do. I mean, I can live with that . . .

Nancy: But you also overplay that, Pete. When you don't want to take me seriously, you go into that act. That's another way of putting me down and not taking me seriously.

Pete: Oh, God! There we go again. Forget about "graduating" from marriage counseling. I think we need a few more visits.

Nancy: You see what I mean? He's laughing at me. I just stated a reasonable complaint. And what's his reaction? To make fun of me.

Pete: Oh, get off it, Nancy. I'm *not* making fun of you. Don't you know me by now? I know I'm wrong. But not because I'm putting you down. I'm not doing that! I'm wrong because when I don't know what to say, I just talk.

Nancy: That makes a lot of sense for Mr. Logic.

Pete: Now, who's putting whom down?

Nancy: I'm sorry. You're right. Go on.

Pete: It's OK. (looking at DLA) I guess this *is* progress, eh? What I mean is that you, Nancy, made a good point. I don't know how to solve that problem. I do recognize that at times I use that crap about your old man as a cop-out. I know it. But I don't know what distinction to make, you know what I mean? When are you reacting to your old man, and when are you really and truly reacting to me? That's what I was trying to say. You understand? What's the answer, Doc?

DLA: (10) My first reaction is, Forget about Nancy's father. Look at yourself, *first*. Be factual. What happened? What did *you* do or say? How did Nancy react? That sort of thing. But all this is nonsense if only *I* say it. You have to find the answer, as you called it, inside of you, in your inner mind. Want to do it now? (Pete nods assent.) You know how to do it by now, Pete. Go inside of you, using your breathing to relax and gently connect with your true self, with your truthful self. You may not know what your true self is all about. But give it a try. Are you with it? (Pete nods.) Be patient and enjoy this moment of peace and calm. Your truthful self has the answer you are looking for. When should you think that Nancy is not reacting to you but to her old man? Still into it? (Pete nods very slowly.) Stay with it . . . maybe Nancy can help you now. Nancy, be his auxiliary ego and say out loud what Pete could say to himself.

Nancy: Oh, he should give me a chance. (*DLA*. Talk as if you were Pete. Talk *for* him.) Oh, OK. "I should give Nancy a chance. I shouldn't assume that she's not reacting to me."

DLA: (to Pete) How does that sound? Can you say that to yourself?

Pete: (still in hypnosis) Yes, good. (*DLA*. Say it to yourself, Pete. "I want to give Nancy a chance. I don't want to assume . . .") I don't want to . . . Yes, I want to give her a chance. (*DLA*. Give yourself all the time you need to assimilate this. Nancy, anything else?)

Nancy: I don't view him as my father.

DLA: Pete says, "You don't view me as your father."

Nancy: Oh, yes, "She doesn't view me as her dad."

DLA: Does that sit well with you, Pete? (He nods.) Would you say that to yourself?

Pete: Yeah, I want to believe that she does not see me as her old man. (*DLA*. Repeat that to yourself. Slowly. Again. Until every cell in your body believes it.) She doesn't see me as her old man. (Very faintly and low.) I want to give her a chance. I want to listen to her. She reacts to me. To me. (*DLA*. Take your time to assimilate this completely, so you feel really good about it. Slowly and feeling good about yourself.)

Nancy: "And if I take her at face value, I'll be happy and she'll be happy."

DLA: What about that, Pete?

Pete: Yeah. I want to take her at face value. Reacting to me. Forget about her old man. It's Nancy and me; me and Nancy.

DLA: (11) Now, Nancy, you can be yourself again and, while Pete is coming back to the ordinary way of using his mind, tell him how you feel about his taking you for yourself and believing that it is you and him when you are dealing with each other.

Nancy: I hope you can do that, Pete. It would make me very happy, less tense, if I know you are not saying to yourself that I'm not reacting to you but to my dad. (Pete is slowly stretching and smiling)

Pete: I liked that. It was weird. When Nancy was talking like me, I wanted her to go on and on . . . I felt very close to her.

DLA: (12) Did you get the answer to your question? You know, about when to take what Nancy does to you as genuinely addressed to you? . . .

Pete: Yes, I guess I knew it all the time. As you said, forget about her old man. We can't communicate if his ghost is between us all the time—or even part of the time, you know.

ENP: (13) I realize that I did open a Pandora's box in a sense, eh? But it turned out to be a benefit. To reinforce what you just did, let's do it a bit differently this time. Pete, you be Nancy and, as expected, Nancy, you take on Pete's character. (Both look a bit puzzled.) In other words, you speak *as if* you were the other person. So (addressing herself to Nancy), How are you today, Pete? (Nancy smiles understandingly. And directing her attention to Pete) Nancy, I love your earrings. They really bring out the color of your eyes. Get it? (Both agree.) OK, who's going to start telling the other something about this issue of relating to each other directly, and so on?

Pete: I can start, I suppose. I'm Nancy, OK? "Pete pisses me off when I'm talking to him and he tells me that I'm really talking to my father. That's not fair."

ENP: (14) (addressing herself to Pete, who is role playing his wife) But Nancy, Pete just went through a hypnotic practice and does not want to continue using your father as an excuse not to take you seriously.

Pete: Yeah, that's true. I hope he can do it.

ENP: What if he slips back?

Pete: I can remind him of what we did here. Yes, I'll do that . . .

ENP: (15) What about you (to Nancy), Pete?

Nancy: (as her husband) I don't really buy this stuff that Nancy is not seeing her old man in me. But I'll give her the benefit of the doubt. I want to give her a chance. I want to forget her dad and really listen to what she wants to tell me—in words or in actions too. (*ENP.* But if you are still convinced that she sees you through the filter of her father, you'll never do it.) Well, I'm not fully convinced. I use that also as a cop-out. When she irritates me, I can look at the real situation or I can *not* look at it and say it's the ghost of her father. I know that, but I want to be honest and truthful now. No more bull . . . I love Nancy and I want to do this for her. I really want to take her seriously, with respect as a person in her own right. That's all. As a real, adult, person.

ENP: (16) You did really good. Now, let's talk about this. Any reactions?

Pete: Oh, plenty. I thought it was so easy to do, but then when I started, I felt so damn self-conscious that I was ready to quit. But then when Nancy played my role, it was fascinating. I felt very good about it.

Nancy: Me, too. That's very interesting and strange in a way. I really felt in Pete's shoes. Very good method. We can do this by ourselves too. It'll be fun.

DLA: (17) (looking at his watch) Well, let's wrap this up. We talked earlier about graduating from family therapy. I also mentioned that we want to have a follow-up session in no more than two months. Esther and I have not yet said goodbye to the children. So let's go over all this for a minute or so. OK?

The rest of the session dealt with the practical aspects of preparing for termination. Another appointment was made for three weeks in the future. This session would include the children. The follow-up session, mentioned before, was postponed for after the next visit.

Comments

The main theme of this session, at least outwardly, was the issue of Nancy's paternal transference. The couple had done the assigned homework and reported improved communication in #2. Even though Pete referred to ''good things'' they had found out in that one instance of a good conversation, neither of us followed up on it. Esther proposed the Subjective Biofeedback exercise (see Araoz, 1984c) as a means to review their gains. In this sense, then, the lack of attention to "the good things" Pete had mentioned was remedied. In the review, as reported in #4, the theme of the previous session regarding Nancy's reaction to her father and husband (see Second Session, #8) was used therapeutically. However, later in the session (#9) ENP helped refine that notion so that it did not become a justification for Pete's possible lack of attention to Nancy.

The involvement of the therapists in the current experience of the clients, either through a discussion between the therapists in front of the client (Second Session, #9, 10) or through direct participation in the hypnotic experience (#3–5) is effective as a means of directly becoming part of the family system only when it happens spontaneously. However, when the family is feeling good and positive about the way things are going, this involvement may tempt the therapist to stay there, as happened toward the end of #8. Thanks to ENP bringing up the transferential issue of Nancy's father again, the session moved on to a more active level of interaction. When Nancy took this opportunity to point to Pete's abuse of the transferential concept, he was ready for a fight, but quickly reverted to himself and, in spite of Nancy's sarcasm, continued his introspection (#9). His request for an "answer" was met with a direct reply from DLA (#10), who used this moment to lead him into a hypnotic experience that made his introspection even more meaningful. As a way of undoing the irritation caused by Nancy's earlier sarcasm, DLA used a technique from hypnodrama and encouraged Nancy to become an auxiliary ego for Pete. Nancy seemed to have been waiting for this opportunity, as her getting into it shows (#10). With some coaxing, this practice became useful for both (#11 at the end).

The technique of role reversal is by nature hypnotic. The more each gets into the other person's role, the more they leave the ordinary reality orientation and become involved in right hemispheric activity. ENP started in a light way (#13) and got Pete and Nancy to check what they had accomplished earlier. By means of role reversal (another hypnodramatic technique) the "Check" step in our OLD C therapeutic model is taken (see Introduction). This practice reinforced the gains made earlier, as #13–15 show. We find, gen-

erally, that role reversal is most effective when applied as a reinforcing method, after the family or couple has already shifted
points of view or attitudes toward a particular issue, as this example demonstrates.

Regarding the learning that took place during the four family
therapy sessions, Pete gave us a few indications. For a "family that
knew too much," after so many years of individual therapy, the experience of viewing problems systemically rather than intrapsych-
ically accelerated their resolution. If a problem existed when the
family realistically wanted something to happen but was actually
experiencing something else, the Cronan family had resolved their
problem. The constructive communication they wanted was not an
unrealistic fantasy. However, things were in the way of their actually enjoying it. These "things" included yelling and anger,
which Pete recognized as "bull" in #6. His introspective comments
at that point indicated that he had recognized his previous behavior as immature and childish. His reflections in #9 seemed to be the
combined outcome of his individual *and* family therapy: when confused, he talked nonsense and therefore his wife needed to keep
this in mind in order to react differently to him. In #13 Pete clarified
at a practical level of understanding Nancy's transferential conflict,
which had colored their relationship.

Nancy too enjoyed her new awareness of her husband (#10, 16)
in a practical way. Now she knew that she could experience the type
of communication with her husband that she desired and perceived as possible. Because these "insights" must be translated
into practice, we decided not to "graduate" them, as Nancy had
suggested earlier (#1), but agreed on having another meeting, this
time involving the children, before ending our therapeutic contact
with the family. A follow-up meeting was mentioned so that the
clients get ready for a final visit (#8) about two months after the last
"therapy" session.

FIFTH SESSION

Nancy: We almost didn't make it on time today. (laughing) It must
be that we're getting so good but we almost forgot that we had

an appointment. Actually it was Rusty who reminded me. Then I had to call Pete and get the children ready. It was a mad rush but we made it.

Pete: I thought of it several times in the last few weeks but Nancy is right; I also forgot all about it.

ENP: (1) I think you're right. We have succeeded when we make ourselves useless. I suppose you are doing so well that we have become useless to you. (*DLA:* What Esther is saying is really a compliment to you *and* to us. We feel very good when we become useless, as Esther just said. That's the whole purpose of therapy; to get you quickly to the point where you don't need us. [to the children] And how have *you* been? Haven't seen you in quite a while.)

Annie: Mom said you wanted to say goodbye to us . . .

Rusty: I thought that was weird.

Annie: . . . and I wanted to say goodbye to you too.

Rusty: I thought we had said goodbye last time we were here.

Annie: Oh, shut up, Rusty!

DLA: (2) Well, Rusty is right in a sense; we said goodbye but not *really* goodbye. So Esther and I suggested that your parents bring you once more to say goodbye really, you know?

Rusty: Well, I still think that's weird. Why would you want to say goodbye to us? We've only seen each other a couple of times. (Annie makes disapproving sounds in the background.)

Pete: Rusty, we wanted to bring you here because you two are part of this family. Remember, we came to see . . . to family therapy because we had problems . . . your mother and I had problems about you . . . I mean about . . . we didn't agree on how to deal with you . . . we got into fights, remember? So we came to family therapy together and we think we should finish it together also. You understand now? That's why we brought you here today. OK? (Rusty mumbles approval.)

DLA: (3) Pete is right. The family is one. What has improved with family therapy is good for all. I suggest that all of you get in touch with this feeling of being one. Want to do it? (Sounds of approval from the family members.) It's rather simple. Let's do it and then we can talk about it. Just feel as comfortable as you can while you are sitting there. Close your eyes whenever you want, and pay attention to your breathing until it becomes very comfortable and relaxed. Then, slowly, think of a situation where you are all together, as a family, having a good time. Be together. It may be at home; it may be someplace else. But be sure to focus on having a good time. You feel very good being with your family. You love every minute of it. You are relaxed and happy. Really get into it. What you are doing; where you are; the time of day; whether it is cold or hot; how you are dressed; whether you are hungry or thirsty. Pay attention to every detail—every color, every sound, every sensation, every awareness of temperature changes, every smell, everything. Enjoy! Enjoy being there. Feel your love for your family. How secure you are with the others. There is real love flowing from you to the others. Flowing from each of the others to you. Take your time and just savor, enjoy, taste this wonderful feeling. You are part of your family. Your family gives you good feelings and you give your family what you are. Good feelings and a comfortable sense of belonging. I belong here. They belong here. No rush in enjoying this. And when you want to, you can come back to the ordinary way of thinking, so we can talk about this whole thing with each other.

ENP: (4) Take your time to come back. We are in no hurry and you may want to stay longer, enjoying your mental pictures. Very slowly and feeling very good.

Rusty: (enthusiastically) That was cool. (Nancy and Annie open their eyes but Pete stays with eyes closed.) I liked it a lot. I was saying to myself that even when they fight, we love each other.

Annie: Silly. They haven't fought like that for a while now.

Rusty: All right, Annie. You always have to boss me around. And I still say that the main thing is that we as a family love each other, regardless. OK, Annie?

Pete: I was still far away when I heard the children argue. It was as if it didn't bother me at all. And usually, I go bananas when they start that nasty bickering. This time I was like floating in that love that Rusty mentioned. Love had become a concrete reality. It was really different and very nice.

Nancy: I'm glad we are here, sort of practicing this. You know, when you started with this mental exercise, I sort of got mad at both of you. I felt that we really had finished and that you were going to drag things out so you could charge us instead of dismissing us after 10 minutes. But when you started with that soft voice I said to myself, "What the heck! We are here, I might as well get into it." But as soon as I got into it, all the anger disappeared, like magic, and I started to feel, you know, a true, a sort of very deep, sense of peace. I guess it was that love and security you kept talking about. I'm sorry I was mad at both of you but I feel terrific now.

Pete: And you are right. We are finished. So now we know things we didn't know before.

ENP: (5) What are the things that you know now that you didn't know before, Pete?

Pete: The minute I said that, I looked at you. You noticed that, eh? I knew you were going to ask me that. But I don't mind. I can only speak for myself. I know now that letting it all out is not necessarily good. I also know that trying to analyze and understand everything is not always the first thing to do. I know now that going through this unconscious, what do you call it?, unconscious searching or getting into, that's it, getting into, having the experience in one's unconscious . . . what was I saying? I don't know. I guess I was trying to say that this stuff we have been doing here works. Thinking unconsciously has merit. Not just thinking logically. Is that it?

ENP: (6) Sounds great to me. Does that make sense to you, Nancy?

Nancy: Most definitely. I believe this has been a tremendous experience for Pete. He's always so analytical. I can't believe my ears when I hear him saying that unconscious thinking has merit and all that. Yeah, definitely, it sits well with me. I'm very pleased.

Annie: I don't know what you're talking about. But I feel good anyway. Both of you guys seem to be so . . . I don't know, you're OK. I'm happy, too.

DLA: (7) So, what do you say, Rusty? Should we now really say goodbye?
Rusty: I think so. Mom is right. We have finished . . .

The rest of the session was spent in chitchat while everybody said goodbye to the two therapists.

Comments

This last session was, indeed, shorter in duration than the previous sessions. Focusing our therapeutic interventions on the effective functioning of the family system, we used this last session to make sure that the original "malfunction" had been corrected. We also sincerely wanted to say goodbye to the family as a whole. This is not merely a polite or sentimental move. It comes from our experience that often children contribute significantly to the healthy functioning of the family system by the insights and comments offered at the conclusion of family therapy. In this case Rusty (#4) shared with us a wisdom far beyond his age: that family love can transcend external alterations of family harmony. Even after divorce, families can remain bonded by love despite the different postdivorce structure of the family.

The self-hypnosis practice proposed by DLA (#3) helped to recapitulate the gains made during the weeks of family therapy. Thanks to ENP (#5), Pete gave a succinct summary of what family therapy had meant to him, to the pleasant surprise of his wife.

Even though at the time DLA would have denied it, the transcript (#7) shows his eagerness to bring this session to an end. Looking into this intervention, the therapists realized that they were pleased with the turn of events and both—not only DLA—were eager to end the session on a positive note. That ENP shared DLA's desire to end at this point is clear from the fact that she did not (as on previous occasions, even in this session at #5) ask what scenes each formed in their minds during the hypnotic practice. In retrospect, we believe that our neglect was not damaging to the family. On the contrary, it may have conveyed an important lesson: hypnosis is an aid to bring forth feelings to help us; through it, we can change our feelings for our personal and family benefit; the "content" of our imaginative involvement is really less important than the process of inner change achieved through hypnosis.

From our follow-up contact with this family, two months after the fifth session, we know that what was important for them was the newly learned ability to use one's mind to improve oneself and to function more productively. This aspect of hypnosis was learned by the Cronans.

FOLLOW-UP SESSION

ENP: (1) It has been a long time. Feels like ages since the last time we saw each other.

DLA: Yeah. I have the same feeling.

Rusty: I got a PC for my birthday.

Annie: That's all he cares about. Spends all day playing with that silly computer. He even talks to it. I heard him say goodnight the other evening. Can you believe it? To be so silly?

Rusty: Just ignore her. I love it. You should come and visit us soon, so I can show it to you.

Nancy: Yes, the computer was a great gift for Rusty. He's very happy with it. But, for that matter, we're all doing very well. Pete and I were talking about the fact that we really didn't have to come to see you today. This computer thing is a good example of our improvement.

Pete: Yeah, we discussed it together before we finally decided to spend the money.

Nancy: Yeah (laughing), we are so good. But what is even better, we're feeling great about each other. So what do we do now?

DLA: (2) We have a couple of things we'd like to do today so that we can really say goodbye. First, we want to teach you again how to use self-hypnosis any time you need to. Then we would like to ask you to spend a few moments together, as a family, discussing your experience of family therapy. Finally, one of you will—we hope—fill out a form writing down your reactions as a family. This will be very helpful to us. We are always gathering information on what we do. Only way we can know if it is really working or not, you know.

Nancy: OK, I'm game.

Pete: Yeah. Me, too. Let's get going, eh?

Nancy: Are the children going to be part of this too?

ENP: Yes, by all means. We also want them to be able to use self-hypnosis any time they need it.

Nancy: So, Rusty, sit down and stop moving.

Rusty: What are we going to do?

Nancy: Just sit down and pay attention.

ENP: (3) Let's start with self-hypnosis. But before we start, each one of you think of a beautiful place—better outdoors—where you are having a great time. Maybe a beach, the mountains, a quiet meadow. Do you have a place like that in mind? (All indicate that they do.) All right. At this point, after you have practiced self-hypnosis with us so many times, we want to give you a quick and easy way of doing it alone. To remember the steps to go through, think of the word BRIMS. Five steps. "B" means breathing slowly, naturally. Start now, if you want, OK? Breathing leads to relaxation—the "R" in BRIMS. Allow your breathing to start relaxing your muscles. In your shoulders and in your back; in your legs and in your arms. All your muscles can benefit from your slow, natural breathing. And your eyes are closed so you can relax even better. Remember, take your time. Don't rush. Especially in the beginning, go slowly. Are you still paying attention to your breathing? Notice how it can relax all your muscles. You can feel so comfortable and nice . . . . And now, you can use your relaxation to move on to the third step, imagination, or the "I" in BRIMS. Imagine your muscles as being still tense. What do they look like in your mind's eye? Don't tell me now. But simply let the mental picture of your tense muscles form clearly in your mind. Concentrate on one set of muscles. Where do you still feel the tension? You got it? OK. Now imagine that the tension starts to go away. Your muscles now start to look less tense in your mind's eye. The muscles start becoming untense. Look at them in the picture you have formed in your mind. And enjoy the nice

feeling. Are you enjoying the lack of tension now? Fine. Beautiful. Now use your imagination again, but this time to see
yourself relaxing as you're now in that beautiful place you
thought about before we started doing self-hypnosis. Place
yourself there. Be there. Enjoy its beauty. Pay attention to all
the good sounds. Listen carefully. Be there. Smell the air: so
nice and cool and pure. Take a deep breath if you want to. Very
comfortably. Feeling more and more comfortable with every
breath. And enjoy everything you see, every sound you hear,
every scent you smell. Feel the nice temperature, the beautiful
sun. Imagine yourself sort of dozing in your beautiful place.
How wonderful to be here. Safe. Relaxed. Happy. No rush.
Nothing else to do. And here in your beautiful place you can
move now to the "M" in BRIMS. You give yourself a good message. Remind yourself that you can do what you want to be
better. Enjoying your relaxation, you can give yourself a loving
message. You may want to say something like this: "I'm OK
and I can always be better. I can imagine myself accomplishing
what I want. I can feel more positive about myself. I can take
better care of my health, of my individual needs, including my
needs as a family person. I'm OK and I want to keep this in
mind. I want to love myself, respect myself, and enjoy life as
much as possible. This I want for myself. I also want to love the
people who are important to me so we can give to each other
and become richer as human beings." You may say other
things to yourself. Whatever they are, make them true and
positive. Give yourself messages for your own benefit. Messages that are true and positive while you are in your beautiful
place, enjoying yourself. And here you may want to stay for a
while until you are ready to stop—the "S" in BRIMS—and return to the ordinary way of using your mind. While you are
stopping your self-hypnosis, tell yourself that you want to try
this again and again, until you master it completely. And
slowly you get yourself ready to change back to the ordinary
mental channel. Slowly, comfortably, feeling terrific.

DLA: (4) So this is our BRIMS method. Yes, stretch and smile. Feel
good, eh? Now, before you say anything else, tell us, How was

it? Did you have any problems doing the BRIMS? (General comments are made, basically positive, except for the mother, who reported many distractions initially but later was able to enjoy self-hypnosis.) Now let me suggest that you go through the BRIMS again but this time on your own. Try it, let's say for about five minutes. Want to do it? (General agreement. For the next eight minutes, the family practiced self-hypnosis on their own. We had mounted the five steps written on a piece of paper on the wall and had suggested that if they forgot what came next, they could open their eyes and look at the next step before continuing their own self-hypnosis practice.)

DLA: (5) So how are you feeling now?

Nancy: I felt better. Not so many distractions. I did what you told me before. I imagined my mind like a room with open windows and the breeze blowing right through it. So my distractions did not have a chance to stay put. I feel pretty good now. (The others make similar comments in a positive vein.)

DLA: (6) This is it. Now you can practice this as much as you want and when you come to the "M" give yourself any constructive message you need. All right?

ENP: (7) So now that you learned to do self-hypnosis on your own, let's move on to the next thing. For the next 10 or 15 minutes, we'll leave you alone. In that time, you can discuss this form (the research questions mentioned in the Introduction) and then you decide who will write the answers on the paper. If you finish earlier, we'll be just outside and then we'll rejoin you and talk about it if you want. OK?

They all agreed to spend a few minutes working on the evaluation form. After about 15 minutes, we reentered the consultation room. They had assigned the father to write down their reactions to family hypnotherapy and he was doing just that. The rest of the session was spent in goodbyes and small talk.

Comments

We used this follow-up session to help the family recapitulate what family hypnotherapy had meant to them. Before that, we went over a five-step method of self-hypnosis and made sure they had learned it well enough to practice it by themselves. From other families that we had seen, we knew that they might not practice this immediately. Months later, if they remembered to do it, they might call us to ask questions regarding the five steps of BRIMS.

Looking back on this session, we may indicate that ENP led the family through a general, practical method of self-hypnosis. She could have integrated some of the individualized experiences of the family members into this "induction," such as Rusty's computer enthusiasm or Pete's new concepts about expressing anger. However, we have found that with a family (as well as with a group) it is better to avoid mentioning specific items belonging to one or another member. It seems that, unless the therapist prepares very carefully, one or another person in the family or group will be disappointed. This may happen either because his or her particular item was not mentioned, or because it was not given enough time, or because what was mentioned was not the specific thing the individual person had in mind. As a consequence, we have decided to make the self-hypnosis practice for the whole family (as well as for groups) general rather than specific, as ENP did in this case. No "induction" is perfect and in ENP's the omission of preparing the family for possible distractions is a good example of "what should have been done." But, as we notice in the process, it was remedied later. When Nancy referred to the room with open windows, according to what DLA had told her (#5), she was going back to what was part of the discussion mentioned in #4 but not recorded verbatim.

As can be noticed, at this point we kept referring to self-hypnosis. This was to emphasize the fact that they could do it themselves and that they did not need us to practice hypnosis. Usually self-hypnosis is less threatening to people than is hypnosis.

GENERAL COMMENTS

Now we want to look at the case as a whole, from beginning to end. As we stressed in the Introduction and throughout the text, our intention is not to build theory about family interactions or about family therapy. We have a more modest goal in this book. We simply want to show how hypnosis can be applied to family therapy in a rather simple and spontaneous manner. Consequently, at this point, we would like to enumerate the hypnotic techniques we used and the advantages of having used them.*

Since we are interested in simplifying the hypnotic method rather than in complicating it, as traditional hypnosis did, trying to apply to therapy what were experimental and laboratory parameters, we started in Session One (#8) with Goal Attainment, one of the two modalities of Mental Rehearsal, as explained in Chapter 2. This was used both as a diagnostic tool and as a warm-up for other hypnotic activities that we wanted to engage the family in subsequently. The diagnostic aspect of Goal Attainment is important in any human condition where change is appropriate. If a person cannot visualize or experience internally the change he consciously wants, the clinician can safely assume that there *are* nonconscious dynamics at work. If this is the case, the hypnotic technique called Activation of Personality Parts, also discussed in Chapter 2, may be employed with good results.

In spite of Pete's objections (1, from #9 to 24), we used his spontaneous mental image (in the snowmobile) to "deepen" his hypnotic experience, as the traditional hypnotists would put it (1, #25–28). Only then was Pete given a rational explanation of the pragmatic value of hypnosis.

At this point, we had proven the value of hypnotherapy. Therefore we moved on (1, #30) into another Mental Rehearsal, this time focusing concretely on one of the difficult issues at hand between the couple. This was a mixture of Goal Attainment and Change Process (see Chapter 2). We finally ended the session with the body check, according to our OLD C model, explained in the Introduction.

In the second session we built on what they had experienced

---

*In this first case study, the use of hypnotic techniques is indicated in detail to facilitate the understanding of our approach. In the other two cases, we shall assume that the reader is already familiar with our clinical method.

during our first contact with them. To do this, we asked them to describe in detail how they had practiced self-hypnosis after the first session (2, #6–8), and we used Pete's images to practice right there in the session. Here we used Mental Rehearsal once more. The reason for repeating the same technique several times in different ways is purely didactic. However, in 3, #17 we introduced Inner Wisdom in combination with Activation of Personality Parts. Pete's wise "part" appeared to him as an old man—he being an old man. We led him to take as much advantage of this mental image as possible at this point, as shown in the following exchanges, from #18 to 21.

The process so far led us to an experiential way of considering "the problem" with the children. So in 2, #25, using another Mental Rehearsal, the Cronans were able to compare their nonconscious images of what they want the children to be. This leads to a possibly constructive action geared to solve their problem (2, #29).

The third session, with the children, did not get into hypnotic work right away. After the first segment of this session, we suggested Past Accomplishments (see Chapter 2) to help the family recognize the value of not "letting it all out," as the father believed disagreements should be handled. This was also done to justify our "rule" about *not* shouting and yelling in anger during the therapy sessions. In #8, Past Accomplishments was practiced again so that they could learn to use it in the future. Incidentally, this mind exercise led spontaneously (3, #8) to a practical insight on the part of the wife. She wanted to make this insight operative in her life and requested that her husband and children help her to change. Honoring her request, we suggested Mental Rehearsal once more for the family to become ready to help the mother. Again, the same hypnotic technique was used with the father and the mother individually (3, #16 and #17). The last hypnosis technique used in this session (3, #23) was a body check (the "C" in the OLD C model, see Introduction), which we find helpful to integrate right and left brain functions and to connect the mind with the body.

The hypnotic review suggested and directed by ENP is a form of Positive Outlook (see Chapter 2), which usually helps families find positive aspects in their problems. This is effectively done when the problem which brought them into therapy seems to have been solved. It works then as either a confirmation and reinforcement of the solutions found or as a way of realizing that the solution is not adequate. In the latter case, we would have to go back to the beginning. Again, in the sequence of Session Four, #3–7, the progression from right hemispheric to left hemispheric activity was followed—discussion comes after experience and integrates it. Pete's report of his experience (4, #8) is a good example of the spontaneous emergence of diverse personality parts. Because of this, DLA felt safe enough to invite Pete to find the answer he was looking for inside of himself (4, #10). This he did well, using again, spontaneously, a combination of some of the hypnosis techniques learned in the previous sessions. These techniques are Mental Rehearsal, Activation of Personality Parts, Inner Wisdom, and Positive Outlook.

The employment of psychodramatic approaches in this section is all hypnotic and as such can be labeled hypnodrama (Moreno, 1950) or even more specifically one of the adaptations of hypnodrama (see Greenberg, 1977). Because of the great flexibility of hypnodrama, family therapists interested in using hypnosis can benefit from learning this modality (see Araoz, 1986).

The fifth session, shorter in duration, was used to review hypnotically the gains made during family therapy. This was a form of Past Accomplishments, practiced to reinforce the progress made by the family. Therefore, in this sense, it was also Mental Rehearsal to help the couple continue their satisfactory interaction in the future. Note that *satisfactory* is defined in terms of their own evaluation, not necessarily that of the therapists.

Finally in the follow-up session we taught the family self-hypnosis in a structured way: as a technique for them to use from now on. The practice of asking them to repeat the self-hypnosis routine after they had gone through it with us made them more confident about using it and gave them the opportunity to ask questions, as was the case with the mother and her distractions during our exercise (#4), which she was able to overcome after our instructions, as shown in #5.

To summarize, then, of the five master techniques described in Chapter 2, we used mostly Mental Rehearsal, only initially in its pure form. This and the other four techniques were always applied according to the need of the moment, without strict adherence to any predetermined formula. One characteristic of the New Hypnosis is the flexibility that appears in our use of hypnotic techniques with the Cronan family. We always consider the techniques a means to an end. The end is to help the family resolve, to their satisfaction, the problem that brought them to us. The end is to help the family. Period. Therefore, unlike the concern of the experimenter using hypnosis in a laboratory, our clinical interest is to establish new, more effective, interaction among family members. And the hypnotic techniques we used are modified, twisted, and arranged in order to attain that end. Whereas the experimenter (from whom traditional hypnosis took many practices) is intent on respecting variables and finding averages, our use of hypnosis is always in the service of the client. To apply hypnosis for the sevice of the family, we often must "contaminate" variables, disregard averages, and alter the initial design.

Whereas in experimental work the subject is subordinated (subjected!) to the design, in clinical work the method is at the service of the individual, or family in our case. Because of this, as Chapter 6 explains, clinical evaluation and assessment *must* refuse the research methods of experimental (exact) science. The scientific method is simply inadequate in clinical research.

The Cronans, then, gave us the opportunity to apply hypnotic methods *for their benefit*. We subordinated (subjected!) hypnosis to their needs, to their readiness, with appropriate timing but always working within the framework of right hemispheric activation. Our bias in this direction—subjecting analysis to inner experience, and thus refusing to intellectualize until the family has had new inner experiences—comes from our own evidence gathered through the years and from extensive research, mentioned throughout this book, especially that conducted by those at the Mental Research Institute in Palo Alto, California. But even with this clear bias, we use right hemispheric methods with elasticity and flexibility. The experience of the Cronans is a good example of their usefulness.

8

The Silent Family

The unfriendly male voice over the telephone asked to see "the therapist" as soon as possible. When told that the two therapists worked together as a team, he ignored this information and repeated his question curtly, "When can we see you?" Before giving an appointment, ENP inquired who had recommended us to him. His annoyed response was, "Just give me a date and hour. We'll talk then." Unremittingly, ENP asked him about the constitution of the family, to which he answered, "Just a regular family. You'll meet us." But ENP did not give up yet, and he finally replied, "Myself, my wife, my mother, and my son."

The appointment was set for 10 days hence in spite of his insistence to be seen immediately. He was told that our instructions would be mailed right away (see Appendix).

The morning of the appointment Joe Denton (not his real name) called to confirm the appointment. The message left in our answering machine was, "We'll be there at 3:00 P.M. today. This is Mr. Denton. Let me know immediately if there is any change. If not, we'll be there." The family arrived at 2:10 P.M. for the appointment. We were busy and could not see them earlier than 2:55.

The receptionist reported that while they were waiting, Mr. Denton showed signs of annoyance, looking at magazines without reading anything, pacing the floor several times, and either refusing to answer to comments from the others or responding without looking at them, curtly and in an annoyed manner. He looked at his watch many times and asked the receptionist two times whether "the Doctor" was still "engaged." The receptionist offered him a cup of coffee, which he refused. When his wife Mary and mother were asked if they wanted tea or coffee, he answered for them saying, "Forget it. Let's not waste time."

FIRST SESSION

Joe: We came all the way from X-town. We have been waiting here for an hour. And my mother here, she's not a well woman.

Mother: It's OK. I don't mind.

Joe: I mind (loud and angrily). I don't like to wait. First we wait 10 days to see the doctor and then we wait one hour sitting here doing nothing.

DLA: (1) Mr. Denton, I'm glad to meet you. This is my associate, Ms. Negley-Parker. Please, sit down anyplace you want. Would you please introduce your family to us?

Joe: My mother, my wife, my son.

DLA: Sorry you had to wait so long. You must be a very good driver to have found this place without getting lost. Many people get lost the first time. Do you have the papers we mailed you?

Joe: What do you mean, the papers? I mailed them to you a week ago. Don't tell me you didn't get them? (to his wife) You mailed that envelope, didn't you? (She assents quickly and adds, "Bobby did," at which point the son nods his head nervously.) You sure you mailed that envelope, Bobby (in a threatening voice)?

Bobby: Yes, Dad, I did.

DLA: (2) (interrupting) Mr. Denton, the papers are not that important. You are here and you will tell us in a few minutes everything we need to know in order to assist you.

Joe: What do you mean, they are not important? If that's the case, why did I waste time filling them out?

DLA: You are more important than the papers. You are here and we really don't *need* the papers. They can be of help but they are not essential. So let's start. All right with you? (Joe nods still looking angrily at his son.)

ENP: (3) First, tell us who gave you our names.

Joe: You asked that over the phone. I told you I really don't know. Someone she (pointing at his wife) works with. (Mary keeps nodding.) You see what I mean? All this information was in the papers that you didn't get.

ENP: All right, Mr. Denton, would you tell me in your own words what brings you to seek family therapy?

Joe: (to his wife) You tell them.

Mary: You are better with words, Joe, go ahead.

Joe: You were nagging me about "the problem." So here we are, doing what *you* wanted to do, "Seeking help," as if I didn't know how to run this family. *You* tell'm.

Mary: Well, you see, Joe is a good man, a good husband, a good provider, he's good with his mother, whom I love dearly.

Joe: Oh, Mary, get on with it.

ENP: (4) (smiling) May I call you Joe? By the way, I'm Esther. Joe, we're in no rush now. I'm interested in what Mary has to say and in the way she says it. So, may I hear her out without interruptions?

Joe: (mumbling) You got yourself an ally.

ENP: (still smiling) Joe, one rule we must use here is that each person has a chance to talk. When you talk, we won't want others to interrupt you either. So, Mary, please, go on.

Mary: Well you see. Joe is too rough with everybody, but especially with Bobby here. Joe doesn't agree, but I don't like to see the way he treats Bobby. Now Bobby is failing four subjects in school. He's a smart kid, you see? A senior already but he's not doing well in school. And I talked to the school principal . . .

Joe: Behind my back. (mumbling) Then you complain that I get angry.

Mary: Well, I went to see him because they sent this note and Joe, of course, wasn't going to go to talk to anybody in that school. You know, he has never been inside that building in three and a half years that Bobby has been there?

Joe: I'm a busy man, you know that.

ENP: (5) What do you do for a living, Joe?

Joe: General contractor, commercial building, you know.

ENP: What about you, Mary?

Mary: I'm a secretary at a small private clinic in X-town.

ENP: So, go on, Mary. You saw the principal and what happened?

Mary: He told me that Bobby is extremely bright . . .

Joe: They tell all parents the same thing.

Mary: . . . and that something is bothering him . . .

Joe: They always blame the family when *they* fail.

Mary: . . . and I agree. I see how Joe treats Bobby.

Joe: Oh, come on, Mary, he's not a baby. What do you want him to be? A ballet dancer?

Mary: Joe wants Bobby to watch football and baseball with him. But Bobby likes other things, artistic, you know? Even his mother, here, complains about the way Joe treats Bobby.

Mother: Yes, Doctor, Mary is right. I wanted to come with them to see you. Joe is too rough.

Joe: Come off it, ma.

Mother: Now, Joe, quit interrupting. Your heard Mrs., I forgot your name.

ENP: Esther is fine. Please, call me Esther.

Mother: You heard Esther. So, let me talk now.

Joe: OK, ma. You know you are exaggerating. But go on, ma, go on.

Mother: As Mary said, Joe is a good person, I could not want for a better son. But when it comes to Bobby, he's just too rough. I've told him, Mary's told him, but he thinks he's right. He's the man, you know, and he knows how to treat boys. I feel very bad because he's just acting the way my late husband, God rest his soul, you know, he's as rough with Bobby as my husband was with him. He forgets. Joe hated his father. He doesn't want to remember. How he feared him. How many times he said to me he wanted to kill him.

Joe: Ma, that's enough already. Stop it, eh?

Mother: No, Joe. You have to remember, so your son does not end up hating you, too. I mean it. And that's why we came here, isn't it? To tell the truth. You know what I mean, Joe.

DLA: (6) Joe, I have a son also and looking back I realize I could've done better when he was younger. No one is a perfect father. But the problem is that our children would want us to be perfect, as we wanted our parents to be perfect. Remember? (Joe makes sounds of approval.) Try something interesting now. Be your son. Put yourself in his shoes, as it were, and talk as if you were Bobby. What do you think of your old man, Bobby (to father)?

Joe: I can't do this. This is strange. You want me to be Bobby? I mean, to talk as if . . . as if I were he? I can't do it.

DLA: (7) I'll help you. Just try. It will make a big difference, you'll see. What would Bobby say about his father. Put his thoughts into words. Come on, Joe. Try.

Joe: I guess he'll say . . . I don't know. Forget it, OK?

DLA: (8) OK. You win. But just for the time being. As a matter of fact, Joe, you really lost. You lost badly.

Joe: What do you mean? I didn't lose. I'm not a loser.

DLA: No, you're not a loser. But by not getting into that role reversal with your son—you acting and speaking as if you were Bobby—you lost the chance to experience something new. Something you have not experienced before in terms of your relationship with your son. In that sense, you lost.

Joe: It wasn't a big loss, don't worry.

DLA: All right, I grant you that. So, let's get to the point here. How is Joe too rough on Bobby? Mrs. Denton, would you like to be more concrete?

Mother: Yes, I can. Joe never spends any time with Bobby. He keeps asking him to watch the games on TV. When Bobby shows lack of interest, Joe puts him down, calls him sissy and other nasty names. He laughs at the things Bobby likes. You know, classical music, ballet, operas, and all that sort of thing.

DLA: (9) Thank you, Mrs. Denton. That's helpful. Not to put Joe on the spot but to have clear and concrete goals to work at. Tell me another thing, Mrs. Denton. Did your husband put Joe down when he was a boy?

Mother: All the time. You see, my husband was not an educated man. Very hard-working man, he was. Also in construction, but not like Joe. He was a mason, a carpenter. Worked 15 hours a day. He did, poor man. But he never learned that people were different from bricks. He treated everybody like bricks. They had to fit where he wanted them to fit. No arguments. No questions. And he was not a very smart man, either. He wanted Joe to become a bricklayer also. I fought. I fought hard for Joe to go to school, to finish high school, and then to go to college. His father made fun of books. Every time Joe was studying, he would mock him and call him names.

Joe: It didn't bother me after a while.

Mother: Nonsense, Joe. You know you hated it. It did bother you. A lot!

Mary: I didn't know that. You never told me that, Joe.

Mother: He wants to forget the whole thing. But now he's being just like his father with his own son. And as long as I live in their house, I won't let that happen. It was enough to go through this type of thing once in my life. Not again, Joe. I had enough with your father.

Joe: OK, then. What do you want me to do? What do you want from me, Bobby? You are not a child any more. You can talk for yourself.

Bobby: I have nothing to say.

Joe: I have nothing to say (mockingly). I have nothing to say either. So let's go home.

Mary: Joe, you're not being fair.

Joe: Fair, fair, fair. I'm sick and tired of this fair crap. Nothing is fair in life. Why should I be the exception. "Joe, you're not being fair." I'm sick of it.

Mother: You see what happens. They never get to talk to each other. And I hate to say it, but it's Joe's fault. He doesn't let people start to talk. This is a silent family. A lot of noise but . . . but no talk. No real communication. This was a good example. You see?

Joe: Ma, you wanted to come here but you're really making me mad. What's that about it being my fault? You know I don't like to talk about nonsense. So what's there to talk about? I asked him what he wanted from me. He said, nothing. So I said no more talk. What's so crazy about that? Then Mary comes in with that "being fair" crap. I am mad, ma! And it's good you are here. Otherwise you know I'd be screaming at the top of my head.

Mother: Talk about your father, Joe.

Joe: What's there to say? He was a bum. He was no good to you. You did the right thing leaving him. I know it was no picnic for you. I was 18, a little older than Bob here, and Jeane was only 4. I always admired you for what you did. You left with six children. So I became the man of the household. Yes, my dad was a drunk and a failure. He never kept a job for more than two or three weeks. But we didn't come here to talk about my father. I'm not like him and that's that. I just want what's best for my son. I'm interested in him, not like my father. I don't want him to waste time. I had to waste time with all the fighting and crap that went on till ma, here, left him. I can't believe her guts. I was 18, Eileen was 16, Tony was 14, Andy 12, Rosie was only 9, and Jeane 4. I was so proud of you ma. I still get all funny inside when I think of it. That's why it hurts when you tell me I'm like him. And Mary here, talking about fair. I never screamed at you, Mary; never touched you. Ask ma, here. She really had it hard.

Mother: Yes, Joe. I was beaten. I was hurt. But I'm proud I left that man. You know? When he died, a few years ago, I didn't shed a tear. In my mind he had died many years ago.

ENP: (10) What's your first name, Mrs. Denton?

Mother: Rose Mary.

ENP: Rose Mary, I feel so warm toward you. You are a heroine. And now I understand why you are so concerned about Bobby.

Mary: Let me say something here. I know how good you are, Joe. That's what I said at the very beginning. But you wanted to cut me off. You act crazy, you know? You complain that I don't appreciate you, but when I mention something good about you, you don't like it. You realize how crazy you are?

Joe: I know what you mean. You are right. I guess I have to learn how to be a good father. Much as I hated the way my dad treated me, I don't know any other way of doing it. I guess that's it, you think?

Mary: I didn't mean you are crazy, Joe, you know. But you don't make too much sense at times. I'm not here to accuse you of anything. I think you're terrific.

Joe: Cut it out, will you?

Mary: You see? There you go again. You can't take praise. You only feel comfortable when others insult you. Then you can fight back. When they show that they like you, you become nervous.

DLA: Go back to what you were saying, Mary, about not meaning that Joe is crazy.

Mary: Oh, yes. No. I don't mean crazy crazy, you know. I mean, Joe, you . . . he contradicts himself. Yes, you do. I'm glad you said what you said about your father. You see (to the therapists) that's the problem with Joe. He never talks about anything. I guess my mother-in-law is right. We *are* the silent family. But anyway. I'm glad he said what he did . . . I mean I'm happy you did, Joe. That's all there is to it. The reason we came here for this family therapy.

Joe: What do you mean?

Mary: I want you to have a good relationship with your son. That's all. And I think you need help.

Joe: What do you mean I need help?

Mary: We all need help at one time or another. I think you need help to treat your son better, different from your father.

Mother: Yes. I agree with Mary. You can be a good father, but you are too rough and have made Bobby afraid of you. Mary is right.

Joe: OK, OK. I get the idea. What do you want me to do?

ENP: (11) Try this for a start, Joe. Close your eyes and go back to those years before your mother had the courage to leave your father. Remember how you felt. Be there again. You can do it. All this is still in your mind. Like looking at an old picture album. Remember. Be there! Forget everything else. You are back, before your mother left your father. Get in touch with the way you feel . . . about the fights, about his drinking, about his violence, about the shouting and the tension and the little kids crying, and you being the oldest. Be there. Are you there?

Joe: (very faint) Yes. My stomach. It hurts. It always hurts when the kids cry. I wish I could stop him.

ENP: OK, Joe. Now say to yourself, "I'll never make my son afraid of me. I'll never scare him. I'll be a *good* father, not like my old man." Keep saying this to yourself. And feel good about it. Feel really good. Because you know you'll be a good father. You won't put your son through the same hell he put you and your brothers and sisters through. Feel really good about it. You are not your father. You *are* different. Bobby won't have to go through all this hell. Never! Never! Stay with that for a little while. Feel good about yourself. You can be a good father and you will be a good father. Let your whole being—body and soul—take this in. Feel good about it. Just like that. OK? . . . And when you're ready, you can join us again, still feeling very good about yourself. Relaxed and comfortable. Ready to return to the ordinary way of using your mind.

DLA: (12) How did it feel to go back like that, Joe?

Joe: Strange. It was a strange thing. As if I were . . . as if I was a kid again. It was terrible. Yes, I know. He was a bastard, a no-good bastard, my father was.

Bobby: I got . . . forget it.

ENP: You got what, Bobby?

Bobby: No, nothing . . .

DLA: Your dad was sort of out of it, eh?

Bobby: Yeah. I sort of got scared. He seemed to be out of it.

Joe: I wasn't out of it at all. I, I don't know. It was strange.

Bobby: I had never seen my dad like that. You know, I was afraid he would faint or something. He's right. It *was* strange.

Joe: You know, when I was doing this, I did think of Bobby. I realized that I've scared him, too, like my father scared us but, you know what? I'm going to tell you what. That's life. Those are the breaks. I scared you, Bobby, as my father scared me. Big deal! I didn't turn out that bad after all, did I? Did I?

Mother: There you go again, Joe. Nobody questions everything you've done, all your successes. You are great and we all know it. But maybe . . . that you had to work so hard and all that . . . maybe it had something to do with all the pain you went through growing up. If we know that, why not make things easier for Bobby? Just because your dad made mistakes with you, you don't have to make the same mistakes with Bobby, do you?

Mary: Your mother is right, Joe. You suffered and that's why Bobby has to suffer? You can't mean that, Joe. I don't believe it. What's wrong with others making the breaks of life easier for us? Life brings enough surprises. You can make life easier for Bobby.

Joe: Ma, you know I love you. And I know that you made things easier for me. I always listen to you, you know that . . .

DLA: Joe, please, stay with that for a moment. Close your eyes and listen again to what your mother just said. Rose Mary, please, say again what you told Joe a moment ago.

Mother: (Joe, with eyes closed, is sitting back on the chair.) Joe, you've always been a good son. You can also be a good father. Be honest with yourself. Stop kidding yourself, Joe. You are a good man. You don't have to be a bad father like your father was. Bobby can be proud of you as his father, like you never were proud of your father.

Joe: (opening his eyes) You're right, ma. Yes, I hated him. He scared us all. And I felt bad about it. Who am I kidding? I felt horrible about it! (to his son) I'll make it up to you, Bob, I will. I realized that you're OK.

Bobby: You know, dad. This is the first time you tell me I'm OK. I can't believe it.

Joe: Believe it, Bobby, believe it. You're OK. You're a good kid. I have to stop trying to make you into something you're not. What you are is OK. Who the hell am I to make fun of your music and ballet and all that stuff? You have to be your own person. I said it before. You're not a kid anymore. So, be yourself! With my blessings. No more trying . . . I mean, trying to make you into what you're not. Don't like baseball and football and sports. Like what you like. I want you to be yourself. (The son is crying out loud.) And it's OK for you to cry, too. I wish I had cried more in my life. But I couldn't. I had to be tough. For my mother and for my sisters and brothers. I was the oldest. I had to be strong. I was the man in the family after we left that bum. But you can cry, Bob, cry and be a man crying.

DLA: (13) Let's be quiet for a moment, all of us. Let's . . . all this to go inside, deep inside of us. Just for a little while. (Silence for about a minute and a half.)

Bobby: It's OK now. I believe my father. Yes, I know he's a good father. I didn't know all this about his father. God! No wonder you were such a grouch, dad.

Joe: (gets up and puts his hand on Bobby's shoulder) You're a good kid, son. I mean it, you are. And I'm proud of you. Forget everything bad I said about you. Believe this now: You are OK.

Bobby: You are OK too, dad. It's that I've never seen you like this. I never knew all this. Now everything will be different. You are a good father.

Mother: I can't believe my ears. I'm so glad you went back in your mind, Joe. Yes, you were my strength. I'll never forget it. Without you I couldn't have left your father. You're right. It wasn't easy with six kids. But you were practically a man. And you supported all of us. You worked hard. Without you, we would have starved . . . I'm so glad you talked to Bobby the way you did. (to the therapists) I'm glad you are taping this so I can hear it again.

Joe: Forget it, ma. Don't exaggerate now, OK, ma?

ENP: (14) This was a good beginning. Now, let's see what we can get out of it for the following days. I think that you, Bobby, should tell your dad many times—only when you truly feel like it—that he is a good father. You, Joe, should first of all tell yourself that Bobby is OK, that he should be his own person, that he does not have to like everything you like. You know what I mean?

Joe: Yeah. It makes sense to me.

Bobby: I'll try.

ENP: So, you two have something very important to practice in the next few days, until we meet again.

DLA: (15) What about Rose Mary and Mary? (to ENP) I'm really at a loss . . . I guess, caught up with all this emotion. But what do you think we could suggest that they do in the next week or so? They were very helpful here and without them we would never had gotten as far as we did, but I can't think of anything they could practice. What do you think?

ENP: (16) I think they can do a couple of things. First, not to bring up what happened today. When you leave this office, leave what you watched in this room. Don't mention it to Joe. Talk about it *only* if he brings it up. Does that make sense to you? (Both women agree.) The second thing that I think Mary and Rose Mary can do is help Joe to be the father he wants to be and the father he can be. How? Just by reminding him when he starts to be rough again. Can we think of some clue or password that you can agree on, so that you can use it when Joe starts being rough? What about you, Joe? Can you think of some clue or password that can serve as a reminder?

Joe: Beats me. I don't know.

ENP: What about "F.T." for family therapy? Every time Joe goes off, one of you can simply say, "F.T." That'll be enough to bring back to his mind what he experienced here in the family therapy session. What do you think?

Joe: OK with me. You mean, they should just say "F.T.," nothing more?

ENP: Yes, exactly. Just a reminder that may trigger all the good feelings you experienced here when you were practicing what you did.

DLA: (17) That's a great idea! So, the first thing for Mary and Rose Mary is not to bring any of this up unless Joe does. And the second is to use a password, "F.T.," to remind Joe of the type of father he wants to be and he knows he can be. Is that OK with you? (General assent.)

ENP: (18) As I said before, this was a very good beginning. I get the feeling that we have come to the end of this session. What time is it anyhow? Oh, it is almost time to quit. So, let's talk about the next appointment, the fee, and all that.

The rest of the session was spent in the practical matters mentioned last by ENP.

Comments

What started as an antagonistic encounter could have become even more tense if DLA had responded to Joe's complaints. His antagonism grew with the realization that we had not received the papers (Appendix) which we often send prior to the first session to gather some basic information. As it turned out, the needed information comes out when it is appropriate. Examples of it are #3 regarding the referral source, #5 regarding their occupation and work, and #9 regarding Joe's familty of origin.

In ENP's trying to diffuse the issue (#3) Joe found another reason to be annoyed and continued to show his mood with ENP and with his wife. ENP's explanation of the "rule" regarding verbal interruptions (#4) helped everyone to finally start focusing on the issue that brought the family for therapy. The trigger had been Bobby's failing four subjects and the school authorities calling this to the parents' attention. But the cause of Bobby's poor school performance, according to the wife and the grandmother, was the way Joe treated Bobby (#4, 5). Joe's mother and wife formed a complex alliance of support and criticism: they recognized his merits but they also disagreed with the way he treated his son.

The older woman zeroed in on a point that Joe would have wanted unmentioned (#5), as he said on two occasions. But thanks to her bringing it up, the wife and the son learned new things about Joe (#9, 12, and 13). Joe's initial denials of his father's character were discontinued later (compare #5, when "mother" is talking, and #9, when Joe is talking) and became the core of his hypnotic experience in #13.

The presenting problem (#4) as described by the wife was too vague to work on. It was made more concrete in #8 by the mother, who drew a parallel between her husband's treatment of Joe when he was a child and Joe's treatment of Bobby now.

Regarding the hypnotic techniques in this first session, DLA's first attempt (#6, 7) failed, while ENP's use of regression to a childhood experience (#11) became Joe's first successful hypnotic exercise. Even though this session is mostly "nonhypnotic," our intention in recording it here is to show that we introduce hypnotic elements when possible and that our "hypnotherapy" is not a rigid, constant approach which disavows regular—left hemispheric—conversation. We also want to stress that hypnosis can be used "naturalistically," as was attempted in #6 and was accomplished in #9. The invitation to silence and inner centering in #13 was a way of solidifying whatever inner experiences people had had during Joe's practice. That this experience was not limited to the family but touched the therapists also was expressed by DLA in #15. We find that sharing spontaneously our reaction with the family (#10, 15) is generally helpful. When it comes to talking about other experiences of the therapists outside the immediacy of the session, we believe that it can be beneficial (as in #6) when done very briefly and in passing.

The change in the way father and son related was evident (#9, father talking, 12, and 13). Joe's change of attitude toward the therapeutic work was also noticeable (#9, father speaking, and 10, end).

Believing as we do that most of the progress toward change occurs between the therapy sessions, we found tasks or assignments for each of the four family members (#14, 15). The assignments act as posthypnotic suggestions in the sense that they usually come from what happened during the hypnotic experience. This is evident in #14. ENP's prudent warning against bringing up Joe's experience was to protect him. It is easy, as we all know, in a moment of annoyance or anger to refer to that positive event and thus make it less positive. The final task for the women, to remind Joe when he started to slip back into his old bad habit of abusing his son, was artitrary in its form, not in its content. Everyone had agreed that the issue about Joe's treatment of Bobby was real. Now ENP selected "F.T." as a clue to remind Joe of his desire to change. The clue was arbitrary; any other password could have accomplished the same purpose. But the content came directly from the family' work at hand.

Finally, our designation of this family as "silent" came from the mother in #9, and was accepted by the wife in #10. The mention of this characteristic in the first session would give us the opportunity of focusing on communication issues in later encounters. The mother contributed greatly to helping Joe "speak" by her frankness (#5, 8) and her direct injunction to Joe to speak about his father (#8). The wife's complaint (#10) that "he never speaks about anything important" started to be addressed in this first session.

There was one crucial incident that could have changed the whole course of the session. In #8, DLA started with annoyance and was ready to confront Joe. This would have led to more anger and antagonism on the latter's part. The family might have discontinued therapy. Fortunately, DLA avoided the confrontation and explained that Joe had lost "the chance to experience something new" (#8). When Joe half agreed by saying that this had not been a big loss, DLA's response was conciliatory. The fact that the successful hypnotic experience Joe had later (#11) was guided by ENP may not have been by chance. This is a good example of the difficulty in conducting clinical research. We are not sure of what would have happened had DLA conducted Joe's hypnosis—and we have no way of being sure.

The important point here is that the therapist had the future of the session and of the whole further contact with this family on the balance in this transaction. His annoyance could have ruined any chance of continuation. His sudden awareness of his negative feelings toward Joe made him change his tone and attitude, thus salvaging the session and further contacts with this family.

SECOND SESSION

DLA: (1) How did the week go, Joe?

Joe: Not bad, considering. OK, I guess.

DLA: What about you, Bobby?

Bobby: Much better. Can't complain at all.

DLA: What about you Rose Mary and Mary? Did you have to remind Joe many times using the "F.T." password?

Mary: A few times. You know? It worked really well! And Joe was a real champ. When we talked about it last time, I thought he'd

get mad every time we would call his attention to it. But, I can't
believe it. He was real good about it.

Joe: I said I would do it, didn't I?

Mary: Yes, you did, Joe, but still, I think it must have been hard for
you to do it.

Joe: Not hard at all. I just did what I said I would.

Mary: Even so, I'm impressed and . . .

Mother: I also have to say that Joe was a prince. I used that trick with
him several times and he always stopped the way he was acting toward Bobby. I'm also impressed and feel very proud of
my son. I told you he was the best.

Joe: Ma, will you cut the crap, please? I learned something important last week here. That's all. I'm a quick learner. What you
don't know is that Bob here and me had a good conversation.
The kid came to me and he asked me, he wanted to know, you
know?, more about my father. So I told him. We talked for
about, how long was it Bob? An hour you'd say? About an
hour we kept talking. We, when we were through, you know,
Bob here made me realize, it was the first, yes the first, time
we had talked like that. Ever. It made me feel good and bad.
Better late than never, I said to myself. It felt good. That's
when he said he wanted to change his name, not really
change, but he liked to be called Bob, not Bobby. I guess Bobby
is too, you know what I mean?, too like a little kid. I told him
I'll never call him Bobby again. Did you know that ma? I guess
Mary knew it already, no?

Mary: Yes, Bobby—I mean, Bob—told me the day after your big
talk. He's happier; he is even studying more. He had a test and
he said that he did very well. Isn't it so, Bobby? Sorry, don't
get mad, I have to get used to Bob.

ENP: (2) I'm very glad to hear that things are much better. So, you
(looking at the two women) did not bring up Joe's self-hypnosis of last week.

Joe: That wasn't hypnosis. I wasn't hypnotized.

ENP: You are right. We don't believe in the hypnosis of the movies
and television. That was a beginning state of hypnosis,
though. And you did very well. You see, now, we don't believe

that hypnosis is being out of it. It's just a special way of using one's mind, a very special way of thinking, with more concentration and attention to one's inner experiences. And you were right there, not in the ordinary way of thinking.

Joe: That's for sure.

ENP: That's all I mean. So, you didn't talk about it, did you? (Both women say they didn't.) And you Bob—it *is* Bob!—tell us more about your reaction to that important conversation with your father.

Bob: I don't know. There is nothing to tell. I guess I understand dad better now. I know where he's coming from, what he had to put up with, and all that. Yeah, I feel good that we talked. That's all. What else can I say?

ENP: (3) That's great, Bob. I'm really glad things turned out as they did. Your wife said that you find it difficult to accept praise and compliments, Joe, remember? (He makes sounds of agreement.) We'll get back to that in a moment. But for now, please, Joe, be patient. I want Bob, your wife, and your mother to tell us concretely what you did well. You deal with a lot of skillful people in your work and you know that unless they know exactly what they do well, they could not be the excellent craftsmen that they are. Agree? So, who wants to start? Tell us what Joe did well.

Mother: As I said, a few times he started to be impatient with Bobby, I mean Bob—you know, I like Bob better than Bobby . . . I do—and when I reminded him, he changed right away. A couple of times I overheard Joe saying something to Bob, nothing important mind you, just general talk, but he sounded different, you know, sort of patient and I guess happy. Before, it was always sort of barking, giving orders. Now it was different. Much better.

Mary: Yes, Joe. I agree with mom. You sounded less angry in general and especially with Bob—I almost said Bobby, so don't think I'm not trying, OK? You sounded much better. I felt less tense than before every time you two talked together. What about you, Bob?

Bob: I told you before. I sort of feel that dad and I can be friends now.

Joe: That's a nice thing to say. I always felt I wanted, I would have wished, but I wanted to be friends, or to have a father I could be a friend to.

Bob: I mean it. You never told me before that you were proud of me and all that. But you did last week. And I told you that I'm proud of you, too. You had quite a bitch of a life dad! Here I am, 17 already, and I never knew it. My own father, and I never knew it . . . I'm glad I do now, though. . .

ENP: (4) So, Joe. How were you feeling when these three important people in your life were saying all these nice things about you? . . . . Take your time, Joe. Go inside of you, if you want. But get in touch with the way you were feeling when you heard all these nice things about yourself from your mother, from your wife, and from your son. Get in touch with your true feelings. Then, if you want to, you can tell us how it felt . . .

Joe: I'm not used to this. I always believed that all this nice stuff was for girls. Not for men. I don't know. I felt funny. Sort of liking to hear it, but also, at the same time, how can I put it? . . . embarrassed? I suppose so, sort of embarrassed, uncomfortable. That's it, uncomfortable, sort of tense, waiting for you to finish it, to stop it, you know? I guess that's how I felt when you were talking about me. I'm not used to it. That's all.

Mary: That's what I told you before, when was it? Last time, I think, that you can't take compliments. Now that I think of it, you're generous and give to everybody else but you don't want to get. Even for your birthday or Christmas, you do look embarrassed when you get gifts.

DLA: (5) Let me interrupt at this moment. We are here sort of at a turning point in the road. You came to see us for one specific reason. That problem seems to have been solved. Now another issue comes up: Joe's reaction to praise and to receiving gifts, and so on, from others. I suggest that we all think together, first, to decide whether this issue is affecting the family functioning one way or another and second, whether you want to get into it here, and do something about it. You get my point?

ENP: (6) To put it in my own words, you feel that this family has solved the problem they brought to us. You also see that a new issue has been brought up now, I mean, Joe's reaction to others doing good things for him. And, finally, you want the family's opinion—and consent, I guess—to get into this new issue. But before we do so, you want to know how they perceive this: Is this issue a family issue or merely Joe's issue? Is that it?

DLA: Yeah. Exactly. You summarized it perfectly. So what about you, people? What do you say?

Mother: I don't know. I feel very good about the changes I've seen this week. I know that Bob has been like a different person. But . . . I don't know. I think it's too soon.

Joe: Too soon? For what ma? What do you mean?

Mother: Too soon, too quick, you know, the change. I don't know. I think that, not that I don't trust you, Joe, you know, but, how can I put it? You may slip back. That's what I mean, you know?

Joe: Come off it, ma. I said I would do something and I did it. It's that simple. You know, ma, I'm a man of my word. Always have been. I don't understand you, ma.

Mother: You see what I mean. He thinks I don't trust him. It's not that . . .

Joe: So, OK, ma. What do you want me to do, eh?

Mother: I don't know. I'm just answering Esther here. She asked the question, didn't she?

DLA: (7) I'm on your side, Rose Mary. People don't change overnight. You want to be sure that the changes you saw and liked this last week are not just . . . superficial? Cosmetic is the word that comes to my mind. Is that it?

Mother: Yes, yes. That's it. I'm, I don't know. I don't believe the problem can be solved so easily, so quickly.

DLA: (8) (to all) Let's apply a little bit of that powerful self-hypnosis Joe practiced last week. Will you? (They all sound relieved and agree.) (to ENP) What I'm thinking of is to work on Joe's statement, his being a man of his word. Also on Bob's feeling of, you know, that he can be a friend to his father. Then, at the same time, I'd like to work on Rose Mary's concern and on

Mary, so that she can enjoy more the new changes she sees in the relationship between Joe and Bob. What do you think?

ENP: (9) That's a mouthful if you ask me. But, yes, I agree. Sounds good to me. Let's do it together, both of us leading them.

DLA: Yeah, I was going to ask you to do it together. Let's go.

ENP: All right. You heard what we want to do. Any questions?

Joe: I know you explained this hypnosis thing before but I guess I don't like the idea.

ENP: I know what you mean. I'll give you something to read about it. So, let's forget about hypnosis. Remember what you did the other day here in the office. Go over it first. In your own mind. You don't need to say anything out loud. Remember what you did. You used your memory and your imagination. You were back there, when you were a child. Yes, close your eyes to remember better. Your father. He's yelling. He's angry. You are a young child. You're afraid. He may hurt your mother. He may hurt your brothers and sisters. You want to protect them all from your father. But you're afraid. That was then, in the past. Now you're a father yourself. And you know you won't be like your father. Your son will never be afraid of you again. You feel good about it. You are the father your father never was. You *are* a good father. You feel good about it. Stay with this good feeling . . .

DLA: (10) Did it come back?

Joe: What d'you mean?

DLA: I mean, did you go back to the experience you had last time?

Joe: Sort of. It wasn't the same. But I get the idea. You want us all to get into this mental frame. You do, eh?

DLA: Yes. As Esther said, memory and imagination, a very special way of using your mind, of thinking: thinking with special attention and concentration on what's happening inside of one's mind. That's all.

Joe: Yeah. I get it. I know what you mean.

DLA: So, you'll all join Joe this time, will you? (General assent.)

ENP: (11) Make yourselves as comfortable as you can in your seats. Be ready to let your eyes close so you can pay close, close attention, very close attention to your inner mind, close to what's going on inside you. And your breathing brings you a sense of general relaxation. Your whole body, feeling less and less tense with every breath you take. More relaxed with your eyes closed. Feeling good all over . . .

DLA: (12) Feeling very good, very relaxed. Think of this experience as a gift you're giving yourself. This sense of relaxation, of inner peace, is your gift to yourself. Stay with that thought for a little while . . . and don't worry about distractions. Let them come and go. Don't fight them but don't hold on to them. Distracting thoughts, distracting sounds, distracting awareness or sensations. They can simply go away the same way they entered your mind. You are relaxing. Focusing on what's happening inside of you, in your inner mind.

ENP: (13) And while we are talking to one of you, the others can simply go on, feeling more relaxed and at peace with yourselves. Each one has something to concentrate on. Joe will be thinking of the fact that he is a man of his word. He has reasons to be proud of it, to feel good about it. You can let your mind focus on your being a man of your word in relation to the way you want to be a father to your son. While Bob, you can let your mind go to that idea of being friends with your dad. (Son starts to say something.) You don't have to say anything right now. We'll talk about it later. Just relax and focus on being friends with your dad. The more relaxed you are, the more you let your inner mind—as if you were dreaming—help your conscious mind. And Rose Mary, your inner mind can review all the good things Joe has done in his life. This review will help you feel comfortable with his present change. The way he has started to change with Bob. Review Joe's accomplishments to reassure yourself that this new change is real, is possible. This will be another one of Joe's accomplishments. Stay with that and feel good about your son. Mary, you're so nicely relaxed. Use this time to assure yourself that your son is a great kid. Imagine more of the things that started happening this week between Bob and Joe. Even Bob's change of name is a sign. A new chapter in his life. A new beginning in the way Joe and Bob relate with each other. And also, feel good about it. Let your mind go over these thoughts gently, effortlessly, nicely. Very relaxed . . .

DLA: (14) Taking your time. This is a gift you're giving yourself. To feel great about your family, to start a new chapter in your family life. With greater peace, inner peace. With more joy. Enjoying your family more than ever before. Feeling good about being part of this family . . .

ENP: (15) Take your time. breathing very nicely and slowly. Yes, take a deep breath when you feel like it. And staying in this relaxed, comfortable state while your mind is reviewing, each one, reviewing gently, comfortably, what is in your mind right now. And in a few minutes, we'll talk about all this; about anything *you* want to talk about . . .

DLA: (16) There is no rush. We have plenty of time. Just stay with your inner concentration. A very natural concentration. Without effort. Letting distractions go away while you get more and more involved. Reviewing what you are reviewing in your innermost mind. Each one very comfortable and relaxed . . . . We'll be quiet now for just a brief moment, so that you can really get into the good feelings you're having now. And while we are quiet, let those good feelings spill over into every part of your body. So that body and mind can benefit from this practice (silence for about 75 seconds).

ENP: (17) And at your own pace, without any hurry, you can get ready to return to the ordinary way of thinking. No rush at all. Very slowly. So that when you are ready to go back to the ordinary channel in your mind, you'll be back here, with all the ordinary sensations in every part of your body. Feeling relaxed, feeling good all over, mind and body. Happy with yourself. At peace with yourself. Slowly changing mental channels, so that we can all talk about your own personal experience. . .

DLA: (18) And if anyone wants to stay in it a little longer, that's fine. While the others start talking, you can still stay with your inner experience and then return to the ordinary mental activity. No rush. Feeling very good in mind and body—all over—from the top of your head to the tip of your toes . . .

Mother: Ah, that was good. I feel so relaxed. But I wasn't asleep. My mind was very active but in a good way. I was enjoying every minute of it. That was great.

Mary: Me, too. I was having a good time, sort of watching Joe and Bob be friends. It was a good feeling. It made me feel very good inside. I liked it.

Joe: (stretching with guttural sound) What time is it? God, I can't believe it! I thought I was gone for an hour!

Bob: I enjoyed this, too. You know, first I thought . . .

Joe: I didn't know I could get . . .

Mother: Joe, F.T., remember?

Joe: What do you mean, ma?

Mother: Bob started to say something and you just ignored it . . .

Joe: (annoyed) Oh, for god's sakes, ma. I can't talk now?

Bob: Dad. I was talking and you did interrupt me. I felt annoyed but not too, you know. I guess Nana is trying to remind you, as we had agreed. That's all.

Joe: OK, OK. I interrupted (still annoyed), I'm sorry. I'm not perfect, OK? I don't see the point of this, at all. What's the big deal?

Mother: It's not a big deal. It's just that . . . you know. You have to listen to Bob here.

Joe: I was listening. Oh, forget it! Let's go on.

DLA: (19) I enjoyed this last interaction. Joe is right, that this is not a big deal. But one aspect of these meetings is that they become like laboratory, where we can analyze what goes on between family members. I guess Rose Mary felt that interrupting Bob, when you interrupted Bob, Joe, that's nothing big in itself, but it may be a sign of your not respecting, is that the right concept? that you don't show enough respect for your son. That's all.

Joe: OK. I get it. Yeah. I see your point. Let's go on now, OK?

Mary: I was enjoying this, too. I like the idea of a laboratory to analyze our actions here. I find it helpful. Perhaps not too pleasant, but helpful. And interesting too. That's what we had agreed on doing with that T.F. or it is F.T. Yeah, F.T.

ENP: (20) (laughing) It gets confusing, doesn't it? When I first started working this way, I felt uncomfortable stopping people at every turn. Then I realized that, yes, this is a laboratory and so, the only way to improve, to change for the better, is to do it, to interrupt, even if it isn't pleasant.

Joe: It's OK now. (smiling) I really don't mind. I just got annoyed, that's all.

ENP: So let's go back to the practice you did before. Will you? I'm curious, going back to the very beginning, when I was helping you, Joe, to go over what you did the first time, remember? What happened then?

Joe: It was OK. I was sort of less, what is it? . . . less, vivid, I guess, than the first time. But it was good also.

ENP: (21) Thanks, I was curious because when Daniel asked you, you didn't sound too enthused.

Joe: It was a good way of getting back into the mood of this thing, this imagination, you know.

ENP: Fine, thank you. All right, let's get to what you all did together. Who wants to be first?

Mary: It's about time I start the conversation around here (with a smile). For a silent family, I don't know. I seem to be the only one quiet here. OK. I, as I said, it was good for me to think of the positive side, Joe and Bob being friends, as it were. I always tend to think the worst. It calmed me down to watch them in my imagination being friendly, Bob feeling comfortable around Joe and all that.

ENP: (22) Sorry, Bob. I forgot that you were about to talk when we got into this whole thing of our sessions being a laboratory and all that stuff. Will you tell us what happened in your mind?

Bob: (laughing) As I was saying a few hours ago, when we first started this, I was sure I couldn't get into it. But something happened when you said, Esther, something about watching myself being friends with dad. All sorts of good . . . like a movie in my head, you know? I was sort of watching him and me, kind of talking the way we did the other day. I was really into it. Like a very intense daydream. That's what it was. A great daydream . . .

ENP: (23) Who else was going to say something?

Mother: I guess we all did, except Joe, really.

Joe: You don't have to make up to me, ma. You know I love you, kid. But you're right, I wanted to say something before I was so rudely interrupted (laughing). It's hard to put into words but, thinking in that way, you know? . . . using my imagination and not my logic, I guess, I sort of—this will sound weird and crazy—but it's as if I've found another piece of myself. You know what I mean? I had forgotten how rotten my father really was. It was like a time machine. Going back there I sort of said to myself—I shouted to myself—I said, "I'd rather be dead than be like my father." Yeah, I'd be dead. Sounds weird, I know. But I'm not crazy. It's that, as if, you know . . . for so many years I'd tried to forget about him, I never realized I could be like him. And, believe me, I don't want that. It was a strange thing. But it was good. And I want you, you too, Bob, to remind me, you know that stuff about F.T. If I've been anything like my father, I can't stand it. It's as if I want to show him—it's weird!—I guess I still want to show him how bad he was. I mean, him in my head. But, the hell with him! I want it for myself. I'm going to be the father he never was, the bum! That's heavy stuff (breathing heavily).

ENP: (24) Take a minute to relax, Joe. Go back inside of yourself. Yes, close your eyes, concentrate on your breathing, and relax. Maybe you can now leave the past behind. Completely. You have nothing to do with your father any more. You are you. Different! You're a good father. Your son will never be afraid of you, like you were afraid of your father. Relax with these thoughts until you really feel good about yourself. Take a moment or two and, as if you take over completely. No more influence from your father in your life. That's past. Finished. You. The person you are. Different from anybody else, including your father. Just like that, more and more relaxed. Good. Very good indeed. Take as long as you want and while we continue talking, you may want to come back to the ordinary mental channel. Take your time and feel very good about yourself.

DLA: (25) Joe can be himself. Joe can separate himself from his father and be the father he can be (as if speaking to the others but not to anyone in particular). I really think that you have enough to work on without us. We usually see the family one more time in two months or so for what we call follow-up. (to Joe, who is stretching with guttural sounds) Welcome back Joe. How are you doing?

Joe: Great. I feel great.

DLA: We were saying that at this point we can stop these sessions. You have enough to work on. In two months we'll meet again and see how things are going. What do you think of that?

Joe: It's OK with me. You see, when Mary here talked about this family therapy thing, she explained to me that it would not be too long. But, honestly, I thought we'd be coming here for several weeks. It's OK with me. I agree that this has been like a turning point in the road. I, especially, learned something very important. I can never go back, as if I hadn't learned what I did. So, we'll come back once more, you say?

ENP: (26) It's like a final checkup. You may have some questions, you know? To really put an end to our family therapy contact.

Mother: It's funny. We've seen each other only two times but I feel as if I had known you for a long time. It was very nice to meet both of you. I felt more, it's funny to say this since I've lived with Mary and Joe since they were married, but I feel even more a part of the family. I've always been part of the family but being here, talking about all this, makes me feel even more so. I don't know. I thought I'd say that, anyway.

Mary: I'm glad you said that, mom. I always feel very close to you, as you know. We are true friends besides being related through marriage. But having you here was very important. I believe that if you had refused to come—remember, at first you didn't want to come?—if you had refused, we would have never, you know, nothing would have happened.

Mother: That's a little too much, Mary. But I know what you mean. I'm glad I came.

Mary: So we'll come back in two months. Thank you, Esther.

The rest of the session was spent saying goodbye and making arrangements for the follow-up session.

Comments

Changes had taken place. Father and son had started a new relationship. The son's change of name, from Bobby to Bob, was a symbol of his more mature view of self. The initial review (#2, 3) could sound like a "flight into health." The mother voiced this concern in #6 and it gave the therapist the opportunity to reinforce the alleged gains in #9.

After the glamorous report on the preceding week, it sounded as if everything was resolved. However, in #5 and 6 the therapists proposed the direction in which this session could go. It's interesting that the issue of Joe's difficulty receiving praise was not addressed at this point or later. Thinking about it after the session was over, we decided that this was not a real issue—at least not an important enough issue with which to spend time in family therapy. The fact that ENP repeated what DLA had just stated clarified for the family members what we intended to do next: to be sure that the changes observed after the first session were real and lasting.

DLA's mention of "powerful self-hypnosis" was probably a mistake in the sense that it did not serve any purpose. Nevertheless, it helped to explain (#9) our understanding of hypnosis—the New Hypnosis (Araoz, 1985)—and provided an opportunity to give the family "something to read." (This was a reprint of Chapter 1, "What Is Hypnosis," from Araoz and Bleck's book [1982], which many clients have found useful to understand the modern view of clinical hypnosis.) ENP then proceeded with the application of hypnosis. Her "induction," as traditionalists would call it, was brief, naturalistic, and to the point, based on the summary of goals to be attained, mentioned in #8. Although at this point she was focusing on Joe, this exercise served as a model for the others, to be convinced that the practice was perfectly "normal" and safe. It also served the purpose of getting Joe in the mood for hypnosis, based on what he had experienced the week before.

The discussion following Joe's brief hypnotic experience also acted as a preliminary to the hypnotic practice that was to follow for the whole family. Joe's lukewarm response was picked up later (#21), when the whole family was discussing their experience. Only after these preparations, disguised as they were, did ENP start the practice for the whole family. We have found it effective to guide the family through the hypnosis experience as cotherapists, spontaneously sharing the hypnotic chatter, as demonstrated in this session. In #13 ENP set the hypnotic stage for each family member. This provided the content for each person's hypnotic involvement. Usually it is not necessary to keep repeating it after it has been mentioned once. Note, however, that in this case, the family had been prepared left hemispherically (#8) for this mental focusing, which at this point (#13) can be designated as right hemispheric.

The concept of using hypnosis (the opposite of the "ordinary" mental channel) as a "gift" to oneself came up in #12 and 14, in the hopes that the Dentons would value this activity as something very special for them. In this respect, the difference between hypnosis and ordinary mental functioning came up again in the comparison with dreaming (#13), which, interestingly enough, Bob seemed to have picked up, as he commented in #22.

ENP used an indirect suggestion for Joe in addressing herself to his mother (#13) when she mentioned Joe's accomplishments and good qualities. The concept of indirection has great applicability in family therapy since the therapist can always address one family member through another, as DLA did in #25.

The reference to the "good feelings you're having now," in #16, is based on the careful observation of the general demeanor of the people involved in the hypnotic experience.

In #23 Joe verbalized what he had experienced before. Sensing his emotionality, ENP (#24) led him again into a hypnotic experience. This also reinforced his resolve to "rather be dead than be like his father."

Toward the end of the session, we realized that the family had achieved its goal: they had found an effective solution for the problem that brought them to family therapy. Consequently, we made arrangements for a follow-up session, as we usually do when we finish with a family.

Reflection on this session can teach us from a practical, clinical point of view the value of hypnosis for family work. After the glowing report of #2 and 3, the session could have become shallow and meaningless, had we looked for nonhypnotic ways of reinforcing the gains made or, on the other hand, if we had looked for new areas "to work on." Our hypnosis orientation helped to bypass meaningless talk in #4, allowing Joe to get in touch with his inner self and thus to deepen the experience he had had the previous week. What happened in #4 was a spontaneous preparation for what Joe experienced later in #9 and again in #11–18. Whenever there is an opportunity, we introduce right hemispheric elements or, better still, we *induce* right hemispheric functioning. But notice that this "induction" has nothing to do with the artificially contrived inductions that traditionalists treasure and their tyros collect like recipes. The "inductions" of the New Hypnosis always come from what is going on at the time between the family members or between them and the therapists(s). Examples of this modality include #4, where Joe was encouraged to get in touch with whatever was going on inside of him when he found it difficult to react to all the positive things his mother and his wife expressed about him. Another instance of this naturalistic manner of introducing hypnosis is #24, also with Joe.

The main "group hypnosis" exercise in #11–18 evolved spontaneously from the consciously listed goals in #8. Once the family agreed to these goals, as their lack of questions implied, we proceeded, encouraging imaginative involvement and thus "depotentiating," as Rossi (1980) expresses it, other non-right hemispheric activities, such as logical thinking and analysis.

FOLLOW-UP SESSION (TWO MONTHS LATER)

After the preliminary greetings, everybody takes a seat and the tape recorder is turned on.

Joe: I was looking forward to this visit for a long time.

ENP: (1) How come? How did things go since last time?

Joe: Oh, very good. But I wanted a booster shot from you guys.

ENP: (2) Does everybody agree that things have been going quite well in the last two months?

Mary: Yes, they have. Bob can tell you for himself, but I'm so proud of him. He's doing so well in school. Better than ever. He may even get a great scholarship for college. He can tell you himself.

Bob: Oh, mom, it's not that great. Big deal! But I am proud of it. Only 10 percent of my graduating class qualified for it. Things have been quite good since last time. Dad and I are, what can I say? I think we are becoming real buddies. I'm even learning about football. What do you think of that? I never thought I'd get to like the game, but . . . well, things have changed quite a bit.

Mother: What can I tell you? I can't believe the change that has taken place. Everybody around the house is friendlier, happier. It's just a pleasure. We kid Joe that it was all his fault. Then he had that conversion, you know like St. Paul being thrown out on the ground. And now he's a different person.

DLA: (3) I don't know about it. But I get the feeling that all this is too good to be true. This is starting to sound like *The Brady Bunch* or *Little House on the Prairie*. How do you explain this, Joe? You started with us by being a grouch, a rough diamond. Then, is it like St. Paul's conversion, which your mother mentioned? Then you become the model of fatherhood, with "the milk of human kindness by the quart in every vein," as Professor Higgins in *My Fair Lady* said of himself. I feel almost sick to my stomach with all this goodness. What's really going on? You tell me.

Joe: Nothing to tell, Doc. What are you getting all wound up about? It's true! Sorry we won't be coming back to pay your inflated fee any more. But that's the way it is. I want a booster shot and then I won't see your face no more. So, get to work if you will.

DLA: (4) You mean to tell me that you got cured in one session? You had that big experience, realizing that you were becoming as much a bastard as your father, you decided to stop it—and that's it. You became the model father. Magic, man, magic!

Joe: Call it what you want. That's the way it happened. I had not realized that I could be, that I was becoming, a bastard with Bob here. I realized that I was being like my father, putting the fear of God in my son, the way he scared me. And I stopped. What's so magical about that, eh? When I decide to do something I do it. That's all there is to it. That's my nature.

ENP: (5) I'm glad you're holding your ground, Joe. Yours is an exceptional story. But I believe you, even though Daniel doesn't.

DLA: We'll see. We'll see.

ENP: Tell us now, please, how do *you* interpret the big change everybody is so happy about?

Joe: I think I said it last time, somehow. But, you see, I had tried to forget about my father so much, that I was becoming like him. No, that's not it. Put it this way: When you taught me to get inside of myself or whatever you call that, it was as if a lid was open. The whole misery of my father came up and hit me in the face. I don't know. It somehow made me realize what . . . what I . . . what was going on here, you see?

DLA: (6) All right, Joe. I believe you. I give up. If you were able to keep this up for the last two months, I don't care whether it's real or fake, it's working. And, you know what? I don't think it's fake. I do think you had a thing like St. Paul. That experience during our first session changed your view of yourself. It took only that one important experience to change your whole perspective. And because you changed your view of yourself, you changed the way you act toward Bob. Yes, it's that simple—and that complicated.

ENP: (7) Now, tell us, Joe, what did you mean by a booster shot?

Joe: Oh, that. Yes, I think it would be good, I don't know, to learn how to do this imagination thing sort of regularly. You know what I mean? To do it when I feel like it?

The next part of the session was spent in teaching them the BRIMS method of self-hypnosis, much as it was taught to the Cronan family (see Chapter 7, Follow-Up Session). Finally, the last goodbyes were said.

Comments

DLA's reaction to the very positive report of the family's inter-action in the previous two months was sincere. He felt that they were overly complimentary of the father and of the improvement between him and the son. However, his reaction also served to stir up any insincerity that might have been hidden. The father's reac-tion, as ENP pointed out, was satisfactory. He explained how he understood the dynamics of change. And DLA rested his case. Once this was clarified, it was time to respond to the father's wish for a "booster shot."

GENERAL COMMENTS

This case shows the effectiveness of applying hypnosis for change. If one were to speculate on what would have happened had we *not* used hypnosis, one would readily surmise that the fath-er's initial resistance would have taken longer to yield. Joe was fa-miliar with argument, controversy, and debate. By switching mental channels, as we did, his defensive maneuvers became ino-perative and he had to either refuse to work with us (against what he had promised his wife he would do) or allow himself to experi-ence a new way of dealing with his inner realities. The first choice was not possible for a man who prided himself on keeping his word. The second choice led him to a regressed state of mind. This became a good instance of "regression in the service of the ego," as Kris (1952) succinctly put it. ENP used this dynamic when she in-vited Joe in the first session, #11, to recall—hypnotically—his childhood experiences with his violent and unreasonable father. Caught, as it were, outside his familiar left hemispheric ways of dealing with his world, he "went back," as DLA in the first session, #12, put it, and had a meaningful inner experience. It was fasci-nating to note that his mother likened Joe's experience to the bibl-ical record of Saul of Tarsus' conversion to Christianity. For Joe it was rather immediate—both in time and emotional distance— and a new experience of himself. Once he "found that piece" of him-self, as he described it in the second session, #23, it was impossible not to change his behavior toward his son. Because he realized internally that he was acting like his father, to whom he owed so much of his childhood misery, he had to stop. Thanks to the help he obtained from his family, the process of change did not have to be prolonged. His family became the support network that would facilitate his behavioral change, once the attitudinal change had taken place in the hypnotic experience.

This family therapy case is also useful for understanding the power plays in a family. Joe, obviously, externally had most of the power. But the two women in the family had a hidden power that led him to change. First, Joe's wife "nagged" him (#1, #3) into seeking family therapy. Then, his mother (1, #5 and #9) confronted him with his denial about his feelings toward his father and prodded him to "talk about your father, Joe." Though Bob, the son, outwardly had little power (if any at all), his not doing well in school precipitated the chain of events that led to a favorable change.

In our approach, we typically do not deal with psychodynamic issues unless our first attempt at effecting change does not work out. We use the most economical model, namely, focusing first on the presenting problem, as the strategists (see Haley, 1976; Madanes, 1981), the behaviorists (see Stuart, 1980), and the brief therapy advocates (see de Shazer, 1985), have taught. Only when this approach is not effective do we attempt to deal with psychodynamics, first within the system and only last within the individuals. At all of these levels we apply hypnotic techniques for effectiveness. In the next chapter we present a case in which the three levels of our intervention are dealt with.

We avoided intellectual arguments and logical confrontations with Joe. Reason, as a left hemispheric function helps in the process of chage only *after* the person has had a new inner experience of his own world, as Joe's progression through the sessions demonstrates. We did not "plan" hypnotic techniques for the Dentons but observed carefully any and all possibilities of hypnotherapeutic entry, as explained in the Introduction. We did not need to announce hypnosis or to artificially interrupt the flow of communication between ourselves and the clients in order to change the pace and "get into hypnosis," as it happened spontaneously in the first two sessions with the Denton family.

As we saw in the two families described thus far in this second part, the family facilitates the process of change. The other family members either share an internal event and then compare notes at the discussion step of the process, or they witness what the other family member has gone through and reinforce the experience with their input and reactions to it. With hypnosis, consequently, family therapy can move faster toward the desired goals of the family. What happens in the therapy session—as the Dentons demonstrated—produces changes after the session. Because Joe had a new experience of his father role in the first session, he found it natural to act accordingly at home.

Hypnosis enriches family therapy work and indeed facilitates it because hypnosis reaches the level at which human change actually takes place—the experiential level—naturally and easily.

9

The Vesuvius Family

The mother, Lila, 39, was an executive at a big computer company. In her attempt to avoid the divorce her first husband wanted, she had become pregnant with Wes, who now was a husky 18-year-old football, rugby and racquetball player. Shortly after the rushed divorce (her husband wanted to marry someone else) she met Ted, now 43 and her husband for the last six years. They had dated for 12 years before they finally married.

Lila contacted us when the violence that had erupted in the household between her husband and her son reached the point when they had had several fistfights. She informed us that she had "spent a lot of time" looking for the right therapists to go to. Several times she used the expression "Things have to stop immediately," even though she assured us that the tension and "eruptiveness of the situation," as she called it, had not been worse lately but had been "very bad" for the last four months. Her ambivalence was evident, as was her sense of guilt. A few times she expressed in a tearful voice, "I've tried to stop them from acting like two little boys ever since it started but I don't know what to do next." She also volunteered general information about the family. Wes, the son, had never met his biological father, who had moved to Europe shortly after divorcing Lila and had not contacted her or the son since. Consequently, according to her, Ted was Wes' father for all practical purposes since Ted had been in the picture since before the birth of the son. She added that Ted had been asking for family therapy since the first fistfight four months earlier, but that she believed then that she could persuade them "to go back to the way things were before." The incident that started all this animosity was the fact that the son had not kept his word to Ted regarding calling home from Chicago, where he was with his football team for a special sports event. Ted had overreacted and "one thing led to another," to the point that now neither was talking to the other and the potential for new, violent eruptions was constantly there. Lila's stomach had been very upset since all this started.

FIRST SESSION

DLA: (1) As you probably know, Ted and Wes, Lila had a pretty long conversation with us over the phone. So we have her side of the story, as it were. Can you tell us how you see the family problem that brings you here?

Wes: Yes, I can. I thought I knew Ted after all these years. But I guess I was wrong. He turned out to be a tight-assed, rigid, inflexible, vindictive bastard.

Ted: You heard him! This is the way he addresses me. Then he expects me to be nice.

Wes: (sarcastically) You interrupted me, didn't you?

Ted: Yes, I interrupted you because I agreed to come here, as long as something constructive would come out of it. The first thing you must do is address me with respect. This whole thing started because of your lack of respect.

Wes: Ted, I told you many times. I forgot to call. I was too busy and I, well, also, we were having too good a time to remember to call home.

Ted: You didn't keep your word, Wes. You ignored my request before you left for Chicago. You disobeyed me.

DLA: I'm listening carefully to your conversation. Go on.

Ted: You're the child and I am the adult.

Wes: That's all you care about, Ted. Respect, respect! I'm the child and you are the all-knowing adult. Come on, Ted! You can't let go of this and you'll use it against me for the rest of our natural lives. And then you complain that I call you rigid and vindictive?

ENP: (2) So, Wes, you see the problem as being Ted's inflexibility. And you, Ted, see it as being Wes' lack of respect for you. Correct?

Ted: Not so simple. You see?

Wes: There goes the long explanation (in a very low voice). He drives me crazy when he does that, you see what I mean?

Ted: Yes, I want to explain because it's necessary to have all the facts. Lila is in therapy with Dr. Doe and she consulted with her about this family situation. Dr. Doe does not see families and recommended that we see you.

Wes: What's that have to do with anything?

Ted: I'll get to the point. You are acting like a child, you know? Wes, I mean. I have been around Wes since he was born. I've been the only adult male around. Now, all of a sudden, I'm not his father —biologically true— as if I were some sort of a stranger in his life. Legally he is my son; I adopted him when Lila and I got married. You know, psychologically, he's my son also. Yes, I'm angry at him because all this fighting has made Lila worse than ever —you know, her nerves and tension and all that.

ENP: What's "all that"?

Lila: Oh, he means my . . . I guess I told you over the phone, didn't I? My eating problems. That's one of the main reasons I started with Lorraine —that's Dr. Doe— about 12 years ago. I couldn't bring myself to marry Ted, even though he was the only person, you know, in my life. That's when I developed this problem. But I deal with it with Lorraine. She's been very helpful. What Ted means is that since all this Chicago thing happened, I've been worse. But that's why I'm seeing Lorraine twice a week again.

Wes: Yeah, and Ted blames me and complains about the money he has to spend on mom because of me.

Lila: Oh, come on, Wes. You know that's not true . . .

Wes: What? That Ted said that to me many times?

Lila: Well no, I mean, he doesn't really mean it. He's just upset be-

cause you didn't call him for his birthday. And you said you
would. And now . . .

Ted: I want him to, I don't know. Wes is not a kid anymore and he
can show me that he's responsible.

Wes: How, how can I show you? What do you mean?

DLA: (4) That's a very important question, Wes. Both of you, Ted
and you, can think very seriously about this question: What
do I want from Ted? or from Wes? And don't be general. Be
very specific. Can you think of anything right now?

Ted: No, really. I'm not in the mood. Let him tell you.

DLA: No, we don't have to do it right now. But can you think of it
before we meet again? Perhaps write it on a piece of paper;
one, two, three, and so on, you know? Be as concrete as possible: I want Wes to do this and that when this and that happens. Or I want Ted to stop doing this particular thing when
this specific thing takes place. Very, very concrete, specific,
and to the point. Will you do that for next time we see each
other? (Both give assent.) Now, let's do something to clear the
air, as it were, or to clear the feelings. All right with you? (Both
ask what is meant. Brief mention of relaxation exercise is
made.)

ENP: (5) Concentrate on what you are doing right this minute. For
instance, you're breathing. Pay attention to everything that
takes place in the simple process of breathing. Close your eyes
to become more aware of your breathing. Just like that, yes.
You too, Lila. You'll enjoy it too. Notice how your body moves
while you breathe: your chest, your face, your abdomen. Enjoy all that. And let the natural rhythm of your breathing relax
all your muscles. All muscles benefiting from your breathing,
becoming more and more comfortable with every breath.
Starting to feel good all over. And in your mind too, start to
feel a sense of peace and well-being. Take a moment to really
enjoy being. Just being. And feeling good. In this state of mind
you can truly be yourself. Are you more relaxed than when
you started, a short while ago? (The three give affirmative indications.) Now, imagine all your anger toward each other
cooling down. The anger may still be there but it can stop

bothering you. Does that make sense? (No response.) Take a moment to visualize your anger. People use different expressions about anger: "boiling with anger, ready to explode, hot under the collar." You may have a different mental image. Focus on it now. Visualize your anger. Clearly appearing in your mind's eye. Feel it wherever it is in your body. You can now be in contact with your anger. Are you feeling your anger now? (Wes and Ted assent. Lila gives no response.) Is it active? Is it moving, as it were? (Both males assent.) All right, still aware of your anger in your body, allow it now to calm down, to become less than it is. The anger is still there but not as active as before. Does that happen now? (Both males indicate that it does.) The anger is calming down even though it's still part of you. Does that make sense? (Yes, from both males and from Lila.) Very good now. Relax for a brief moment and stay in this state of inner peace . . . very calm and content. Now let good mental pictures of your life together start to parade across your mental screen . . . since Wes was a baby . . . good pictures . . . as if you were looking at old family movies . . . enjoying the good images . . . so many good times together . . . as if you were paging through an old family album . . . feeling very good about the images you're reviewing. Take your time . . . feeling good all the while . . .

DLA: (6) And after that review of old pictures of your life together, you may want to start thinking of coming back to the ordinary way of using your mind. But take your time . . . no rush at all . . . very relaxed and comfortable so that when your eyes open you feel great all over . . . (First the mother opens her eyes and looks around. She's going to start talking, but we signal to her to wait a moment before starting a conversation. The silence continues for more than 30 seconds.)

Ted: (straightening himself in the chair) Whatever we just did, I feel glorious! (laughing) Wes gets mad when I use glorious. (*Wes:* Not always. I think it's cool at times. So, where are we now?) How do you feel, Wes?

Wes: I feel very good also. This reminds me of a mind-stretch we used to do with this coach, you know. He called it mind-stretch. I think it's great. (*DLA:* What did you use it for?) He was a football coach. A great guy. He believed we had to be happy inside in order to play well. And we used to review— just like we did before—all the good plays of a previous game to psych ourselves up before important games. This was just like it.

ENP: (7) What about you, Lila?

Lila: Well, yes. I was relaxed, sort of. I could not get in touch with any anger. I was just afraid of Ted and Wes getting into one of their fights again. I don't know . . .

DLA: (8) So now that you had a chance to change your feelings a bit, your mood, ask yourself that important question again: What do I want from Wes? What do I want from Ted? The best way to do it now is to go back to that relaxed feeling and . . . yes with your eyes closed and sitting comfortably, and try to be honest with yourself. Picture in your mind what you want from the other. Remember, very concretely. (Both males go back to a state of relaxation while Lila is looking on.) Allow yourself to answer that question in detail. So, afterward, we can talk about it. What do I want from him?

Wes: (after about a minute and a half of silence) I really don't hate Ted, as he has accused me that I do. I just can't stand his rigidity. I'm sorry I called you names, Ted. I'm sorry we struck each other. But what I want is for you to be less rigid. (*DLA:* Too general, Wes.) OK, I understand. Like this whole thing. Can he forget about it? Can he say to me, "OK, Wes, you goofed. I was hurt. Do better next time." Can't he do that?

Ted: Of course I can if you stop treating me like dirt. That's what I want from you. Yes, you are right! I do want respect, or whatever you want to call it. To show me that I'm, yes, I am like your father. I would want you to treat me different from anybody else in the world. Because of the special bond we have with each other. Is that too much to ask?

DLA: (9) Wait. Don't get into any discussion yet. You, Ted, be Wes now. Put yourself in his shoes and tell Ted, right here (pointing to Wes) what you want from Ted. And you, Wes, are Ted now. You'll tell Wes what you—Ted—want from Wes. All right?

Wes: Who'll start?

DLA: Go right ahead. It doesn't make any difference.

Ted: No, let me start.

Wes: Wait, Wes, you're always so impatient. I'm talking—I'm Ted now—and I want to tell you what I want from you, once and for all. No more questions after that, understand? (Ted laughs, saying, "OK, OK, go ahead, Ted.") This may sound crazy, but that's all I want. You know what? Respect. Yes, respect, kid. Something your generation does not have for anybody or anything.

Ted: (serious now) What sort of respect do you mean? Like in the army?

Wes: No, not that. Just to treat me right. To be thoughtful, not selfish. To acknowledge that you are around, that you exist—I mean, I got carried away, I'm supposed to be Ted. I want a . . . not military respect but . . . you know, the type that shows me, Ted, right?, that you care, that I'm not just a piece of garbage around you. I guess that's all he, I mean, I want from you, Wes.

ENP: (10) That was very good, Wes. Now let Ted be you and . . . so that Wes can tell Ted what Wes wants from Ted. Go ahead (to Ted), Wes. Your turn now.

Ted: (as Wes) I want you to forget about that incident in Chicago. I know it's hard for you to do so. Your background and so on. But you, Ted, can do that. You can let go of that damn thing and . . . just let go of it. You know I'm a good kid, I mean a good person. So what's the big deal? I know I should have done it, but I can't turn the clock back. It's done and it's finished. That's what I want from you, to stop harping on that one incident. And also, I want you to stop generalizing from that. Because you did that—oops, I mean, I did that. Because I forgot, I'm not irresponsible, disrespectful, unloving, and all that crap. That's what I want from you, Ted.

Wes: (as Ted) OK, Wes, I accept your apology once and for all. Let's turn the page. I promise I won't bring this up again. And if I forget and I do, please, remind me in a nice way, OK? You just tell me that I'm bringing it up again and I promise you, I'll stop. Is that fair?

Ted: (as himself) Yes, it's fair, Wes. This was constructive. Very interesting, I'll say. You're right, let's turn the page once and for all. I'm willing to leave that behind and not to bring it up again.

Wes: Great! I'm glad. And I do apologize for everything. I'll try. You know what I mean. I'll try to go back to before Chicago—B.C., eh? That's going to be our B.C.

DLA: (11) Lila, could you help us all by summarizing what just happened? You know, can you repeat what Ted and Wes have agreed on doing?

Lila: Well, it sounds very simple. Let's hope it works. They'll forget about the Chicago incident. They won't, rather, Ted won't bring it up again. And if he does, Wes will point it out to him without anger and Ted will drop the issue. In return, Wes will go back to being a loving son to Ted . . . I guess that's it, isn't it? Basically that's it.

ENP: (12) I agree. That's it for now. Is there anything else that you, Lila, would want to add to what Ted and Wes said?

Lila: No, I hope it works. That's all.

The remainder of the session was spent in practical matters, such as payment of fees, next appointment, and so forth, and in answering questions they had after the first session with us.

Comments

From the beginning, we realized that this case had special complications that would require careful observation on our part in order to plan how to proceed. Several issues came up in this first session—all of which were a challenge to our hypnotherapeutic approach: first, the triggering incident between Ted and his adopted son. We asked ourselves questions regarding Ted's expectations. We have found that the adjectives and descriptions one family member uses with another (Wes calling Ted rigid, inflexible, etc.) are useful for us to check whether there is something to it. In this case, the fact that Ted reacted positively to our interventions (#5, 9) seemed to indicate that he was not as inflexible as Wes described him.

The second issue was Lila's "eating problems" (#3), which she had *not* mentioned over the phone before the first session. We kept this in mind for future reference, especially in view of her defensiveness ("I deal with it with Lorraine [her own therapist]".) Were there special dynamics in Lila's delayed decision to get married, after 12 years of dating Ted? Did this have anything to do with her relationship with her son? Again, these were issues that we had to keep in mind for future sessions with this family.

The role reversal exercise (#9) was successful, although too easily and too quickly, if compared to the way other clients respond to our instructions. We decided that Wes' familiarity with hypnotic techniques, thanks to his former football coach, made the role reversal easy. It's interesting that Wes insisted on starting this exercise (#9) and used the opening lines to admonish Ted the way, obviously, the adult male had frequently admonished the son. Although Lila did not participate directly in the exchange between the two males, when asked to summarize what had just gone on (#11), her synthesis, spiced with skepticism and doubt, was adequate, thus indicating her thorough involvement in the action.

To focus more specifically on the hypnotic techniques used, the first intervention (#5) was a result of the two males' inability to verbalize rationally, or left hemispherically (in our pedagogical metaphor used for heuristic purposes), a response to the core question in their relationship. The hypnotic technique was employed as a preparation for the answer to what each wanted of the other. ENP (#5) proceeded from a general relaxation exercise, to an experiential acknowledgment of their anger, to a mental control —if you wish— of its intensity. In agreement with Tavris (1982) we distinguish between *the experience of anger* and *the expression of it*. We have found that in the family therapy sessions, *reporting one's anger* is effective, whereas *aggression, verbal or physical*, is not. ENP was helping the two males acknowledge and experience their anger, so they could express it (report it) later if necessary. As it turned out, neither felt the need in #6 to focus on anger. Tavris (1982) has collected

massive research evidence against the encouragement of free verbal aggression, advocated by the psychology establishment in the
late 1960s and early 1970s. Our clinical experience had led us not to
encourage verbal aggression during therapy, especially with families. Tavris' work justified our clinical conclusion with scientific evidence. Thus, in this instance, without ignoring their anger, ENP
helped Ted and Wes to process it. If "the purpose of anger is to
make a grievance known" (Tavris, 1982, p. 144), our two males were
doing just that and thus making verbal aggression unnecessary.
But because some anger may still remain, ENP used the sentence,
"The anger is calming down even though it's still part of you."
When asked whether that made sense, Lila also agreed. Once the
anger was under control, the good memories could fill their minds
(toward the end of #5).

The following discussion showed that Lila was still concentrating
on her husband and son, rather than on herself (#7). DLA ignored
Lila's comments. Thinking about this in retrospect, we concluded
that it was DLA's lack of attention to Lila. He was interested in
pursuing the two males' relationship and ignored Lila's comments. However, in #11 DLA tried to bring her into the therapeutic
action.

After ENP's hypnotic relaxation and diminution of anger, DLA
again posed the question regarding mutual expections to the two
males. This time, they were able to verbalize clearly what they
wanted from each other. It sounded good but it was still too intellectual. Therefore, DLA led them to a right hemispheric way of expressing what they wanted from each other. The whole sequence
(#9, 10) of the role reversal became the conclusion of the session.
Even though the rational understanding of an issue comes usually
after the hypnotic/experiential awareness of it, in some cases like
this, the latter can be used to confirm and solidify what the per-
son(s) had understood intellectually before.

How the mother's "eating problems" fit into the family system,
as it was operating at this time, was not investigated in this session.
As we shall see, Lila herself brought up the issue in the second
session.

SECOND SESSION

DLA: (1) Ready to start?

Lila: I've been ready for a few days. I talked to Lorraine, my therapist, you know, and she said I should bring it up with the family. (Sounds of encouragement and curiosity from the other
four people in the room.) Well, this is what happened. I was
very fat as a teenager. You wouldn't believe it, would you? Always trying new diets and failing. You know the cycle. Then I
found out through a girl friend that vomiting was a good way
to control my weight. I lost 30 pounds in about two months.
That started the whole problem. Now I could binge and not
worry. This went on and off until I got married. When things
went sour there, I started again. Then the divorce. I was really
bad then. But that's when I met Ted. He was very good to me.
I was happier than I had ever been before. No problem with
food. I was keeping the weight I wanted to have. Wes was a
love also. I never had any problems with this kid. Only satis-
factions. So everything was peachy. But then, after three years
of dating Ted, he wanted to get married and I panicked. It took
me nine years to make up my mind. That year, when he proposed, was probably the worst of my life. That's when I
started seeing Lorraine. She was a tremendous help all
around. She helped me control the eating problem again and
to marry this wonderful man. Am I going too fast?

ENP: No, Lila, go right ahead.

Lila: Well, my marriage to Ted has been wonderful. It really was
great until this thing happened a few months ago. In the six
years we are married, I never had problems with throwing up,
you know, and bingeing and all that. But when this happened,
I started all over again. As if I had no control. That's when I
went back to see Lorraine twice a week. Things *are* much better as compared to when it just happened, you know? So, this
is it. This is what Lorraine said I should bring up here.

ENP: (2) Ted and Wes, let's hear your comments, will you, please?

Wes: You never told me all that. I don't know. It's awesome, what
can I tell you? I guess . . . No, forget it.

ENP: "I guess. . ." Can you finish that sentence, Wes?

Wes: I guess, yes, that's it, that must be it. When mom is upset, this thing hits her right in the face. Yes. She has the problem under control until something bad happens. God! That's miserable. I hope you can get over it because it's miserable. You are vulnerable all the time this way. I'm sorry. I really am.

Ted: Well, I knew the details of the problem. But it just hit me between the eyes. It may sound cruel to say this, Lila, but it sounds as if you are not just vulnerable. I hate to say it, but it sounds as if, you know, when things get very tough, your problem . . . How can I put this? Your problem helps you to change things around you.

Lila: Go on, go on. I want you to tell me what you think, Ted.

Ted: Please, understand me, Lila. I'm not mad at you. I know this is beyond your control. Is this what they call subconscious? You can't help it but you do it, sort of, without realizing that you do. That's it. I don't know. It seems to be clear in my mind but I can't put it any better in words, I mean, than I did . . .

DLA: (3) Sounds pretty clear to me, Ted. You seem to say that Lila's problem serves a purpose. . .

Ted: Yeah, she sort of changes things around her through her problem. You know? We all get upset—I go crazy—and we pay attention to her. Somehow, the energy is redirected and things change.

DLA: I was saying that, according to Ted, Lila's problem seems to serve a purpose. Want to explore this together? (They assent.) Let's limit ourselves to the last incident, all right? So, relax for a moment, get yourselves ready to go inside of yourselves and to be in touch with the true feelings that come up when Lila . . . you know, when her problem acts up. Use your breathing to relax you. Find the most comfortable rhythm of breathing for you and perhaps you want to visualize a 12-inch ruler. Hold that image in your mind's eye. Make it as sharp as you can. Now, decide that 12 is the highest level, the best you can do with this type of mental activity. Still looking at the 12-inch ruler? OK, now allow any number from 1 to 12 to pop up in your mind. Pay attention to your number. If it is 6 or higher, you can proceed. If it is below 6, you need to take a little more time to get into it. What's your number, Lila?

Lila: Six, I guess.

DLA: Imagine the 6 very sharply, very clearly, and stay with it for a while. What about you Ted?

Ted: Eight, very definite.

DLA: And you, Wes?

Wes: Eight also.

DLA: All right, you are all ready. Relax as much as you can for a moment. Very comfortable. Count on distractions coming and going. They don't stick to your mind. They just pass through. Now, focus your inner attention on Lila's problem. Allow yourself to bring back to your mind the way you felt when she started having her problem a few months ago. Go back in time, slowly, with every breath you take, to that day when you realized the problem. You, Lila, be right there when it started again . . . your feelings, your fears, your memories of other times in the past. And you Ted and Wes, put yourselves at the moment when you realized what was going on. Check your feelings and your reactions . . . those things inside of you, you haven't told anyone yet. Be in touch with them. You don't have to talk about them unless you want to. But at this very moment, don't hide your feelings. Lila is having her problem and you are reacting . . . take your time and stay with your reactions, your true feelings, for a little while. Yes, it's *you* reacting to Lila's problem. Give it time. Go slowly but keep focusing on it. Say to yourself, "The truth will bring a new sense of peace. I want to be truthful with myself. I want to be honest. I want to feel right now my true feelings regarding Lila's problem." And stay with these thoughts for a moment or two until they have reached the innermost depth of your very being. You are relaxed but your inner mind is at work, reliving the feelings you experienced when Lila was having her problem. And after a little while you may be ready to return to the ordinary manner of thinking. But take all the time you need before you do return to the day-to-day mental channel . . . (The family stayed quiet for the next minute and a few seconds.) And while you start to return to ordinary consciousness, visualize that 12-inch ruler again and start counting back from 12 all the way to zero. So that when you reach zero your eyes open and you feel terrific. . .

ENP: (4) (after about one minute) How did it go? What feelings came up?

Lila: I felt terrible.

ENP: Yes, both pleasant and painful feelings. So, what happened, Lila?

Lila: Everything that Ted had said before . . . he's right. I've been manipulating my environment with my sickness and my eating and my throwing up. It's very depressing.

ENP: Did this practice help you in any way to understand why you did that?

Lila: Well, as you said, I concentrated on this whole mess since the Chicago incident. And it just hit me: I started all this sickness to stop Ted and Wes from fighting. But when I didn't get what I wanted, I just became worse.

DLA: (5) I think we'll have time to work on this—or to start to work on this—today, Lila. Let's first hear what Ted and Wes have to say. Ted?

Ted: My main feeling was anger. It was very curious. I felt the anger but not at Lila as such. It was as if I was furious at some aspect of her personality. As if I wanted her to let the mature self take over and to squash the other side. I was shouting at that ugly part. I was saying, "Yes, shame on you, you manipulative little bitch," and things like that. I felt a strange mixture of relief and guilt shouting like that in my head. That's what happened to me. . .

Wes: I guess each of us reacted differently. I felt sort of overwhelmed with sadness, you know, for mom. But I was angry also . . . I wasn't shouting, but I was saying to myself, more than to mom, that I felt cheated . . . I suppose that's it. Every time she started her sickness, I felt ashamed of her . . . as if she didn't want to be my mother or something . . . heavy stuff . . . but the overwhelming feeling was feeling sad for mom . . . I felt so sorry for her . . . I still do. . .

Lila: I'm sorry, Wes. I'm really sorry, Ted. I *am* working on this with Lorraine and now . . . this realization . . . I'm sure will help me, you know? . . . help me change.

ENP: (6) Is it fair to say that you feel so responsible for both Wes and Ted that you can't stay out of their conflicts, as it were?

Lila: Yes, I think you're right. I have to defend Ted from Wes and Wes from Ted. It's crazy. I know. . .

ENP: Do just that, Lila, will you, please? Imagine yourself defending Ted or Wes or both. You know how to do it now. Close your eyes and let the images in your mind run like an animated cartoon. Are the images starting to form? Wonderful! You're defending Ted or Wes. Who is it?

Lila: I'm right in the middle.

ENP: See yourself very clearly in the middle of Wes and Ted; what you are doing; feel it; stay with your mental images, like an animated cartoon . . . very active, very involved. And you, Ted and Wes, join Lila and remember how nicely relaxed you felt before, check what images come to *your* mind when you think of Lila defending you. Are you getting into it? Very good. Give it a little time. Allow any images and pictures to appear. Now? Good. Lila defending you . . . no rush . . . letting it happen . . . Lila, you are defending, still between the two? No? What happens now?

Lila: It's OK.

ENP: Fine, get into it even more if you wish . . . and while you are very involved in what is happening right now in your mind . . . take notice of any sensation in your body . . .

DLA: (7) Lila defends . . . she defends you . . . and the images and body sensations may continue or they may not. Later we'll talk. Now, just take your time and stay with the whole scene, Lila defending you . . . or with the many scenes that. . .

Lila: It's OK. (opening her eyes and smiling, while the others are still sitting with their eyes closed.) I don't have to defend either of them. They can handle their problems without me.

ENP: (8) What happened, Lila? You came out of your self-hypnosis so quickly. . .

Lila: I'm fine. (Both males make noises while returning to ordinary consciousness.) It was very interesting to me. It was like a vivid dream. I saw myself very big, hovering over both of you. You, Wes, were still a little child and you, Ted . . . it was funny, but you looked as you did when I first met you . . . I mean when we first met. . .

ENP: Tell us a little more, Lila.

Lila: Well, first I was all upset making sure that Ted would not harm Wes. And that's strange because Ted has always been excellent with Wes. But I guess . . . I must have had a lot of fears that he wasn't going to like being with a baby and all that.

Ted: You know, it's very interesting, but I also had this picture of you pushing me away from Wes. But, of course, we both were our current age. I kept saying to you that I love Wes and you kept crying and yelling, "No, you don't, you don't!" Finally I calmed you down, we embraced, first the two of us and then the three of us. All in all, it was a rather beautiful . . . fantasy? More like a vivid daydream . . . it was so real.

Lila: Wait a sec, Wes. Let me answer before you talk. I forgot to tell you the ending. It's funny. But it was pretty much the way you saw it, Ted. We all embraced and I really believed that you love Wes. But the funny thing is that Wes, at this point, was the young man he's now. That's all I wanted to say, Wes, go on. Sorry I interrupted.

Wes: It's all right. My mind-stretch was different. The first thing that happened was a gruesome picture of us fighting. Much worse than it really happened. But then, mom stepped in and sort of, by magic, we were shaking hands and embracing. Then I saw mom, you know? . . . getting sick, you know. Throwing up. But it was confusing, it seems that she was sick and we stopped . . . then we stopped fighting. Yeah, and then she smiled and . . . you know, a happy ending.

ENP: (9) What about it, Lila? Anything about your sickness in your mind-stretch, as Wes calls it?

Lila: You know, I sort of forgot all about it until Wes mentioned it. I feel so embarrassed . . . it's disgusting . . . but . . . anyway. Yes, I *was* throwing up at one point. But—this *is* awesome— what was coming out of my mouth became like a cloud, something puffy and very soft and nice, and it enveloped Ted and Wes. Really crazy, but I felt very good about it, somehow. I wanted to stay with this whole thing when you said something about ending it . . .

ENP: (10) There is an interesting symbol here. I don't know if I'm sure of what it means, though. Before we lose the mood, can you go back to that scene in your inner minds and check what comes out of it? The cloud, somehow connected to Lila's problem, is a good thing. You know what I mean? Go back, will you now? Just for a few minutes. See what comes up. (The three make themselves comfortable in their seats and close their eyes.) You don't need much direction from me. Build on the picture that Lila described. What came out of her mouth becomes a soft, puffy, cloud that enveloped Ted and Wes . . . your inner mind is very wise . . . there may be an important meaning in this scene. Allow it to become very vivid, to be there, to have the experience of being there . . . your inner mind will let your conscious mind know what it has to know, what it's good to know . . . . The cloud, soft, nice, made out of Lila's . . . what came out of her mouth . . . . Stay with it for a moment . . . you are there and you know . . . being there, you know . . . understand, know from within, while you are there for another moment or so. . .

Lila: It's as Ted said before. But it's more than that, not that simple. Yes, my eating problems have been manipulative. To some extent, very effective. Somehow, what came to me is that I can do the same, I mean, you know, create the family I always wanted—the love, all that. I can do it, not with my vomit—gosh, this is disgusting!—but with my words. It's not clear yet but it has something to do with communication.

Ted: I'm lost here. I didn't really get into that connection between Lila's sickness and the cloud. I suppose I found it sort of repulsive. I just stayed with the soft cloud. It wasn't just Wes and I. Lila was there, too. We were having a ball, jumping as if we were weightless, laughing, just having fun.

Wes: I don't know but I first saw the most disgusting scene. Puke all over. Like a lake of puke. Sorry, mom. Then it went away and the sun was shining. That's when this soft, cottony, cloud appeared. And the three of us were under it. I felt very good about it. Even in the beginning with all the disgusting stuff. Somehow I wasn't upset or anything. I felt good.

DLA: (11) At this point, we may do one of two things: send you home and let your inner mind bring up in your night dreams any other meanings of this cloud—and you'll be surprised when you start dreaming about it tonight or the next night— because your subconscious never sleeps. The other thing we may do is to reinforce what we have been doing so far. I'd like to work on it a little more. What do you think? (Family assents.) So, relax again. Visualize your 12-inch ruler and check now what number comes up. If your number is below 6, show us the number with your fingers . . . You're all at 6 or higher, right? (Agreement from all.) Enjoy the relaxed feeling for a moment more. Let your breathing bring you closer to the truth. And be in the cloud again . . . knowing that it came from Lila . . . and it's a nice, good, cloud now . . . . Be there and let your inner mind find the truth of this . . . what's really there. Go slowly and let it happen . . . are you with it? Good. While your body is relaxing, your inner mind is now at work . . . and it may continue to work on this cloud . . . Lila's cloud, tonight when you're asleep . . . anything you want to know about the cloud, you can know it and in a little while, when we talk about it, you may understand completely the meaning of the cloud . . . very relaxed and comfortable . . . and by now, you may get ready to change back to the ordinary mental channel . . . slowly returning to the day-to-day way of thinking. . .

ENP: (12) Take a minute to reconnect with the world around you . . . You can still keep that sense of inner peace when you talk about what happened just now . . . How did it go?

Wes: I was back in that delicious cloud . . . Nothing negative this time. Mom was there looking very happy. Ted and I were on one side and mom was on the other. We were not touching but felt very happy. I think this means that the problem—mom's problem—can be resolved and we'll all be happy.

Lila: I also have this strong conviction that my eating problem is becoming a thing of the past. . .

Ted: I hope so. I saw that cloud first, but then we were at home and everything was peaceful, quiet. Somehow or other, the cloud was gone and I was happy with it. Don't know . . . as if the cloud was not real. You know, the problem is not the reality we want, but the cloud is also some sort of fiction. I know I'm not making too much sense. But we were at home and everything was all right. I suppose this was also an optimistic insight.

Lila: Yes, I'm sure it was positive. I had a strange thing happen. I saw myself getting rid of my problem, you know—not too nice but not upsetting either—I was throwing up my very problem. And I felt healthy—yeah, that was it—very healthy and strong and happy. It was a very optimistic thing.

Wes: I see that we all had the same kind of mind-stretch. It's great, isn't it? I always loved it but I hadn't done it for a long time. Funny how your mind works. . .

ENP: (13) Well, we didn't get into the issue between Ted and Wes, but I think we touched on something important nevertheless. Tonight, when you're in bed ready to go to sleep, ask your inner mind to go back to this issue. You'll be surprised, as Wes said, how the mind works. Do the same thing every night until we meet again next week.

The session ended after an appointment was made for the following week.

Comments

Family therapy understands human problems systemically, as opposed to the intrapsychic view of other—individual—therapies. This session offers a good example of the interpsychic way of working. Lila made it clear from the very beginning that she wanted the family to concentrate on "her" problem, which was closely related to the presenting problem. Her "eating problems" became, in this way, the focus of this session.

Hypnosis proved itself useful for the exploration of her eating

disorders from the family system point of view. The hypnotic interventions started after Lila had explained how she comprehended
her problem. DLA (#3) suggested that the whole family explore
hypnotically their true feelings regarding Lila's problem. In the ensuing discussion, Lila tended to be negative about her problem
when ENP (#4) asked her to consider whether she had gained
some further understanding of her nonconscious dynamics. Her
response might be the beginning of a change ("I started all this
sickness to stop Ted and Wes from fighting").

After hearing the comments of the two males, ENP (#6) checked
the accuracy of her understanding of Lila's perception of her problem. Using her response about "defending" Ted and Wes, the next
hypnotic technique was introduced (#6). The concept of "defending" was translated into spontaneous mental pictures through the
facilitation of hypnosis. And, incidentally, Lila went back spontaneously to earlier fears she had experienced when she was debating
whether to marry Ted (#8).

On the basis of Lila's report on her previous hypnotic practice,
ENP led the family into another hypnotic experience, this time
based on the cloud Lila had talked about (#10). ENP's intervention
at this point is worth exploring in detail. First, she referred to "a
symbol," thus leaving it open to many possible interpretations.
Then, by referring to "the mood," she took advantage of the previous practices during the same session, in order to get them rapidly into a hypnotic modality. Her suggestions, open and indirect,
presupposed that there was meaning in Lila's cloud (the cloud *is* a
symbol). ENP appealed to their inner wisdom ("your inner mind is
very wise") and to their free choice ("Allow it to become very
vivid. . .") But indirectly, she was also teaching them to use their
inner mind ("Your inner mind will let your conscious mind
know. . ."). Never did she refer to vomit but to "what came out of
her [Lila's] mouth." It is interesting to note that Lila used this lead
later in #10 when she explained that she could do with words what
she had been trying to do with her sickness. ENP's words also
pointed to the integration of right with left hemispheric functions
("important meaning," "understand," "know from within"), always keeping reason as the final arbiter of a person's decisions.

At #11, DLA suggested two possibilities for the rest of the session but showed his bias in favor of continuing the hypnotic work before the session was finished. By returning to the device of the 12-inch ruler, used previously (#3), he helped them to use hypnosis very quickly. To extract the possible meaning of Lila's "cloud," both DLA, during the practice of hypnosis itself, and ENP, afterward, made suggestions to the effect that their night dreams might clarify the issue (#12, 13).

The session focused on what Lila introduced at the very beginning regarding her eating disorder. Because of our understanding of family dynamics, we not only encouraged her "to get into it," as her therapist had recommended, but we made hers a *family* problem, involving the other two family members. This we did in spite of Lila's assurances that her individual therapy was aimed mainly at resolving this problem. At this stage of our therapeutic relationship, our intention was to help the three family members recognize experientially that not merely the symptom-bearer had the eating disorder; the whole family was affected by it.

Regarding the use of hypnosis for anorexia nervosa and bulimia, the literature offers approaches based either on intrapsychic conceptualizations (e.g., Baker & Nash, 1987) or on a systemic orientation (e.g., Yapko, 1986). We definitely took the latter approach.

THIRD SESSION

DLA: (1) What's happening? How are things?

Lila: Everything has been very smooth last week. Ted and Wes got along famously. I haven't had any problems with my problem, you know? And Ted and I have been more relaxed with each other. I think everything has been great.

DLA: (2) I'm glad to hear that. So now we must try to understand what happened. How do you explain the incident of Wes' trip to Chicago and the effects it produced?

Ted: I've been thinking about it all week long. What happened? Why? Whose fault is it? Or was it? I'd really like to go over this here, especially with Wes. You know, somehow I was afraid—

maybe that's too strong a word—I was uncomfortable to bring
this up with Wes alone.

Wes: What d'you mean?

Ted: I was afraid we'd get into a fight again. And things were going
so nicely that I didn't want to take the chance of upsetting
everything with a nasty argument.

Wes: I'm listening.

Ted: Well, that's part of the problem, Wes. And I don't want to
blame you, but I want to find some way of breaking this . . . I
don't know . . . of changing this. You listen but you don't tell
me what's going on in your mind. I can't talk to you. Either
you have nothing to say or when I ask you about things, you
give me general answers as if to say that I'm bugging you.

DLA: (3) Let me interrupt here. Before going on talking, do it hypnotically. Go inside of you, Ted, and you too, Wes. Lila, you
want to join them? Give yourselves a minute to center yourselves, to relax. Yes, with your eyes gently closed and allowing
your breathing to slow down . . . now imagine that beautiful
cloud we had last time. Make it very beautiful and safe so that
both of you, Ted and Wes, are in it, having a good conversation. Both of you talking about something interesting, something that will come to mind now . . . talking in a pleasant,
interested way. Are you getting into it?

ENP: (4) And you feel very comfortable talking to each other. Yes?
. . . Fine. Listen to the other person's voice . . . you're talking
about something that both of you are interested in . . . you enjoy this conversation. This beautiful cloud makes the conversation more enjoyable. Notice where you are. At home?
Outdoors? In the car? And *be* there right now. Listening, answering, thinking . . . a real adult exchange between two people who respect each other, who like each other . . . . Are you
there? Fine! Stay with it for a while . . . still enjoying being together . . . and then, slowly, when you are ready, bring yourselves back to the ordinary mental channel . . . very relaxed
. . . ready to discuss this in a moment.

Wes: (stretching) It's funny but when Ted started talking before, I
was getting very tense. I know you were careful to choose the

right words and all that, but I still felt you were blaming me for not talking. This mind-stretch was a good idea. I relaxed right away and saw myself in the car—you were driving, Ted—and we were talking about cars. I was asking questions and you were really giving me the information I wanted. I was giving you my impressions of models and engines and you were correcting me at times—but in a friendly way—at other times even you were asking me questions . . .

ENP: And you, Ted?

Ted: At first, I got annoyed at Daniel for interrupting me. But then I said to myself, "What the heck! We're not here just to chat. Let's get into it." Then I was fine and followed your directions. I had a completely different picture, though. We were walking along the beach on a winter day. There was some snow on the sand and the cold made me feel energetic. The waves were not big so we were talking without shouting. But we were just commenting on what we were seeing, the birds, a fishing boat in the distance, the clouds, some beautiful shells we found in the sand . . . nothing heavy. But I was feeling very relaxed and happy . . . yeah, I remember now. I was also telling Wes stories of when he was a little child and he was really enjoying them. We were in no rush and feeling very relaxed. That was it.

Lila: May I tell you what came to my mind?

ENP: Yes, of course.

Lila: Nothing like that. I couldn't see them now, you know, Wes being 18, you know. I was watching an old scene. I loved it. Wes was about 13 or 14 and Ted was wrestling with him in the den. They used to do that in the . . .

Ted: (laughing) Yes, until Wes became too strong for me. Then I retired.

Lila: I felt so good watching them. They were having such a good time. I was standing by the den's door. They didn't even see me . . . . That was my scene.

DLA: (5) (to ENP) It's always fascinating to have this happening. The same open suggestions elicit such different pictures but with interesting common elements. (to the others) Let's find the common elements in the three pictures. What do you think?

Ted: You mean, you want us to identify similar . . . what? characteristics, traits, that came up in all our mental scenes?

DLA: Precisely.

Ted: Well, for one thing, we were getting along well.

Wes: That's for sure.

Ted: Other than that . . . let me think . . .

Wes: In mom's picture we weren't talking, but we felt good about each other. I remember wrestling with Ted. I used to love that.

ENP: You felt comfortable with each other, trusting each other?

Wes: Yes, that's it. There was no tension between us . . .

DLA: (6) What other common elements do we find in the three scenes? So far we have: one, getting along; two, trusting each other, and—may I add?—friendly physical contact. Mock fighting?

Ted: Yeah. I was thinking of that. Very important in view of our recent angry fights . . . I hope, never again. Well, another element is that Wes found a common topic of interest. We both love cars but we haven't talked about it in a long time.

Wes: That's right. I thought of that just now. I really admire Ted's knowledge of cars. He has a fantastic memory for that sort of thing . . . I also liked the fact that you were listening to me, Ted.

Ted: We were listening to each other, actually.

Wes: Yes, that's right. This is another thing that we both had in our mind-stretch.

DLA: You're right. Listening to each other clarifies the first common point, getting along.

Wes: And this is the way it was before Chicago. Look, Ted, with all due respect, I believe you made a big deal of this whole thing. Wait, wait, let me finish. I'm not saying that I was right. In fact, I apologize again for not having called you, but you kept at it as if I had murdered someone.

Ted: Well, I don't want to start a fight right now and I know you apologized and all that. But you should know by now that lack of responsibility, in general, drives me bananas.

Lila: OK, Ted, that's exactly the point. I told you this many times. You do overreact. You have some sensitive point about responsibility. Not just with Wes. It's the same with your work, with service people, you know?

DLA: (7) (to ENP) It's obvious that we are up against a difference in *values, don't you think? It's not a matter of right or wrong, objectively speaking, but what they see as right and wrong. What's your reaction to it?

ENP: (8) I would help Ted find out what's underneath his attitude toward responsibility.

DLA: Go ahead.

ENP: Do you know, Ted, why lack of responsibility drives you bananas, as you put it?

Ted: Oh, I think I know. I was in the seminary to become a minister and . . . well, I was very young then . . . my whole thinking was shaped by this . . . you know, we have to answer to—respond, you know—to God. We can't just go through life whistling a happy tune. That's the way I see it. I live by this and I expect others, I mean, adults, to live the same way.

Lila: But most people don't. And you can't accept that. You're still hoping that next time—always next time—people, including me, Wes, your family, the whole world, will live up to your impossible principles.

Ted: Impossible? Why impossible? Many people live up to my ideals.

Lila: Yes, saints! Tell me where you find them. Why didn't you stay in the divinity school and become a preacher? You still sound like one, you know?

Ted: Come on, Lila. You're being unfair. You know why I couldn't become a minister. I never found a satisfactory answer for the key question about the Scriptures being God's Word.

ENP: (9) Ted, can you imagine the worst case of a person not fulfilling his responsibility?

Ted: What d'you mean?

ENP: The worst possible instance of lack of responsibility. Think about it. What is it? What comes to mind?

Ted: All right, yes. The worst to me is not to keep one's word, one's promise.

ENP: So Wes committed the worst possible sin . . .

Ted: Well, there are degrees. But, yes. I still don't think I overreacted. How can I trust anybody? How can I believe him once he has gone back on his word?

DLA: Can a person make up for that?

Ted: That's part of my problem. I don't know how a person can; or how long it would take to undo that damage.

DLA: What about forgiveness on your part, Ted?

Ted: It doesn't have to do with forgiveness. The person cannot be trusted even if I forgive him. Something essential and precious has been broken. Can it be mended? How? That's my dilemma, I admit.

ENP: (10) Go inside of you, Ted, and relax for a moment. Get in touch with all your parts: your reason, yes, but also your compassion; your logic, but also your mercy; your principles, but also your tolerance . . . the whole of you. All right? Fine. Take a moment or so to get in touch with the whole, complex, and rich picture of your personality . . . what appears in your mind?

Ted: A very bright mural.

ENP: Pay attention to that bright mural. Perhaps you can come closer and discover some details. What do you notice?

Ted: Many little pieces. Mosaic. Tiny.

ENP: Look at them . . . . How do you feel looking at them? At the whole mosaic, the mural.

Ted: (laughing with eyes closed) They are paper.

ENP: What is paper?

Ted: The mosaic . . . little pieces of paper.

ENP: Stay there, Ted. Look at this mural, this mosaic, made of tiny pieces of paper. You're amused, are you?

Ted: (crying) Sad . . .

ENP: You are sad, also. Connect with your true feelings, Ted. You're looking at this mosaic of your personality . . .

Ted: My values.

ENP: . . . your values. First you saw them as very bright; then you came closer and discovered the mosaic is made of little pieces of paper. You laughed and then you cried. Take a moment to absorb this thoroughly . . . you're learning something about yourself. Look at the mosaic, at the mural, again. You're learning . . . the truth . . . the truth about yourself. Is the mural still showing your values?

Ted: Yes.

ENP: You may be able to learn a great deal about yourself . . . . Does the mural represent something? Does it show some scene or figure? . . .

Ted: I see myself.

ENP: In the mural?

Ted: Yes. Mosaic . . . very small . . . paper.

ENP: Take your time, Ted. No rush. Check what's coming up right now. You see yourself, in the mosaic?

Ted: Yes, very small.

ENP: You are very small in the mosaic?

Ted: Yes.

ENP: All right. Stay with that for a while. The mosaic represents you, very small?

Ted: Yes . . . paper . . . cheap.

ENP: What's cheap?

Ted: (laughing) Paper principles . . . cheap principles.

ENP: Let that sink into you, Ted. You're learning about yourself. I don't know what it means but your inner mind knows the truth about yourself. Let that truth enrich you. The truth about yourself can become a blessing . . .

Ted: (opening eyes and smiling) Can't . . . I don't know . . . I need time to think. (very grave voice) This is really a shock . . . a good shock. Thank you, Esther. I really have to think about it.

Lila: You worry me, Ted.

Ted: No, darling, nothing to worry. I just think . . . I've discovered something about myself. It's like a conversion, you know? A sudden realization of something very, very heavy. Don't worry. I'm all right. In fact I feel a great sense of peace, of inner calmness.

DLA: (11) All right, Ted. Take your time and if you want to tell us anything about your inner experience in the next few moments, please, interrupt at any time. (to the others) Remember, we started today working on communication. Want to review for a moment how you feel about the communication you had today during our session here? (There is general agreement.) Fine, then, close your eyes and let your mind bring up any points covered today . . . in today's session. Breathing very gently. No mental effort at all . . . just allowing your inner mind to take over and bring up any of the issues, images, feelings, or whatever, that came up during our previous interaction. Take a little time and check what happens. If nothing comes up, that's OK, too. Consciously, you're just focusing on your breathing and the wonderful way your body can feel when it is relaxed . . . your inner mind at work. Is anything coming up? (No response for 30 seconds.) Please, stay relaxed for a moment more and then we'll get back to the ordinary conversation . . .

Lila: You said something about communication just now, remember? I had a very interesting flash. I somehow or other realized that I don't need to get sick—you know, vomit, that's my nice way of saying it—to communicate. I can do it with words. I had a vision of it—don't ask me to explain—a very vivid vision in those few moments just now. It was like . . . I don't want to sound too optimistic . . . but it . . . I knew that I would never vomit again. Don't think I'm crazy. It's like, that's in the past. I'm finished with it . . . I'm still shook up about it, somehow, but I feel good. Something snapped in my mind, in a good sense. I feel I'm finished with my stupid problem.

Ted: I'm so glad to hear that. But I'm frightened, too. What if it happens again?

Lila: I don't think it will.

Ted: I hope so, darling.

Lila: What about you? Did anything come to mind?

Ted: Oh, yes, I forgot. Yes, yes. Remember that "conversion" I spoke about before? I went back to that. I kept hearing—as if I was in a church and a voice—the place was empty—and a voice kept repeating Scripture verses—I kept hearing words from Scripture about my so-called principles. Sort of making me realize that I was missing the boat. All my great principles had drowned the main principle of all, the great commandment of love and respect for others. I felt quite . . . ashamed, I suppose, and saw the whole situation with Wes in a different perspective. For the first time since it happened, I realized that *I* was wrong. Yes, Wes. *I* was wrong. *I* was wrong. I'm sorry . . . I made too much of it. And you're right, I didn't let go of it. Well, now I do. I'm going to take a long weekend off with Bill. Fishing always helps me recover, as it were.

Lila: That's a great idea. (to us) Bill is his best friend and Ted always comes back renewed after one of those weekends.

Ted: Yes, he's like my father confessor and he always lets me have it between the eyes. I need to go over all this with him.

Lila: I'm so glad you decided on this. I hope Bill can take a weekend off soon.

Ted: Oh, he will. You know that if I tell him I need to get away, he'll make the time.

ENP: (12) I guess Bill is a very good friend.

Wes: Bill is my godfather. He's like a member of the family. I call him Uncle Bill. I've gone with them fishing many times.

Lila: Yeah. That's a funny story. When Wes was born, my family was mad at me because of the divorce. I wanted Ted to be Wes' godfather but he—and he was right—he said he wanted to marry me and it would not be a good idea. So he suggested Bill. I had met Bill and he's always been a great friend. Ted and Bill are like brothers, very close. And I love him like a brother, too.

DLA: (13) Well, it sounds as if you, Ted, have found a good way of reinforcing whatever insights you've had here today. I mean, that going over this whole thing about your principles and all that with Bill will crystallize everything for you.

Ted: Yes. I'm sure it will. I had a big realization today and I'm sure it's valid. But I need to get away to allow it to sink in. And, of course, Bill is a big help.

DLA: (14) (to Wes) Did you have anything else to say?

Wes: Not really. I'm glad Ted apologized, but I want to . . . I mean, it wasn't all your fault Ted. I'm also sorry for not calling, for the fights, the insults, the anger. I feel bad about it, too. So this can be a new beginning, eh?

Ted: Yes, I like that.

Wes: The last thing I wanted to say is that at the end, there, when we did our last mind-stretch, I felt very good. I saw in my mind the family I want to have. It's real. This is it. And I felt terrific about it.

DLA: (15) I get the feeling that we have come to the end of this session. I suggest that we make an appointment for two or three weeks. What do you think? So we can be sure that all the gains you made are here to stay. All right? Two weeks then?

The next session was scheduled for three weeks later because Ted remembered that he was going to be busy in two weeks.

Comments

The first comments by Lila were very positive. Therefore, DLA suggested the family focus on understanding what this crisis had been about. This was the time to process what had happened. DLA (#3) used a hypnotic way of doing it, rather than just talking about it. The hypnotic practice (#3–4) was directed by the two therapists, using the "cloud" that the family had found useful during the previous session. Then, after #4, the family discussed what they had experienced during the hypnotic practice (the "D" in the OLD C model). DLA (#5), talking to ENP, commented on the differences reported by the three family members and tried to summarize the gains made by the family. This led to Ted's concern with "responsibility" (#7–8) and his ideals about life. In view of Ted's rigid "principles," ENP helped him hypnotically to review his position. The images that were elicited (mural, mosaic, paper) allowed Ted to obtain a new perspective on his stance. This section (#10) exemplifies hypnotic interaction while exploring attitudes and motives.

The result (just before #11) was that Ted needed time to integrate, with his rational self, what he had just experienced. Respecting Ted's need for time to integrate his inner experiences, DLA (#11) focused on the others, attempting to summarize what had happened in the session thus far, also hypnotically. Even though this was a very brief practice, the family benefited from it. When a family has been working hypnotically, it usually takes a short time to help them get in touch with nonconscious material. The report of Lila (after #11) shows the advantage of encouraging clients to review hypnotically what they have been working at in therapy. Lila had had an inner experience that gave her a sense of security and conviction regarding her eating problem. Only the future would tell whether her current feeling was valid. Ted was apprehensive about Lila's confidence. We purposely avoided detouring into his possible motivation to keep Lila "sick," for whatever secondary gains he may have obtained from her problem. Our rationale to ignore that possibility is based on the total process of the family as a system. Ted's report on his inner experience showed a new awareness of his idealistic stance and principles, which led him to a heart-felt apology to Wes. The latter's response was positive.

The whole session showed a systemic integration. The initial problem was placed in a wider perspective and resolved systemically, not on an individual basis.

The hypnotic techniques used were, as always, naturalistic, uncomplicated, and spontaneous, in accordance with two of the main characteristics of the New Hypnosis: client-centeredness and inner experiencing (Araoz, 1985). When Ted was complaining about his difficulty in talking with Wes, DLA (#3) introduced the image of the beautiful cloud that Lila had initially brought up during the preceding session and which the other two had found beneficial. Had we concentrated on the quality of communication between the two males, we probably would have spent much time in arguments of the "You do this"–"I do not" type. The hypnotic "cloud" had the effect both of relaxing them in order to do productive therapeutic work and of helping them concentrate on the real issues. The images that spontaneously came up for them (the conversation in the car for Wes, the walk on the beach for Ted, and the wrestling in the den for Lila) were conducive to attaining the two effects just mentioned. (People in general find it easier to employ their own images therapeutically.) At #5, DLA could have attempted to work on each separate image. This would have taken more time than available during one session and perhaps would have deemphasized the family unity or system and the commonality of the problem at hand. He chose to move to right hemispheric thinking by seeking the common elements in the three spontaneous mental images. In reviewing the three images, DLA allowed their meaning to become more evident (e.g., #6). Another benefit of this posthypnotic "discussion" (OLD C model) is the emergence of important underlying issues—in this case Ted's idealism and unreasonable expectations of others based on his aloof principles (#7–8).

The discussion between Ted and ENP (#9) could have degenerated into an intellectual debate, had ENP not returned Ted to inner experiencing in #10. Her suggestion regarding Ted's reason and compassion, logic and mercy, led spontaneously to his image of a bright mural. By taking his mental picture seriously and by encouraging him to stay with it experientially—not analytically—ENP helped Ted (#10) to find meaning in his image and to move toward change: the principles which he considered so sturdy and massive are, after all, as weak as paper.

By the end of this session, the family seemed to be in quite a different "mood" than when they first started family therapy. They had connected two important issues in their life as a family: Lila's eating problems and Ted's rigid values. They had become aware of the inner dynamics at work as manifested by these issues. The point to emphasize is that, by working hypnotically, this working process is direct and rapid. Is it effective? In the three weeks given them to "practice" at home what they had discovered during the family therapy sessions, the family would test the validity of this therapeutic work.

In this session, the use of hypnosis to explore and uncover nonconscious dynamics and motivations is exemplified, especially in #10. It should be noted that the transition from dealing with the presenting symptoms to inner exploration is made smoothly and easily when working hypnotically.

The fourth session would be used to reinforce the gains, if they had been maintained, as there was reason to believe that they would be. The final meeting would be a follow-up session, as reported later in this chapter.

FOURTH SESSION

ENP: (1) Even though it has been three weeks, I feel as if we had seen each other only yesterday.

Lila: Yes, now that I'm here, it seems like yesterday. But, let me tell you, a few times I wished we could have come to see you earlier.

ENP: What happened?

Lila: Well, in a sense . . . you know, looking backward, it was all very good. Once or twice I started to feel nervous, because I noticed Ted's efforts to reach Wes and he didn't . . . you know, he wouldn't talk.

DLA: You mean Wes?

Lila: Yes. But what was good about it is that Ted was very patient and was able to joke about it.

Ted: Yes. That's true. Remember that mural I saw last time? It made a big difference. When I started to feel pushy with Wes, I somehow remembered my paper principles and was able to laugh at myself. The interesting thing is that Wes always came through . . . in *his* time, not mine. And then the irritation was over and I felt like a fool for being so impatient. But I'm making progress. I definitely felt a big difference in my attitude.

Wes: (laughing) I'd say that things have been almost perfect. Yeah. I never really got angry at Ted. Never had that crazy anger that led us to fistfights. And not that I was grinding my teeth or feeling tense. Not at all. All of us, isn't it true, were more relaxed with each other? . . .

Ted: I'd say so.

Lila: I guess I was too self-conscious. I still find myself feeling responsible for the way things are going between Ted and Wes. But I've been talking about this with Lorraine. By the way, we went back to once a week instead of two times a week. To me, that's great progress. She thinks so too.

DLA: (2) It sounds as if you don't need us anymore. But even after we are finished, as it were, we request that you come to see us once more, maybe in three months. For us it's a follow-up, to be sure what we did was the right thing. For you, it can be like a booster shot. So, now that you feel you have resolved what you wanted our help with, let me suggest a way of solidifying your progress.

Ted: I don't understand.

DLA: This is our last official session. The next one, in three months, is a follow-up session. We could now keep on talking about the progress you've made, how pleased you are with it, and so on. But I prefer to strengthen that progress as much as we can.

Ted: Sorry, Daniel, I still don't understand.

DLA: All right. Yes, I'm going around in circles. Would you help me, Esther?

ENP: (3) One way of solidifying your progress is to stop talking for a moment. Close your eyes, concentrate on your breathing, and just take it easy. We have plenty of time. You're good at self-hypnosis and you may think of what we're doing as a gift to yourselves. Breathing nicely, slowly . . . and with your breathing becoming aware of your body. Relaxing more and more with every breath . . . you become aware of sensations in your body. Your hands . . . where they are resting . . . your legs . . . the weight of your body on the seat . . . perhaps your pulse . . . perhaps a difference in temperature somewhere in your body. Are you with it? Good! Stay with your body awareness for a moment longer . . . very relaxed. With a wonderful inner calmness . . . peace, comfort, plenty of time to enjoy just being . . . body and mind and soul in perfect harmony . . . at peace and relaxed . . . still with it? . . . All right. Enjoy this sense of being . . . at peace and relaxed. Feeling good all over . . . feeling healthy and happy . . . aware of the life-energy in you. You are aware of your body because you are alive . . . because life is flowing through you. Does that life-energy appear in your mind's eye? Some people see it as a beautiful light . . . others as a force inside . . . others still in different images. Check what's your image . . . life, energy, health . . . in you, flowing through every part of your body . . . giving you a sense of peace and inner balance . . . inner beauty . . . inner harmony. Are you in touch with it? . . . . If not yet, just enjoy the general relaxation and take your time . . . just like that. Very good. Plenty of time . . .

DLA: (4) And now that you are aware of your life-energy, focus gently on only one sensation in your body. Focus on one sensation alone. Just pick one sensation. All right? Fine. Concentrate on that one sensation and allow any and all associations that come up spontaneously when you focus on that one sensation . . . feelings, memories, images . . . anything that comes up . . . still OK? . . . Very good. Don't try to make sense. Just stay with your associations. We'll talk about them later. Whatever comes up is fine . . . and while you are aware of your sensation and . . . whatever comes up in connection with it may have something to do with the progress you've made in the last few weeks as a family . . . let it happen. Still with it? Very fine. Just enjoy the experience. Later, you'll find it useful to continue your progress as a family. Stay with it, very relaxed but very involved in your associations . . . your inner mind at work. After a few moments, we'll return to ordinary thinking and we'll discuss what you are experiencing right now . . . still very relaxed, with a sense of inner peace and well-being . . .

ENP: (5) And now, slowly, gently, allow yourselves to come back— very slowly—to the ordinary way of thinking, to the ordinary mental channel, as it were . . . . How are you doing? (Silence for about half a minute.) Yes, stretch and feel great all over . . . now we can talk about it. What do you think?

Wes: You know, I forgot to tell you. But since we started doing these mind-stretch things, I've done it on my own again, the way my old football coach recommended; and I've improved my concentration, especially in sports, but also reading and studying. I think this is great. And I had stopped doing it for quite a while. I'm glad you brought me back to it.

DLA: What happened just now, Wes?

Wes: Oh, yeah. I became aware of my hands. It was related to the fights with Ted. It was as if I was making sure that my hands would never become fists again, you know, I mean, with Ted. I saw myself touching Ted, you know, like buddies, on the shoulders, on the arms. It felt good.

Ted: That's nice to hear. I had a crazy . . . it was like a dream. I went back to my paper principles. It was as if they were coming out of my body through my ears (laughing). I wonder why my ears. It was like smoke coming out of a valve. Then I felt great, light, relieved . . . I guess I had concentrated on the sensations in my head. I felt a bit hot, like perspiration on my forehead. And I associated that with letting . . . I guess it is my hot air . . . coming out of me. But while this was going on, I was very aware of Wes. As if I felt good that now I could . . . relate to you, Wes, I suppose, without my rigidity. It felt real good . . . . Explain this to me, either one of you. Is this really hypnosis? What we've been doing here with you, I mean.

DLA: (6) Yes, Ted, we consider it self-hypnosis. The New Hypnosis we call it, because it is not as structured and ritualized as the traditional way of practicing hypnosis. But others who we respect a lot disagree with us. Call it what you want, we find this way of working more effective than either mere talking or the traditional hypnosis. But do you mind if I ask Lila what she experienced?

Ted: No, of course not. I'm sorry, Lila. Go ahead.

Lila: (laughing) I was wondering whether you had forgotten me.

Ted: I'm sorry, darling. I guess I took the "plenty of time" they were telling us about seriously. Please, go ahead.

Lila: OK, I'm just kidding. I feel very good, as a matter of fact. The interesting thing to me was that I started thinking of my shoulders relaxing. Ted often massages my shoulders and it feels terrific. I was sort of having that same experience in my mind. But then, I concentrated—not that I wanted to change. It just happened—I concentrated on my stomach, my whole digestive system. I felt a beautiful light inside. It was silvery and bright and beautiful, energizing. I felt my body was healing itself . . . . Again I was sure that my eating problem was in the past. It was a strange feeling. A conviction that I was cured. And that light sort of came out of me, like an aura, and expanded to include Wes and Ted. I still feel that glow. It *was* very peaceful. A wonderful feeling. Better than massage . . . almost a spiritual thing. It's hard to explain but it was wonderful . . .

ENP: (7) I noticed that you, Lila, looked very calm and beautiful. Now that you talk about it, it was like a light, a radiance, coming out of you.

DLA: I agree.

ENP: The three of you looked very relaxed and with a sense of inner peace. I would have to say that it was a positive experience, as you all agree.

Ted: Yes, it was. Definitely!

ENP: So, let's go over this once more. How does this connect with the resolution of your family difficulties? What do you think?

Lila: I'm surprised at my images. This is sort of new to me. But, remember, first it was that cloud that came from my mouth and enveloped everyone. This time it was that light inside of me that, after healing me, came out again to envelop Ted and Wes . . .

Ted: Well, I think it means . . .

DLA: (8) Wait, Ted. Sorry to interrupt. But I'm curious of what Lila makes out of it. Can you wait a moment?

Ted: Yes, of course. Sorry again. I'm really wound up today, am I not? Go ahead, Lila.

Lila: You are! But, you know? It's different. You're not intense, like angry. It's more . . . I don't know . . . and I mean it as a compliment, like a little kid . . . innocentlike. In fact, I love it.

Ted: Don't embarrass me, Lila. Go back to your inner light.

Lila: Ah, yes. My inner light. I don't know. I think it was my awareness of the healing forces in me, but not just physical healing. I guess it was love. That energy was love and it came out of me to embrace the two most important people in my life. I guess that's it. Not too complicated.

Ted: I'm glad you interrupted me, Daniel. That's what I had in mind. I hate to sound maudlin. But I feel your love as a real force. You know what. It's like something I can touch. But it's not from you, it flows between you and me. And Wes has been part of it from the very beginning. (laughing) The old Trinity of my former years.

Lila: You do sound mushy, Ted. But I know what you mean and I agree with you. I guess the light I saw inside of me has a lot to do with love. I like that.

DLA: (9) What do you make of all this, Wes?

Wes: I'm used to it. It used to embarrass me when they started carrying on like that, you know, all that love stuff. But lately . . . I suppose since I have this girl friend, I . . . it even makes me feel good to see that love . . . I don't know. It's complicated. I guess I want to say that I do believe in love. I'm not ashamed of it anymore. It's better than hate, that's for sure.

DLA: (10) So, now that everybody seems to be in agreement, let's do a final body check. Very simple. Close your eyes again; concentrate on your breathing once more and let yourselves relax as much as before or even more . . . very slowly, allowing your breathing to become very relaxed and . . . to relax your whole being. Check how it feels to say to yourself, "We are together," or, "We love each other." Repeat that to yourself and check how your body responds to it . . . you may use any other words you want . . . along the same lines of love, being a family unit . . . any words are all right. Choose a statement, a sentence, like that and repeat it to yourself, slowly, gently, again and again. Now, check your body's reaction. How does it feel? Check your level of relaxation or tension. Say your sentence again and check your reaction to it. Keep doing it for a moment or so . . . and notice the reaction in your body. Your sentence produces like an echo. Allow it to resound inside of you and check whether your body likes it or not . . . Then, after a moment, when you are ready, bring yourselves back to the ordinary mental channel. After this mind-stretch, we'll talk again . . .

Wes: I'm glad you called it mind-stretch. I thought you didn't like that name.

DLA: Oh, no. I think it's a great way to describe it. It's only that I'm not used to calling it that. But I like it. So, what happened to you, Wes?

Wes: Oh, I had a great time. I used your words, "We love each other." They became like a soft music inside of me. I felt great. No tension at all.

ENP: (11) You'll find yourselves using this type of mind-stretch when you need it. What you learned here can be carried with you home. It's a new method to cope with many things that may happen. And the more you do it, the more useful it'll become.

Lila: I felt great also. It was as if my body was agreeing with my mind. No tension at all. Was that what we were checking?

ENP: Yes. A form of integrating body and mind.

Lila: And, as you just said, I can see many good uses for this sort of thing—Wes's mind-stretch.

Ted: I want to thank you both for helping us. I'm convinced these few visits have made a lasting impact on me and on my family. The last body check—was that the name you used?—put everything together for me.

DLA: Can you explain that, Ted?

Ted: It sort of hammered in me the conviction that my change of attitude—you know, the whole thing about my rigid principles and all that—that that is the way to go. I felt stronger, physically I mean. I felt great. As if my whole being was saying, "Right on!" It was a way of capping this whole family therapy. And you're right, Esther, I can see how these exercises—the mind-stretch—will be helpful in many things.

The remaining time of the session was taken up with arrangements for the follow-up session and with further explanation of our understanding of hypnosis.

Comments

After three weeks since the last session, the family reported that the problem for which they had sought professional help had been resolved. Some unrequested indications of lasting gains were volunteered by Lila and Ted: his ability to laugh at situations with Wes which earlier would have built up irritability and her awareness of an exaggerated sense of responsibility with respect to the two males' interaction (#1). Rather than questioning their positive report, we accepted it and used the time of this fourth session to solidify the gains made.

At #2, DLA tried to explain how the session would be employed but found himself unable to do so. ENP, rather than engaging in lengthy explanations, led the family into the hypnotic technique designated "Somatic Bridge" by Araoz (1984c). Repeating the method already familiar to these clients, the hypnotic practice was conducted by both therapists (#4). It seems that the exposure to two voices has a "deepening" effect, as traditional hypnotists would say. This might be due to the inevitable repetition of concepts (as a comparison between #4 and 5 indicates), to the diversity of voices which inevitably elicits different emotional reactions in the family members, to the unconscious message of interest and concern coming from two interested professionals, or to other variables still to be researched.

The ensuing discussion showed the therapists that the mind–body integration sought after had taken place. Ted's curiosity about our method (at the end of #5) was answered briefly and directly, satisfying his interest, at least in part. At the very end of the session, he brought up the same topic and it was explained more fully. Lila, consistent in her imagery (#6), recognized the similarity between her previous "cloud" and her current "healing light." Because the hypnotic practice had been beneficial, ENP invited the family to do the final analysis of what it all meant (#7). This led the family to a maudlin type of exchange, as Ted called it. Overemotional or not, important concepts were brought forth, leading finally to the body check (OLD C model), for which another hypnotic technique was used. This time DLA chose "Subjective Biofeedback" (Araoz, 1984c), based on what had transpired during the previous discussion (#10).

It should be noted that ENP (#11), casually commenting on the practice, was making an indirect hypnotic suggestion to the family who had been in and out of hypnosis.

FOLLOW-UP SESSION

ENP: (1) It *is* nice to see you again. Bring us up to date. How are you doing?

Lila: As a matter of fact, fantastic. Lorraine is already talking about my terminating with her. I feel so proud of myself and of all of us. I'm much more relaxed at home. There is no question in my mind that Ted and Wes can take care of themselves and handle their own problems. Remember we spoke of love last time? And Ted said that he felt he could touch it, remember? Well, this is what happened to me in the last few weeks.

Ted: I was even wondering what we would be doing here this last time. To tell you the truth, I feel a bit foolish; like coming to the teacher for a report card or something like that.

DLA: So, tell us what these last three weeks were like, Ted.

Ted: Oh, there was nothing wrong with it. That's the point. What are we doing here today? You helped us, we thanked you, and we said goodbye.

DLA: (2) Sounds as if you're annoyed at being here today.

Ted: Well, no, but . . .

DLA: You asked me a question and I want to answer you. We have a few things to do. First, we have some papers that we would like you to fill out. This is a questionnaire you can complete in a few minutes. Then we want to give you an easy method of self-hypnosis you can practice every day for your benefit. Finally, we want to have some time to talk a little about the whole experience of family therapy. Does that make sense to you?

Ted: Yeah. It does. I was just trying to tell you that we have been doing quite well since last time.

DLA: I'm glad to hear that. Now, do you have any questions?

Wes: It's final exam time, eh?

Lila: I'm glad you said we'll have time to talk because I want to ask you a couple of questions.

The questionnaire from the Introduction took more than 15 minutes to complete. After that, and while ENP was teaching the family the BRIMS method of self-hypnosis (see end of Chapter 7), DLA went over the responses in the questionnaire, in order to discuss them at the end with the family. The responses were positive, emphasizing the relationship they had established among apparently diverse problems, such as Lila's bulimia, Ted's rigidity, and Wes's anger. They all felt that the mind exercises learned and practiced during our session would be useful in the future and Lila, the one who had more experience with psychotherapy, attributed the rapid progress made to the hypnotic approach. Her questions, at the end of the follow-up session, were related to this. She was afraid that the rapid progress would not be lasting. Chapter 6 refers to some of these concerns.

GENERAL COMMENTS

This was a case in which our intervention moved easily from the symptomatic level to the "insight" level thanks to the exploratory capabilities of hypnosis. More than in most cases, the presenting problem was a cry for help. The whole family was frightened and insecure, feeling guilty and angry. By introducing relaxation very early (Session 1, #5), we framed the therapeutic interaction in terms of inner experiencing, of introspection in the literal sense of the word, and not in terms of talking, reporting, and analyzing.

In so doing, we were also teaching them new skills to deal with old problems such as anger (first session). Again, Lila, familiar with more traditional psychotherapy, interjected her first doubts (Session 1, #11), which would remain till the end in the follow-up session. Because of our experiential bias, we request that people try this method, rather than arguing against long-held beliefs. This approach, both with clients and with colleagues, seems to convey a sense of respect for their beliefs and a trust in their ability to learn, to enlarge their perception, and to grow emotionally.

The fact that Wes had been exposed to mind-stretching, as he called it, and had recognized its value made our hypnotic work more direct than with families who have to be taught what self-hypnosis is. The hypnotic practices we taught this family were relaxation (first session), role reversal (first session), and mood control (Session 1, #5). In the second session we used hypnosis for exploration and uncovering of nonconscious dynamics (#3), a technique we employed again later, especially in the third session (#10). The self-monitoring device of visualizing a 12-inch ruler was also practiced in the second session (#3). Hypnosis also allowed us to bring the family together, as it were, regarding Lila's bulimia, which, so far as we could ascertain, had been considered *her* personal problem. In other words, hypnosis was used to make the family aware of the systemic aspects of their interaction, as explained in Chapter 2.

Also in the second session, Lila's interpretation of her bulimia in terms of "defending" both Ted and Wes was checked and tested through a hypnotic intervention (#6, 7). This function of validating insights through hypnosis proved useful again, also in the second session (#9), when Lila's "cloud" was employed to elicit possible associations and imagery in all the family members. Number 10 in the same session only reinforced that inner investigation. The use of hypnosis to reinforce new insights or alteration of perceptions appeared in this case and again in the third session (#11) and in the fourth session (#3, 4, 10).

Mental rehearsal was used in the third session (#3) in a direct way, although it appeared as part of other processes in several other places.

Keeping in mind that this book is about the *application* of hypnosis to family therapy, we do not study this case from any family theory point of view. Our interventions are essentially strategic, though we do not want to identify with the strategic family therapy school as such. As we have repeatedly stated, we are presenting the clinical practice of hypnosis in family therapy. From this family, we learn the advantage of insisting on the client's inner experiences, using the therapy sessions as a laboratory where they can learn a new way of looking at themselves and thus of understanding themselves. The ultimate goal is "to enrich the patient, to help expand the ego span and to give pride in the ability to cope and master," as Erika Fromm (1981, p. 427) stated so succinctly. Even though we insist on inner experiencing by means of hypnosis, our final goal is to help clients become the masters of their own destinies.

The Vesuvius family teaches us that hypnosis is an effective means to attain that goal.

Appendix

PSYCHOTHERAPY INITIAL DATA AND INFORMATION

Name _____ Date of Birth _____

Address _____

Phones (Home) _____ (Work) _____ (Other) _____

Circle One: Single   Married (# of yrs ____)   Divorced (yrs ____)

　　　　　　　Separated (yrs ____)   Widowed (yrs ____)

Children & Ages: _____

Parents & Ages: _____ Siblings & Ages: _____

Who Else Living in Household: _____

Brief Medical History: _____

_____

_____

Your M.D.'s Name: _____

When Was Your Last Medical Checkup? _____

Cultural Background & Religion: _____

Occupation _____ How Long in Present Job? _____

Education _____ Hobbies & Interests _____

_____

Any Previous Psychotherapy or Counseling? _____ How Long? _____

With Whom? _____ Why Did You Quit? _____

_____

What Did You Get Out of It? _____

Briefly Describe Your Problem _____

_____

When Did This Start? _____

What Have You Done to Cope With or Solve It? _____

_____

Any Other Information That Will Be Useful in Helping You

_____

_____

(Please, use back if necessary. Thank you!)

References

Alexander, J. & Parsons, B. V. (1982) *Functional family therapy.* Monterey: Brooks/ Cole.

Andolfi, M., Angelo, C., Menghi, P., & Nicolo-Corigliano, A. M. (1983) *Behind the family mask.* New York: Brunner/Mazel.

Andolfi, M. & Zwerling, I. (1980) *Dimensions of family therapy.* New York: Guilford.

Araoz, D. L. (1979) Hypnosis in couples group counseling. Paper presented at the American Psychological Association Annual Convention, New York City.

Araoz, D. L. (1981) Negative self-hypnosis. *Journal of Contemporary Psychotherapy,* 12(1), 45–51.

Araoz, D. L. (1982) *Hypnosis and sex therapy.* New York: Brunner/Mazel.

Araoz, D. L. (1983) Transformation techniques of the New Hypnosis. *Medical Hypnoanalysis,* 4(3), 114–124.

Araoz, D. L. (1984a) Hypnosis in family therapy. Paper presented at the American Psychological Association Annual Convention, Toronto, Canada.

Araoz, D. L. (1984b) Hypnosis in management training and development. In W. C. Wester II & A. H. Smith (Eds.), *Clinical hypnosis: A multidisciplinary approach.* Philadelphia: Lippincott.

Araoz, D. L. (1984c) *Self-transformation through the New Hypnosis.* New York: BMA Audio Cassettes Publication (Guilford Press). (4 cassettes and 2 manuals)

Araoz, D. L. (1985) *The New Hypnosis.* New York: Brunner/Mazel.

Araoz, D. L. (1986) Hypnodrama. Third International Congress on Ericksonian Approaches to Hypnosis and Psychotherapy. Phoenix, Arizona. (2 cassettes)

Araoz, D. L. & Bleck, R. T. (1982). *Hypnosex.* New York: Arbor House.

Araoz, D. L. & Negley-Parker, E. (1985) Family hypnotherapy. *American Journal of Family Therapy,* 13(3), 11–15.

Baker, E. L. & Nash, M. P. (1987) Applications of hypnosis in the treatment of anorexia nervosa. *American Journal of Clinical Hypnosis,* 29(3), 185–193.

Bandler, R. & Grinder, J. (1975a) *Patterns of the hypnotic techniques of Milton H. Erickson, M.D.* (Vol. I). Cupertino, California: Meta Publications.

261

Bandler, R. & Grinder, J. (1975b) *The structure of magic* (Vol. I). Palo Alto, California: Science and Behavior Books.

Bandler, R., Grinder, J., & Satir, V. (1976) *Changing with families* (Vol. I). Palo Alto, California: Science and Behavior Books.

Barber, J. & Adrian, C. (1982) *Psychological approaches to the management of pain*. New York: Brunner/Mazel.

Barber, T. X. (1969) *Hypnosis: A scientific approach*. New York: Van Nostrand Reinold. (rpt. 1981, Powers Publishers, South Orange, New Jersey)

Barber, T. X. (1985a) Hypnosuggestive procedures as catalysts for psychotherapies. In S. J. Lynn & J. P. Garske (Eds.), *Contemporary psychotherapies: Models and methods*. Columbus, Ohio: Merrill.

Barber, T. X. (1985b) Preface. In D. L. Araoz, *The New Hypnosis*. New York: Brunner/Mazel.

Bateson, G. (1979) *Mind and nature: A necessary unity*. New York: Dutton.

Baudouin, C. (1922) *Suggestion and autosuggestion*. New York: Dodd, Mead.

Bloch, D. & Weiss, H. (1981) Training facilities in marital and family therapy. *Family Process*. 20(2), 131–196.

Blumenthal, R. A. (1984) Rational suggestion therapy: A subconscious approach to RET. *Medical Hypnoanalysis*, 6(2), 56–60.

Boszormenyi-Nagy, I. & Spark, G. M. (1973) *Invisible loyalties*. Hagerstown, Maryland: Harper & Row.

Bowen, M. (1978) *Family therapy in clinical practice*. New York: Jason Aronson.

Bowers, K. S. (1976) *Hypnosis for the seriously curious*. Monterey: Brooks/Cole.

Braun, B. G. (1984) Hypnosis in family therapy. In W. C. Wester II & A. H. Smith (Eds.), *Clinical hypnosis: A multidisciplinary approach*. Philadelphia: Lippincott.

Calof, D. L. (1985) Hypnosis in marital therapy: Toward a transgenerational approach. In J. K. Zeig (Ed.), *Ericksonian psychotherapy: Vol. II. Clinical applications*. New York: Brunner/Mazel.

Cameron-Bandler, L. (1985) *Solutions: Practical and effective antidotes for sexual and relationship problems*. San Rafael, California: Future Pace.

Coe, W. C. & Sharcoff, J. (1983) An empirical evaluation of the neurolinguistic programming model. Paper presented at the American Psychological Association Annual Convention, Anaheim, California.

Coleman, S. B. (Ed.) (1985) *Failures in family therapy*. New York: Guilford.

Cooper, A., Rampage, C. & Soucy, G. (1981) Family therapy training in clinical psychology programs. *Family Process*, 20(2), 155–166.

Coué, E. (1922) *Self-mastery through conscious autosuggestion*. London: Allen & Unwin.

Dammann, C. A. (1982) Family therapy: Erickson's contribution. In J. K. Zeig (Ed.), *Ericksonian approaches to hypnosis and psychotherapy*. New York: Brunner/Mazel.

de Shazer, S. (1982) *Patterns of brief family therapy: An ecosystemic approach*. New York: Guilford.

de Shazer, S. (1985) *Keys to solution in brief therapy*. New York: Norton.

Diamond, M. J. (1986) Hypnotically augmented psychotherapy: The unique contributions of the hypnotically trained clinician. *American Journal of Clinical Hypnosis*, 29(4), 238-247.

Dinkmeyer, D. & McKay, G. D. (1976) *Systematic training for effective parenting.* Circle Pines, New Mexico: American Guidance Service.

Duhl, B. S. (1982) *From the inside out: A systems thinking approach.* New York: Brunner/Mazel.

Eden, J. (1974) *Animal magnetism and the life energy.* Hicksville, New York: Exposition Press.

Ellis, A. (1985) *Overcoming resistance.* New York: Springer.

Erickson, M. H., Rossi, E. L., & Rossi, S. I. (1976) *Hypnotic realities.* New York: Irvington.

Everett, C. (1979) The master's degree in marriage and family therapy. *Journal of Marital and Family Therapy.* 5(3), 7–19.

Fisch, R, Weakland, J. H., & Segal, L. (1982) *The tactics of change.* San Francisco: Jossey-Bass.

Forsyth, D. R. & Strong, S. R. (1986) The scientific study of counseling and psychotherapy: A unificationist view. *American Psychologist,* 41(2), 113–119.

Framo, J. L. (1982) *Explorations in marital and family therapy.* New York: Springer.

Freud, S. (1915) The unconscious. *Standard edition* (Vol. 14, pp. 159–215). London: Hogarth Press, 1951.

Fromm, E. (1977) An ego-psychological theory of altered states of consciousness. *International Journal of Clinical and Experimental Hypnosis,* 25, 372–387.

Fromm, E. (1981) Values in hypnotherapy. *Psychotherapy: Theory, Research and Practice,* 17, 425–430.

Galin, D. (1974) Implications for psychiatry of left and right specialization: A neurophysiological context for unconscious processes. *Archives of General Psychiatry,* 31, 572–583.

Gazzaniga, M. S. (1970) *The bisected brain.* New York: Appleton-Century-Crofts.

Gelman, D., Finke Greenberg, N., Coppola, V., Burgower, B., Doherty, S., Monroe, A., & Williams, E. (1985, July 15) The single parent. *Newsweek* 42–50.

Golden, W. L. & Friedberg, F. (1986) Cognitive-behaviorial hypnotherapy. In W. Dryden & W. L. Golden (Eds.), *Cognitive-behavioral approaches to psychotherapy.* London: Harper & Row.

Goleman, D. (1985) *Vital lies, simple truths.* New York: Simon & Schuster.

Goodwin, J. S. & Goodwin, J. M. (1984) The tomato effect: Rejection of highly efficacious therapies. *Journal of the American Medical Association,* 251(18) 2387–2390.

Greenberg, I. A. (Ed.) (1977) *Group hypnotherapy and hypnodrama.* Chicago: Nelson-Hall.

Grinder, J. & Bandler, R. (1976) *The structure of magic* (Vol. II). Palo Alto, California: Science and Behavior Books.

Grinder, J., DeLozier, J., & Bandler, R. (1977) *Patterns of the hypnotic technique of Milton H. Erickson, M.D.* (Vol. II). Cupertino, California: Meta Publications.

Gurman, A. S. (Ed.) (1985) *Casebook of marital therapy.* New York: Guilford.

Haley, J. (1973) *Uncommon therapy: The psychiatric techniques of M. H. Erickson.* New York: Norton.

Haley, J. (1976) *Problem solving therapy.* San Francisco: Jossey-Bass.

Haley, J. (1980) *Leaving home.* New York: McGraw-Hill.

Haley, J. (1984) *Ordeal therapy.* San Francisco: Jossey-Bass.

Hansen, J. C. & L'Abate, L. (1982) *Approaches to family therapy.* New York: Macmillan.

Hartland, J. (1971) *Medical and dental hypnosis and its clinical applications* (2nd ed.). Baltimore: Williams & Wilkins.

Hartmann, H. (1939) *Ego psychology and the problem of adaptation.* New York: International Universities Press.

Hilgard, E. R. (1977) *Divided consciousness: Multiple controls in human thought and action.* New York: Wiley.

Hollis, J. & Wantz, R. (1982) *Counselor preparation 1980: Programs, personnel, trends* (9th ed.). Muncie, Indiana: Accelerated Development.

Horney, K. (1945) *Our inner conflicts.* New York: Norton.

Howard, K. I., Kopta, S. M., Krause, M. S., & Orlinsky, D. E. (1986) The dose–effect relationship in psychotherapy. *American Psychologist,* 41(2), 159–164.

Janet, P. (1889) *L'Automatisme psychologique.* Paris: Alcan.

Kempler, W. (1968) Experiential psychotherapy within families. *Family Process,* 7(1), 88–99.

Kempler, W. (1981) *Experiential psychotherapy within families.* New York: Brunner/Mazel.

Kohn, A. (1986) How to succeed without even vying. *Psychology Today,* 20(9), 22–28.

Kopel, S. & Arkowitz, H. (1975) The role of attribution and self-perception in behavior change: Implications for behavior therapy. *Genetic Psychology Monographs,* 92, 175–212.

Kris, E. (1952) *Psychoanalytic explorations in art.* New York: International Universities Press.

Kuhn, T. (1962) *The structure of scientific revolutions.* Chicago: University of Chicago Press.

L'Abate, L. (1983) *Family psychology: Theory, therapy, training.* Washington, D.C.: University Press of America.

L'Abate, L. (1984) Beyond paradox: Issues of control. *American Journal of Family Therapy,* 12(4), 12–20.

L'Abate, L. (Ed.) (1985a) *Handbook of family psychology and therapy.* Homewood, Illinois: Dow Jones–Irwin.

L'Abate, L. (1985b) A training program for family psychology: Evaluation, prevention and therapy. *American Journal of Family Therapy,* 13(4), 7–16.

L'Abate, L. Hansen, J. C. & Ganahl, G. (1985) *Methods of family therapy.* Englewood, New Jersey: Prentice-Hall.

L'Abate, L. & Weeks, G. R. (1978) A bibliography of paradoxical methods in psychotherapy of family systems. *Family Process,* 17, 95–98.

Laing, R. D. (1961) *The self and others: Further studies in sanity and madness.* London: Tavistock Press.

Laing, R. D. (1969) *The politics of the family and other essays.* New York: Pantheon Books.

Laing, R. D. & Esterson, A. (1964) *Sanity, madness and the family.* Harmondsworth, Middlesex, England: Penguin.

Lange, A. (1985) Motivating clients in directive family therapy. In J. K. Zeig (Ed.), *Ericksonian psychotherapy: Vol. II. Clinical applications.* New York: Brunner/Mazel.

Lankton, S. & Lankton, C. (1986) *Enchantment and intervention in family therapy.* New York: Brunner/Mazel.

Lazarus, A. A. (1976) *Multimodal behavior therapy.* New York: Springer.

Levant, R. F. (1984) *Family therapy: A comprehensive overview.* Englewood, New Jersey: Prentice-Hall.

Lieberman, L. R. (1977) Hypnosis research and the limitations of the experimental method. *Annals of the New York Academy of Science,* 296, 60–68.

Loriedo, C. (1985) Tailoring suggestions in family therapy. In J. K. Zeig (Ed.), *Ericksonian psychotherapy: Vol. II. Clinical applications.* New York: Brunner/Mazel.

Mace, D. R. (1983) *Toward family wellness: The need for preventive services.* Beverly Hills: Sage.

Mace, D. R. & Mace, V. C. (1975) Marriage enrichment—Wave of the future? *The Family Coordinator,* 24, 131–135.

Madanes, C. (1981) *Strategic family therapy.* San Francisco: Jossey-Bass.

Madanes, C. (1984) *Behind the one-way mirror.* San Francisco: Jossey-Bass.

Maturana, H. & Varela, F. (1980) *Autopoiesis and cognition: The realization of the living.* Boston: Reidel.

Miller, S., Wackman, D. B., & Nunnally, E. W. (1983) *Talking together.* Minneapolis: Interpersonal Communication Programs.

Minuchin, S. (1974) *Families and family therapy.* Cambridge, Massachusetts: Harvard University Press.

Moreno, J. L. (1950) Hypnodrama and psychodrama. *Group Psychotherapy,* 3(1), 1–10.

Negley-Parker, E. & Araoz, D. L. (1985a) Hypnosis strategies to reduce stress in student nurses. *Cognitive Behaviorist,* 7(2), 15–17.

Negley-Parker, E. & Araoz, D. L. (1985b) New Hypnosis in family therapy. *Medical Hypnoanalysis,* 6(4), 110–117.

Negley-Parker, E. & Araoz, D. L. (1986) Hypnotherapy with families of chronically ill children. *International Journal of Psychosomatics,* 33(2), 9–11.

Olson, D. H. & Dowd, E. T. (1984) Generalization and maintenance of therapeutic change. *Cognitivie Behaviorist,* 6(1), 13–19.

Papp, P. (1977) *Family therapy: Full length case studies.* New York: Gardner Press.

Papp, P. (1984) *The process of change.* New York: Guilford.

Pratt, G. J., Wood, D. P., & Alman, B. M. (1984) *A clinical hypnosis primer.* La Jolla, California: Psychology and Consulting Associates Press.

Ritterman, M. (1983) *Using hypnosis in family therapy.* San Francisco: Jossey-Bass.

Ritterman, M. (1985) Family context, symptom induction and therapeutic counterinduction: Breaking the spell of a dysfunctional rapport. In J. K. Zeig (Ed.), *Ericksonian psychotherapy: Vol. II. Clinical applications.* New York: Brunner/Mazel.

Rogers, C. R. (1951) *Client-centered therapy.* Boston: Houghton Mifflin.

Rossi, E. L. (Ed.) (1980) *Innovative hypnotherapy by M. H. Erickson. The collected papers of M. H. Erickson* (Vol. IV). New York: Irvington.

Roy, L. & Sawyers, J. K. (1986) The double bind: An empirical study of responses to inconsistent communications. *Journal of Marital and Family Therapy,* 12(4), 395–402.

Rubin, T. I. (1983) *One to one: Understanding personal relationships.* New York: Pinnacle Books.

Sacerdote, P. (1978) *Induced dreams.* New York: Gaus.

Salin, L. (1985) We are O.K., they are O.K. *Family Therapy Networker,* 9(4), 31–37.

Sargent, G. A. (1986) Family systems and family hypnotherapy. In E. T. Dowd & J. M. Healy (Eds.) *Case studies in hypnotherapy.* New York: Guilford.

Satir, V. (1967) *Conjoint family therapy.* Palo Alto, California: Science and Behavior Books.

Satir, V. (1972) *Peoplemaking.* Palo Alto, California: Science and Behavior Books.

Schwartz, R. & Perrotta, P. (1985) Let us sell no intervention before its time. *Family Therapy Networker,* 9(4), 18–25.

Selvini Palazzoli, M. S., Boscolo, L., Cecchin, C., & Prata, J. (1978) *Paradox and counterparadox.* New York: Jason Aronson.

Sherman, R. & Fredman, N. (1986) *Handbook of structured techniques in marriage and family therapy.* New York: Brunner/Mazel.

Shields, C. G. (1986a) Critiquing the new epistemologies: Toward minimum requirements for a scientific theory of family therapy. *Journal of Marital and Family Therapy,* 12(4), 359–372.

Shields, C. G. (1986b) Family therapy research and practice: Constructs, measurement and testing. *Journal of Marital and Family Therapy,* 12(4), 379–382.

Singer, J. L. & McCraven, V. (1961) Some characteristics of adult daydreaming. *Journal of Psychology,* 51, 151–164.

Singer, J. L. & Pope, K. S. (1978) *The power of human imagination.* New York: Plenum.

Smith, A. H. (1981) Object relations theory and family systems: toward a reconceptualization of the hypnotic relationship. *Psychotherapy: Theory, Research and Practice,* 18, 64–67.

Smith, A. H. (1984) Sources of efficacy in the hypnotic relationship: An object relations approach. In W. C. Wester II & A. H. Smith (Eds.) *Clinical hypnosis: A multidisciplinary approach.* Philadelphia: Lippincott.

Stiles, W. B., Shapiro, D. A., & Elliott, R. (1986) Are all psychotherapies equivalent? *American Psychologist,* 41(2), 165–180.

Stone, G. (1985) Family structure as metaphor. In J. K. Zeig (Ed.), *Ericksonian psychotherapy: Vol. II. Clinical applications.* New York: Brunner/Mazel.

Stuart, R. B. (1980) *Helping couples change.* New York: Guilford.

Tavris, C. (1982) *Anger: The misunderstood emotion.* New York: Simon & Schuster.

Tomm, K. (1986) On incorporating the therapist in a scientific theory of family therapy. *Journal of Marital and Family Therapy,* 12(4), 373–378.

Walters, M. (1985) Where have all the flowers gone? *Family Therapy Networker,* 9(4), 38–41.

Watkins, J. G. (1971) The affect bridge: A psychoanalytical technique. *International Journal of Clinical and Experimental Hypnosis,* 19(1), 21–27.

Watkins, J. G. & Watkins, H. (1979) The theory and practice of ego state therapy. In H. Grayson (Ed.), *Short-term approaches to psychotherapy.* New York: National Institute for the Psychotherapies/Human Sciences Press.

Watkins, J. G. & Watkins, H. (1981) Ego state therapy. In R. J. Corsini (Ed.), *Handbook of innovative psychotherapies.* New York: Wiley.

Watkins, J. G. & Watkins, H. (1982) Ego-state therapy. In L. E. Abt & I. R. Stuarts (Eds.), *The newer therapies: A handbook.* New York: Van Nostrand Reinhold.

Watzlawick, P. (1978) *The language of change.* New York: Basic Books.

Watzlawick, P. (1984) *The invented reality.* New York: Norton.

Watzlawick, P., Beavin, J. H., & Jackson, D. D. (1967) *Pragmatics of human communication.* New York: Norton.

Watzlawick, P., Weakland, J. H., & Fisch, R. (1974) *Change: Principles of problem formation and problem resolution.* New York: Norton.

Weakland, J. H. (1976) Communication theory and clinical change. In P. J. Guerin (Ed.), *Family therapy: Theory and practice*. New York: Gardner.

Weakland, J. H., Fisch, R., Watzlawick, P., & Bodin, A. (1974) Brief therapy: Focused problem resolution. *Family Process*. 13(2), 142–166.

Weeks, G. R. & L'Abate, L. (1982) *Paradoxical psychotherapy: Theory and practice with individuals, couples and families*. New York: Brunner/Mazel.

Weisinger, H. D. (1985) *Dr. Weisinger's anger workbook*. New York: William Morrow.

Weitzenhoffer, A. M. (1957) *General techniques of hypnotism*. New York: Grune & Stratton.

Wells, R. A., Dilkes, T. C. & Trivelli, N. (1972) The results of family therapy: A critical review of the literature. *Family Process*, 11, 189–207.

Wester, W. C., II (1987) *Clinical hypnosis: A case management approach*. Cincinnati: Behavorial Science Center Publications.

Whitaker, C. A. (1976a) A family is a four-dimensional relationship. In P. J. Guerin, Jr. (Ed.), *Family therapy: Theory and practice*. New York: Gardner.

Whitaker, C. A. (1976b) *Process techniques of family therapy*. Unpublished manuscript available from Boston Society for Family Therapy and Research, 94 Lewis Road, Belmont, MA 02178.

Winnicott, D. W. (1971) *Playing and reality*. New York: Basic Books.

Wright, S. (1985) A little less magic, please. *Family Therapy Networker,* 9(4), 27–29.

Yapko, M. (1986) Hypnotic and strategic interventions in the treatment of anorexia nervosa. *American Journal of Clinical Hypnosis*, 28(4), 224–232.

Zeig, J. K. (1980) *Teaching seminar with Milton H. Erickson, M.D.* New York: Brunner/Mazel.

Zeig, J. K. (1982) *Ericksonian approaches to hypnosis and psychotherapy*. New York: Brunner/Mazel.

Zilbergeld, B. (1983) *The shrinking of America: Myths of psychological change*. Boston: Little, Brown.

Zilbergeld, B. (1986) Using result imagery with sex problems. In Zilbergeld, B., Edelsien, M. G. & Araoz, D. L. (Eds.) *Hypnosis Questions and Answers*. New York: Norton.

Zilbergeld, B., Edelstien, M. G., & Araoz, D. L. (Eds.) (1986) *Hypnosis questions and answers*. New York: Norton.

Name Index

269

Subject Index

272